HARD FEELINGS

HARD FEELINGS

The Moral Psychology of Contempt

Macalester Bell

UNIVERSITY PRESS

Oxford University Press is a department of the University of Oxford. It furthers the University's objective of excellence in research, scholarship, and education by publishing worldwide. Oxford is a registered trade mark of Oxford University Press in the UK and certain other countries.

Published in the United States of America by Oxford University Press
198 Madison Avenue, New York, NY 10016, United States of America.

© Oxford University Press 2013

First issued as an Oxford University Press paperback, 2019

All rights reserved. No part of this publication may be reproduced, stored in a retrieval system, or transmitted, in any form or by any means, without the prior permission in writing of Oxford University Press, or as expressly permitted by law, by license, or under terms agreed with the appropriate reproduction rights organization. Inquiries concerning reproduction outside the scope of the above should be sent to the Rights Department, Oxford University Press, at the address above.

You must not circulate this work in any other form
and you must impose this same condition on any acquirer.

Library of Congress Cataloging-in-Publication Data
Bell, Macalester.
Hard feelings : the moral psychology of
contempt / by Macalester Bell.
p. cm.
Includes bibliographical references (p.).
ISBN 978-0-19-979414-0 (hardcover); 978-0-19-092955-8 (paperback)
1. Contempt (Attitude)   I. Title.
BF575.R35B45 2013
152.4—dc23
2012037390

CONTENTS

Acknowledgments	ix
Introduction: The Moral Importance of Contempt	1
1. What Is Contempt?	25
1.1 Contempt and Feeling Theories of Emotion	26
1.2 Intentionality, Rationality, and Cognitive Theories of Emotion	33
1.3 Contempt's Evaluative Presentation	37
1.4 Active and Passive Contempt	48
1.5 Contempt, Hatred, and Disgust	51
1.5.1 Contempt and Disgust	52
1.5.2 Contempt and Hatred	55
1.6 Potential Problem Cases	59
1.6.1 Contempt for Non-Persons	59
1.6.2 Self-Contempt	61

CONTENTS

2. Contempt as a Fitting Globalist Emotion	64
2.1 Can Contempt Ever Fit Its Target?	65
2.2 Defending Contempt against the Fittingness Objection	73
2.3 Fitting Evaluative Prioritizations	78
2.4 Relationships, Fittingness, and Fitting Attitude Accounts of Value	89
3. Contempt and the Vices of Superiority	96
3.1 Superbia and Vices of Superiority	97
3.2 Hypocrisy and Arrogance	110
3.3 Contempt as an Answer to Vices of Superiority	126
3.4 Cowardice, Stupidity, and Lightheartedness	132
4. The Moral Value of Contempt	137
4.1 Passive Contempt in Aristotle and Nietzsche	138
4.2 Contempt's Aptness Conditions	147
4.3 Contempt's Moral Value	151
4.3.1 Contempt's Instrumental Value	152
4.3.2 Contempt's Non-Instrumental Value	160
4.4 Challenges to an Ethic of Contempt	165
4.4.1 Contempt's Globalism and Aptness	165
4.4.2 Respect-Based Arguments against Contempt	168
4.4.3 Contempt and Comparisons	177
4.4.4 Withdrawal and Moral Address	183
4.5 Do We Have an Obligation to Contemn?	189

CONTENTS

5. Contempt, Racism, and Civility's Limits	197
5.1 Contempt and Anti-Black Racism: The Case of the Obama Bucks Cartoon	198
5.2 Race-Based Contempt as a Vice	200
5.3 Race-Based Contempt as Unfitting	208
5.4 Race-Based Contempt as Inapt	213
5.5 Contempt and Civility	217
6. Contempt, Forgiveness, and Reconciliation	227
6.1 A Problem with the Standard Account of Forgiveness	228
6.2 The Fundamental Features of Forgiveness	235
6.3 The Standard Account of Our Reasons to Forgive	238
6.3.1 Repentance	240
6.3.2 Excuses and Good Intentions	242
6.4 Reasons to Overcome Contempt through Forgiveness	245
6.4.1 Character Transformation	245
6.4.2 Shame	249
6.5 Do We Genuinely Forgive in Overcoming Contempt?	254
6.6 Contempt, Symbolic Reparations, and Social Reconciliation	259
Conclusion: "Contempt Is Not a Thing to be Despised"	272
Bibliography	277
Index	289

ACKNOWLEDGMENTS

Many have supported me through the process of writing this book. I am grateful to my colleagues at Columbia University for their feedback and support. Akeel Bilgrami, Philip Kitcher, Carol Rovane, and Achille Varzi provided helpful comments on the manuscript, and I am indebted to each for their assistance over the years. Pat Kitcher, Carol Rovane, and Achille Varzi have been very helpful department chairs. Lydia Goehr, Wolfgang Mann, and Christia Mercer have been generous with their time, advice, and good cheer. Emma Winter has been an amazing friend and source of encouragement since the afternoon we struck up a conversation during a CC coursewide lecture in 2005.

This book began as a dissertation at the University of North Carolina at Chapel Hill. I had the great good fortune of a wonderful dissertation committee, and I am indebted to Tom Hill, Susan Wolf, Bernie Boxill, Jerry Postema, and Jesse Prinz. Tom was an ideal advisor, and I am forever grateful to him for his calm guidance and intellectual generosity. I may not have gotten through graduate school at all without the friendship and support of Jan Boxill and Robin Hill.

ACKNOWLEDGMENTS

I have given a number of talks on themes drawn from this book. I am grateful to audiences at the American Philosophical Association, Columbia University, Occidental College, Ohio State, Princeton University, University of Michigan, Temple University, and York University for their astute comments and questions. Amy Coplan and Andrea Westlund served as commentators at two APA sessions, and I learned a great deal from their remarks. For additional comments and discussion, I am indebted to Stephanie Beardman, Larry Blum, Justin D'Arms, Matt Evans, Jorge Garcia, Charles L. Griswold, Liz Harman, Nancy Lawrence, Chris Lewis, Michelle Mason, Howard McGary, Dana Miller, Nishi Shah, and Sigrún Svavarsdóttir.

Several institutions have supported my work on this project. A Royster fellowship from the University of North Carolina at Chapel Hill and a Ford Foundation fellowship from the National Research Council helped fund my work in graduate school. I am indebted to Vice President Nick Dirks and my colleagues in Columbia's philosophy department for providing me with a Chamberlain Fellowship and teaching leave that allowed me to bring the book to completion.

I am endlessly grateful to Peter Ohlin, and I cannot imagine a more encouraging and efficient editor. I've benefited from anonymous referees who read the manuscript with great care and offered insightful criticisms and useful suggestions. Lucy Randall has been a great help in answering my questions about the production process, and I am indebted to Molly Morrison and Mary Sutherland for their patience and assistance with copyediting.

Portions of the book draw on previously published essays. The majority of chapter 5 was originally published as "Forgiving Someone for Who They Are (and Not Just What They've Done)," *Philosophy and Phenomenological Research*, 77, 3, 2008, pp. 625–658. Much of chapter 2 was published as "Globalist Attitudes and the Fittingness Objection," *Philosophical Quarterly*, 61, 244, 2011, pp. 449–472. Finally, parts of chapters 2 and 4 appeared in "A Woman's Scorn: Toward a Feminist Defense of Contempt as a Moral Emotion," *Hypatia*, 20, 4, 2005, pp. 80–93. I am grateful to Wiley for granting permission to reproduce this material.

HARD FEELINGS

Introduction

The Moral Importance of Contempt

The subject of ethics is how we ought to live; and that is not reducible to what we ought to do or try to do, and what we ought to cause or produce. It includes just as fundamentally what we should be for and against in our hearts, what and how we ought to love and hate. It matters morally what we are for and what we are against, even if we do not have the power to do much for it or against it, and even if it was not by trying that we came to be for it or against it.

Robert Adams

A kind Providence has placed in our breasts a hatred of the unjust and cruel; in order that we may preserve ourselves from cruelty and injustice. They, who bear cruelty, are accomplices in it. The pretended gentleness, which excludes that charitable rancour, produces an indifference, which is half an approbation. They never will love where they ought to love, who do not hate where they ought to hate.

Edmund Burke

Injustice and vice are widespread and call for some response; moral agents should, at the very least, *stand against* injustice and vice, and cultivate attitudes of resistance. As the epigraphs above bring out, what we love and hate are important aspects of the moral life, and when it comes to standing against immorality, it matters who and how we hate.¹ Hatred is, however, a rather blunt instrument. There are many different attitudes that may play a role in standing against someone or something, and other so-called "negative emotions" also offer ways of confronting immorality.² In this book I explore contempt's role in standing against a range of faults. Contempt certainly has its dangers, and inapt contempt is at the heart of several vices, but it also has an important defensive role to play in our moral lives.

Over the past thirty years, philosophers have become increasingly interested in the emotions, yet contempt has garnered relatively little philosophical attention.³ This neglect may be due to the widely held assumption that it is a "nasty" or "immoral" emotion that we ought to strive to extirpate as much as is possible. Moreover, contempt strikes some as a bit passé; discussions of the morality of contempt may seem more at home in the novels of Jane Austen than in current debates within moral psychology.⁴

---

1. Aristotle articulated a similar idea: "[E]njoying and hating the right things seems to be most important for virtue of character." *Nicomachean Ethics*, trans. Terence Irwin (Indianapolis: Hackett Publishing Company, 1999), 1172a.

2. Kristján Kristjánsson argues that the term "negative emotion" has six distinct senses. See "On the Very Idea of 'Negative Emotions,'" *Journal for the Theory of Social Behavior* 33, no. 4 (2003): 356–357. I use the term to refer to a certain class of emotions that are, as Kristjánsson puts it, "generally evaluated negatively" (357). Contempt is clearly a negative emotion in this sense. But I argue that contempt is not a negative emotion in the sense that it is always irrational, unfitting, or morally inappropriate. For skepticism about the usefulness of distinguishing between negative and positive emotions, see Robert Solomon and Lori D. Stone, "On 'Positive' and 'Negative' Emotions," *Journal for the Theory of Social Behavior* 32, no. 4 (2002): 417–435.

3. Three notable exceptions are Michelle Mason, "Contempt as a Moral Attitude," *Ethics* 113, no. 2 (2003): 234–272; Kate Abramson, "A Sentimentalist's Defense of Contempt, Shame, and Disdain," in *The Oxford Handbook of Philosophy of Emotion*, ed. Peter Goldie (Oxford: Oxford University Press, 2009); and William Ian Miller, who has written on the topic of "upward contempt" and democracy in *The Anatomy of Disgust* (Cambridge, MA: Harvard University Press, 1997).

4. As Abramson points out, philosophers have not always been reticent to include contempt in the class of "moral emotions"; sentimentalists such as Hume and

INTRODUCTION

I hope to show that contemporary philosophers have been remiss in ignoring contempt. While it may seem old fashioned, and while some varieties certainly deserve their nasty reputations, contempt has an important role to play in how we live our lives today. We should abhor those who are overly contemptuous or contemptuous for the wrong reasons, and we ought to be mindful of contempt's dark side, but we should also recognize contempt's virtues and value. Contempt is the best response to a range of faults that have the potential to impair our personal and moral relations. If we refrain from cultivating apt contempt, we will be unable to stand against these faults.

What is contempt? And what distinguishes the kind of contempt that has a positive role to play in our moral lives from the kind of contempt that is morally abhorrent? If, as many now think, we owe all persons respect qua persons, how could contempt ever be apt? What implications does a defense of the moral value of contempt have for our understanding of the virtue of civility? Do we ever have good reason to overcome contempt through a process of forgiveness? These are some of the questions that I take up in this book.

Contempt is very much at home in, and helps to sustain, rigidly hierarchical societies. If this hierarchy should begin to break down, concerns about the moral propriety of showing contempt are often raised. We can find examples of this across history and cultures. For example, as the West became increasingly egalitarian, we see a marked increase in expressed anxiety about the dangerous consequences of revealing one's contempt for another. Over and over again in his celebrated correspondence with his

---

Shaftesbury characterize contempt as an important mode of disapprobation. However, these philosophers do not offer much by way of an analysis of the nature of contempt, nor do they take up the question of what contempt does or when it has (or lacks) moral value.

son, Lord Chesterfield cautions the young man about the dangers of inadvertently showing his contempt:

> However frivolous a company may be, still, while you are among them, do not show them, by your inattention, that you think them so; but rather take their tone, and conform in some degree to their weakness, instead of manifesting your contempt for them. There is nothing that people bear more impatiently, or forgive less, than contempt; and an injury is much sooner forgotten than an insult.[5]

And a bit later Chesterfield notes:

> Wrongs are often forgiven but contempt never is. Our pride remembers it forever. It implies a discovery of weaknesses, which we are much more careful to conceal than crimes.[6]

Contempt must be concealed since it has the power to rupture the bonds that help hold society together. Reputed to be a rather contemptuous man himself, Chesterfield clearly takes contempt seriously, and he recognizes both its temptations and its dangers.

Since contemporary Western societies are significantly less socially stratified than Chesterfield's eighteenth century Great Britain, one might have thought that contempt would have, over the years, become less common and less important. But even in relatively egalitarian societies we still harbor, express, fear, and occasionally cheer on contempt. Contempt-talk may have receded

---

5. *Lord Chesterfield's Letters*, ed. David Roberts (Oxford: Oxford University Press, 1998), 46–47. Also quoted in Miller, *Anatomy of Disgust*, 216.

6. Ibid., 85. The first two sentences are also quoted in Miller, *Anatomy of Disgust*, 295, n. 16.

from the vernacular (people today are more likely to refer to being "dissed" than "contemned"), but contempt and concerns about its expression have not faded away. Many of our everyday moral pronouncements and aesthetic criticisms are expressions of contempt (e.g., "He is such a loser," or "What a jerk," or "He's a tool!" or "Whatever!"), and while psychologists have discovered that American test subjects have difficulty providing a precise definition of the word "contempt," the same subjects have no trouble matching contempt's characteristic facial expression to the appropriate situational antecedents.[7]

The dangers of contempt are familiar, and as Chesterfield astutely warned his son more than 250 years ago, we often negatively assess those who are inaptly contemptuous of others. In the 2004 presidential campaign, for example, several pundits remarked upon George W. Bush's smirk. Commentators were troubled by Bush's half-smile because this particular facial expression is characteristic of contempt. Daniel Hill, a psychologist specializing in the analysis of facial expressions, remarked, "the conundrum for Bush is that on one hand he smiles genuinely quite commonly, which is nice and upbeat, but it's combined often with contempt. You can see that either as cockiness or as smugness, depending on how you're oriented to him."[8]

As in Chesterfield's time, expressing contempt for the wrong person or group can have serious repercussions. In a case that received a great deal of media attention, the radio personality Don Imus lost his job after making what some saw as egregiously contemptuous comments about the Rutgers women's basketball

---

7. Erika L. Rosenberg and Paul Ekman, "Conceptual and Methodological Issues in the Judgment of Facial Expressions of Emotion," *Motivation and Emotion* 19, no. 2 (1995): 111–138.

8. John Tierney, "Of Smiles and Sneers," *New York Times*, July 18, 2004, http://www.nytimes.com/2004/07/18/politics/races/18points.html.

team, referring to them as "nappy-headed hos." In an editorial in the *New York Times*, Frank Rich writes:

> What Imus said about the Rutgers team landed differently, not least because his slur was aimed at young women who had no standing in the world of celebrity, and who had done nothing in public except behave as exemplary student athletes. The spectacle of a media star verbally assaulting them, and with a creepy, dismissive laugh, as if the whole thing were merely a disposable joke, was ugly. You couldn't watch it without feeling that some kind of crime had been committed. That was true even before the world met his victims. So while I still don't now whether Imus is a bigot, there was an *inhuman contempt* in the moment that sounded like hate to me.[9]

For many, Imus's expression of inapt and unmotivated contempt was so reprehensible that it justified CBS's decision to cancel his radio show.

While many people remarked on the calm and measured way in which the Rutgers women's basketball team responded to Imus's derogatory remarks, we know all too well that targets may strike back at their contemnors in highly destructive ways. In 2005 the world watched with horror as people around the globe were killed in protests after a Dutch newspaper printed cartoons depicting the Prophet Muhammad as a terrorist with a bomb hidden in his turban. Many Muslims were of the opinion that the cartoons expressed contempt for them as Muslims and even for the Prophet himself. This feeling of offence led to violent protests that resulted in the deaths of more than one hundred people.

---

9. Frank Rich, "Everybody Hates Don Imus," *New York Times*, April 15, 2007, http://www.nytimes.com/2007/04/15/opinion/15rich.html?scp=1&sq=Everybody%20Hates%20Don%20Imus&st=cse (emphasis added).

INTRODUCTION

Our sensitivity to expressions of contempt is reflected in many legal systems. The oldest legal prohibition of hatred and contempt comes from the law of seditious libel that prohibits "all writings...which tend to bring into hatred or contempt the king, the Government, or the constitution as by law established."[10] In our own legal system, those who express contempt for a presiding judge or for the court more generally can be charged with contempt. Those held in contempt face fines and incarceration. In Great Britain, blasphemy and blasphemous libel were only recently abolished. And while the First Amendment protects expressions of contempt in the United States, a person defamed by contemptuous speech can seek damages through the courts.

But while we are cognizant of its dangers, contempt does sometimes seem to be a *morally apt* response. On February 10, 2011, the Egyptian president Hosni Mubarak addressed his nation and the world in a highly anticipated speech. Mubarak's address came after three weeks of national protest, following a successful revolution in Tunisia. Egyptian protesters called on Mubarak to step down, and demanded free and fair elections. Throughout the day, it was widely reported that Mubarak's speech would include a declaration of his resignation, but in what some saw as a moment of arrogance and defiance, he boldly proclaimed his unwillingness to heed the protesters' calls for his resignation:

> I say again that I lived for the sake of this country, preserving its responsibility and trust. Egypt will remain above all and above everyone. It will remain so until I hand over this trust and pole. This is the goal, the objective, the responsibility and

---

10. Henry Coleman Folkard, *The Law of Slander and Libel*, 7th ed. (London: Butterworth & Co., 1908), 371. Quoted in Robert Post "Hate Speech," in *Extreme Speech and Democracy*, ed. Ivan Hare and James Weinstein (New York: Oxford University Press, 2009), 124.

the duty. It is the beginning of life, its journey, and its end. It will remain a country dear to my heart. It will not part with me and I will not part with it until my passing.[11]

Many of those gathered in Tahrir Square responded by waving their shoes in the air, and people around the world cheered on what they saw as the crowd's apt response to an arrogant and defiant dictator. In Egypt, as in much of the world, to show someone the sole of your shoe is a paradigmatic gesture of contempt. While those gathered to hear the speech likely felt a complex mixture of emotions, what stood out most clearly was the protesters' scorn for Mubarak and his administration.

Were the protesters right to dismiss Mubarak with contempt? Was it appropriate for others to cheer on the protesters' contempt? Contempt can be a positive moral accomplishment insofar as it answers certain faults, and many seemed to think that Mubarak's arrogance and defiance merited the people's contempt. However, it is difficult to account for contempt's positive value using the tools of contemporary moral theory. Contempt, contemporary critics allege, has no role to play in our moral lives. Ethicists writing today emphasize egalitarian values: everyone, no matter what their gender, race, social position, or history of moral improprieties and vice must be accorded the same kind of basic consideration and regard; everyone has dignity and is owed a modicum of respect. Since contempt is a dismissive and insulting attitude that manifests *disregard* for its target, it has, according to these critics, absolutely no role to play in modern moral theory or in contemporary life more broadly.

I stand with the shoe wavers and their champions, and I will defend an *ethic of contempt* in this book. I will argue that contempt

---

11. "Egypt unrest: Full text of Hosni Mubarak's speech," BBC News, February 10, 2011, http://www.bbc.co.uk/news/mobile/world-middle-east-12427091.

is an apt response to those who evince what I will call the "vices of superiority." These vices impair our personal and moral relations, and contempt offers the best way of *answering* the damage wrought by these vices. While contempt may not seem to have a home amid the egalitarian values characteristic of contemporary moral theories, this shows the limitations of the standard interpretations of these theories. As moral agents, we must confront all kinds of immorality, and in some circumstances, we *ought* to harbor (and show) contempt for persons.[12]

Some will resist this conclusion and insist upon an *anti-contempt ethic*. These critics vociferously deny that contempt has any positive role to play in our moral lives. Those who defend an anti-contempt ethic may do so for a number of reasons: some may argue that all emotions are capricious and irrational, and therefore have no place in our moral lives; others may argue that seemingly "positive" emotions like love and gratitude are necessary components of an adequate moral psychology, but "negative" emotions like contempt ought to be driven out. However, these are now minority positions. Many of those who defend an anti-contempt ethic think that other negative emotions, particularly resentment and indignation, do have positive roles to play in confronting injustice. We might describe these theorists as defending an "ethic of resentment" and rejecting an ethic of contempt.[13] Those who subscribe to an ethic of resentment need not maintain that resentment structures all of morality, but they

---

12. Or, more precisely, we ought to strive to *cultivate* feelings of apt contempt. I acknowledge that we cannot, though sheer force of will, immediately come to have (or eradicate) particular emotions; we are, to some degree, passive subjects of emotion. If ought implies can, then we shouldn't say that people ought to feel (or eliminate) their emotions. Nevertheless, we do have control over whether we choose to cultivate certain emotions, and I aim to show that we ought to strive to cultivate apt contempt.

13. Defenders of an ethic of resentment include R. Jay Wallace, *Responsibility and the Moral Sentiments* (Cambridge, MA: Harvard University Press, 1994); and Allan Gibbard, *Wise Choices, Apt Feelings: A Theory of Normative Judgment* (Cambridge,

do see it as having a crucial role to play in an adequate normative system. According to its defenders, resentment is a way of addressing a claim or making a demand: if you intentionally step on my foot and I respond with resentment, I am making a claim about how I deserve to be treated and, through my resentment, I address this claim to you.[14] My resentment presupposes that you are the kind of creature that can be held accountable for your actions, that I am the kind of being that can be wronged, and that in intentionally stepping on my foot, you have wronged me. My resentment seeks an exculpating explanation of your behavior or contrition and reparation for the wrong done. In short, resentment is partially constitutive of the stance of holding people responsible for their wrongdoing.

Defenders of an ethic of resentment are right to stress resentment's important role in holding people accountable for their actions. But an ethic of resentment cannot, by itself, offer a way to confront all forms of immorality. We ought to hold people accountable for who they are as well as for what they've done, and an ethic of contempt offers the best way of answering a range of vices.

The vast majority of those who defend an ethic of resentment consider contempt a pernicious emotion lacking any redeeming features. Why is contempt dismissed even by those who defend an ethic of resentment?

Many think that contempt is always disvaluable because of its tendency to bring about negative consequences; indeed, some persons respond to contempt with violence, and political

---

MA: Harvard University Press, 1992). Stephen Darwall argues that resentment has a special role to play in the second-personal stance characteristic of morality, but he suggests that other emotions may also be second-personal forms of address. See *The Second-Person Standpoint: Morality, Respect, and Accountability* (Cambridge, MA: Harvard University Press, 2006).

14. See Darwall, *Second-Person Standpoint*, 72.

theorists have long cautioned their readers to be wary of the dangerous consequences of contempt. Niccolò Machiavelli, for example, warns that a "a ruler must avoid contempt as if it were a reef."[15] Thomas Hobbes was also troubled by contempt. Subjects who hold their rulers in contempt have the potential to topple the monarchy, and given Hobbes's emphasis on the importance of stability, he saw contempt as an especially dangerous emotion. In fact, Hobbes went so far as to declare it a law of nature that contempt should never be expressed:

> But because all signs of hatred and contempt provoke most of all to brawling and fighting, insomuch as most men would rather lose their lives (that I say not, their peace) than suffer slander; it follows in the seventh place, that it is prescribed by the law of nature, that no man, either by deeds or words, countenance or laughter, *do declare himself to hate or scorn another*. The breach of which law is called *reproach*.[16]

We are, Hobbes notes, extremely sensitive to perceived slights. Signs of contempt can be felt in "a word, a smile, a different opinion,

---

15. Niccolò Machiavelli, *The Prince*, ed. Quentin Skinner and Russell Prince (Cambridge: Cambridge University Press, 1988), 64. Machiavelli's argument here echoes Aristotle's arguments in the *Politics*: Aristotle argues that new monarchies fail when their rulers come to be viewed with contempt or hatred. See *Politics*, trans. C. D. C. Reeve (Indianapolis: Hackett Publishing Company, 1998), 1312b.

16. Hobbes, *De Cive*, in *The English Works of Thomas Hobbes of Malmesbury*, vol. 2, ed. William Molesworth (London: John Bohn, 1839), chap. 3, sec. 12. Emphasis in original. Hobbes describes the dangers of contempt in the *Leviathan* as follows: "Again, men have no pleasure, but on the contrary a great deal of grief, in keeping company, where there is no power able to over-awe them all. For every man looketh that his companion should value him at the same rate he sets upon himself, and upon all signs of contempt, or undervaluing, naturally endeavours, as far as he dares (which amongst them that have no common power to keep them in quiet, is far enough to make them destroy each other), to extort a greater value from his contemners, by damage, and from others, by the example." *Leviathan: With Selected Variants from the Latin Edition of 1668*, ed. Edwin Curley (Indianapolis: Hackett, 1994) pt. 1, chap. 13.

and any other sign of undervalue, either direct in their Persons, or by reflexion in the Kindred, their Friends, their Nation, their Profession, or their Name."[17] Given our sensitivity to signs of contempt and its tendency to lead to social strife, we ought to do all that we can to avoid expressing contempt for others.

It is not just political philosophers who worry about contempt's negative consequences. Recently, the psychologist John Gottman has shown that married partners who respond to each other with contempt during arguments are far more likely to separate than those who express anger or frustration.[18] Wives whose husbands showed contempt for them believed that their marital problems were severe and could not be worked out, and were more likely to become ill over the course of the study.

Others argue that contempt is intrinsically disvaluable since it is incompatible with the respect we owe all persons as persons. Those who take this position often appeal to Immanuel Kant's criticism of contempt in *The Metaphysics of Morals*: "To be *contemptuous* of others (*contemnere*), that is, to deny them the respect owed to human beings in general, is in every case contrary to duty; for they are human beings."[19] Kant is worried about the types of gruesome punishments that express contempt, such as drawing and quartering, and letting people be torn to pieces by dogs.[20]

---

17. Hobbes, *Leviathan*, pt. 1, chap. 13.
18. See John Gottman and Robert Levenson, "How Stable is Marital Interaction Over Time?" *Family Process* 38, no. 2 (1999): 159–165; John Gottman, Robert Levenson, and Erica Woodin, "Facial Expressions During Marital Conflict," *Journal of Family Communication* 1, no. 1 (2001): 37–57; and John Gottman, *What Predicts Divorce?: The Relationship Between Marital Processes and Marital Outcomes* (Hillsdale, NJ: Lawrence Erlbaum Associates, 1994).
19. Immanuel Kant, *The Metaphysics of Morals*, trans. and ed. Mary Gregor, with an introduction by Roger J. Sullivan (Cambridge: Cambridge University Press, 1996), AP463. Emphasis in original. As I argue in chap. 4, Kant's own position on the moral propriety of contempt is far more nuanced than this passage suggests. There is, I hope to show, room for apt contempt within a Kantian moral system.
20. Ibid.

INTRODUCTION

Contemporary Kantians are troubled by the fact that contempt involves downward-looking comparative evaluations that appear to threaten the dignity of the target of contempt. Some commentators have insisted that a fully autonomous person ought to be unconcerned with the status of others within the moral community; according to these theorists, it is contrary to duty to look down on some persons in comparison to others.[21]

Other critics have argued against contempt's moral propriety because they claim it is essentially an *anti-social* emotion.[22] While anger tends to motivate direct confrontation with the offender, which can lead to social change, contempt tends to motivate psychological disengagement from the target and thus seems to stand as a formidable impediment to social progress. Given the withdrawal and disengagement characteristic of contempt, some have questioned whether contempt can ever serve as a form of *moral address*.[23]

Still others object to the way contempt presents its target. Contempt takes as its object *whole persons* and not simply persons' actions; it presents its targets as low and as all of one piece. Some see contempt's totalizing quality as a reason to dismiss it as always objectionable: since persons are multifaceted and complex, globalist emotions like contempt would seem to never *fit* their targets.[24]

Finally, there is a worry that members of stigmatized groups are especially vulnerable to the pain of being held in contempt.

---

21. Allen Wood, *Kant's Ethical Thought* (Cambridge: Cambridge University Press, 1999), 135.

22. See, for example, Jonathan Haidt, "The Moral Emotions," in *Handbook of Affective Sciences*, ed. Richard J. Davidson, L. Klaus R. Scherer, and H. Hill Goldsmith (Oxford: Oxford University Press, 2003), 859.

23. Stephen Darwall raises this issue in *Second-Person Standpoint*, 67.

24. See, for example, John M. Doris, *Lack of Character: Personality and Moral Behavior* (Cambridge: Cambridge University Press, 2005).

In fact, some have argued that contempt is at the heart of racist, sexist, and heterosexist systems of oppression.[25] Insofar as members of stigmatized groups are especially vulnerable to the pain associated with being a target of contempt, contempt would seem to have no place in the psychological repertoire of the morally mature.

Given these concerns about the apparent disvalue of contempt, it might seem reasonable to defend an anti-contempt ethic and strive to drive out all feelings of contempt. Against this, I argue that contempt—like resentment—has a crucially important role to play in the practice of morality. We must confront injustice and vice, and we should do so in a way that best mitigates their damage; given the way in which some vices impair moral relations, we ought to adopt an ethic of resentment as well as an ethic of contempt.[26]

What do critics of contempt mean when they claim it is inappropriate? We assess and criticize emotions along a number of distinct dimensions, and it may be helpful to distinguish these different forms of assessment:[27] first, emotions may be criticized when they do not *fit* their targets: you may, for example, be open to criticism for feeling fear in the absence of danger.[28] Unfitting emotions fail to correctly present the world. Second, an emotion may

---

25. See for example, David Haekwon Kim, "Contempt and Ordinary Inequality," in *Racism and Philosophy*, ed. Susan E. Babbitt and Sue Campbell (Ithaca, NY: Cornell University Press, 1999); and J. L. A. Garcia, "The Heart of Racism," *Journal of Social Philosophy* 27, no. 1 (1996): 5–45.

26. Nor is there any principled reason why we should exclude other hard feelings from our moral lives.

27. For a similar mapping of the terrain employing somewhat different terminology, see Karen Jones, "Emotional Rationality as Practical Rationality," in *Setting the Moral Compass: Essays by Women Philosophers*, ed. Cheshire Calhoun (New York: Oxford University Press, 2004).

28. For a discussion of the different forms of affective appropriateness see Justin D' Arms and Daniel Jacobson, "The Moralistic Fallacy: On the 'Appropriateness' of Emotions," *Philosophy and Phenomenological Research* 61, no.1 (2000): 65–90. As they point out, our emotions can be unfitting in terms of "size" or "shape" (73): an emotion

be open to criticism when it is not based on good evidence or is *unreasonable*. Consider, for example, the person who suffers from arachnophobia: given that most spiders are not dangerous, this person's fear is both unreasonable and unfitting. But even fitting emotions may be unreasonable. One may, for example, be terrified of brown recluse spiders because one believes that they have the capacity to cast spells on people. In this case, one's fear is fitting—brown recluses are very dangerous—yet the fear is unreasonable since it is not based on good reasons. Third, an emotion may be criticized because it isn't *prudent* to feel. We might warn a new parrot owner not to show fear when interacting with their bird since a dominance-seeking parrot can sense fear and will be more difficult to control; fear in this case may be reasonable and fitting given the parrot's powerful beak yet still criticizable as imprudent. Finally, we may condemn emotions as morally disvaluable because of the unacceptable way in which they present their targets. One may, for example, argue that schadenfreude is morally objectionable because it presents the pain of another person as risible.

Against those who criticize it as always inappropriate, I argue that contempt offers, in some circumstances, the best way of responding to persons: it may be a fitting, reasonable, prudent, and morally valuable emotion. Without contempt, we would be ill equipped to stand against what I will call the "vices of superiority", and they would wreak havoc on our personal and moral relations. Contempt can, of course, go horribly wrong and be directed toward those who don't merit it, harbored for the wrong reasons, or maintained for too long, and so on. But rather than dismiss contempt *tout court,* we should carefully consider the conditions under which it does and does not have value.

---

that is unfitting in terms of its size is excessive or muted. An emotion that is unfitting in terms of its shape presents its target as having qualities that the target does not, in fact, have.

Why is it that contemporary moral theorists have written so little about contempt? Many think that contempt's unique features make it particularly pernicious. In addition, there are several other, more general, reasons why contempt has received little attention in moral psychology.

First, for many years, what we might term "the ethics of action" dominated contemporary moral theory. According to this position, moral assessment ought to be restricted to the *actions* of moral agents: what ethicists ought to do is come up with normative, action-guiding principles, and what we ought to evaluate are agents' actions.[29] If one accepts this position, then one may conclude that the only emotions that have a role to play in our moral lives are those that directly motivate subjects to act and those that take as their objects persons' actions.[30]

If we accept the ethics of action, then we may be tempted to conclude that contempt has no role to play in our moral lives. For contempt is focused on what we might call "badbeing" as opposed to "wrongdoing." That is, contempt is directed toward *persons* and not simply persons' *actions*. I don't think we should assess the value of emotions solely in terms of the actions they motivate. Very often there isn't much that we can *do* about serious immorality and injustice other than cultivate apt attitudes toward it. Moreover, in at least some cases, figuring out what attitude

---

29. This is, of course, a simplification of a complex variety of positions. There are moral theorists who might subscribe to the ethics of action yet maintain a strong emphasis on character judgments. Humeans, for example, think that we ought to evaluate actions in terms of what they express about a person's character. Nevertheless, most theorists who subscribe to the ethics of action do not advocate this kind of mixed view, and their emphasis on action comes at the expense of considerations of character.

30. Consider, for example, what Allan Gibbard says about the relationship between emotion and action: "Emotions, in evolutionary terms, cash out in action: in the actions to which they lead and in the actions they elicit in others. It is through actions that reproductive prospects are enhanced or diminished." *Wise Choices, Apt Feelings*, 139.

to adopt is actually a precondition for determining what to do. Our actions and practices have affectively expressive dimensions, and because of this, determining the right thing to do cannot be cleanly separated from determining how to feel.

Many moral theorists now recognize that action assessment is not the only type of moral assessment, and even paradigmatic "guilt moralists" have written approvingly of shame.[31] As part of the practice of morality, we can (and should) assess the motives, attitudes, and character traits of persons, and this assessment involves coming to have a range of positive and negative attitudes toward persons and their actions.[32]

Second, philosophers have only recently begun to focus attention on the moral psychology of confronting immorality. There is, of course, a huge literature on moral responsibility and an equally large literature on punishment, but participants in these debates have paid relatively little attention to how moral failings may impair our relationships and what attitudes we should cultivate to respond appropriately to this damage. In the literature on moral responsibly, for example, much of the focus has been on the offender and the conditions under which he is blameworthy for his actions. Whether a person is blameworthy is often thought to depend on answers to familiar metaphysical questions such as whether the truth of determinism is compatible with the kind of freedom thought to be required for responsibility. In focusing on the metaphysical status of the wrongdoer, not enough attention has been paid to the ways in which wrongdoing and badbeing

---

31. For a discussion of the role of shame in Kant's moral theory see David Sussman, "Shame and Punishment in Kant's *Doctrine of Right*," *Philosophical Quarterly* 58, no. 231 (2008): 299–317. The ethics of action generally favors a focus on guilt since guilt takes as its object the target's actions whereas shame takes as its object the target herself. Sussman convincingly argues that shame plays a much larger role in Kant's ethics than is standardly acknowledged.

32. Robert Adams forcefully makes this point in the passage that serves as an epigraph to this introduction.

impairs relationships and how best to respond, attitudinally, to this damage.[33] The literature on punishment tends to focus on the offender and the kinds of considerations that could justify depriving persons of their liberty. Philosophical discussions of punishment tend to gloss over the issue of how immorality threatens our moral relations and how we, as moral agents, ought to respond to these threats.

Third, contempt's neglect may be due to the fact that it is commonly associated with "shame" or "honor" moralities as opposed to "guilt" or "respect" moralities. The distinction between these types of moral systems has its genealogy in anthropology, but many moral psychologists have uncritically accepted this distinction. The mark of a shame culture is, according to Ruth Benedict, the role that external sanctions play in regulating behavior: "True shame cultures rely on external sanctions for good behavior, not, as true guilt cultures do, on an internalized conviction of sin. Shame is a reaction to other people's criticism. A man is shamed either by being openly ridiculed and rejected or by fantasying to himself that he has been made ridiculous. In either case it is a potent sanction. But it requires an audience or at least a man's fantasy of an audience. Guilt does not."[34] If one accepts a sharp distinction between shame and guilt moralities, the lack of attention paid to contempt may not be surprising. An ethic of contempt is conceptually connected to honor codes and shame moralities since it is often thought to be a fitting response to dishonor. For this reason, many believe that contempt has no role to play in our contemporary moral lives. We have been told that moral

---

33. Of course, not everyone participating in these debates has focused their attention on these metaphysical issues; my own approach to the moral psychology of wrongdoing and repair owes a debt to P. F. Strawson's treatment of moral responsibility in "Freedom and Resentment," *Proceedings of the British Academy* 48 (1962).

34. Ruth Benedict, *The Chrysanthemum and the Sword* (Wilmington: Mariner Books, 2006), 223.

systems in the West are guilt moralities, and many insist that we have made moral progress in leaving our former shame moralities behind.[35] In part, my project aims to cast doubt on the supposedly sharp distinction between shame and guilt moralities.[36] An acceptable morality will be one that recognizes the importance of a wide variety of hard feelings including guilt and resentment on the one hand and shame and contempt on the other; these emotions do very different things and answer distinct types of threats. They all have a role to play in our moral psychological lives.

Nevertheless, there are important differences between ethical systems that emphasize guilt and resentment as compared to those that emphasize shame and contempt. The former

---

35. Not all contemporary ethicists are dismissive of honor and shame. Kwame Anthony Appiah has recently argued that honor has an important role to play in moral revolutions. Progressive social change such as the rejection of chattel slavery was, according to Appiah's argument, driven primarily by concerns about what was *honorable*, rather than by reflection upon what was *right*. While he doesn't emphasize the point, contempt—and anxiety about being the target of contempt—does much of the motivational work in the moral revolutions Appiah discusses; disdain for those who participate in and defend practices like dueling, foot binding, and chattel slavery, rather than an abstract concern regarding one's honor, is what precipitates the moral progress that he describes. If we accept the story Appiah tells about social progress, then an anti-contempt ethic would deprive us of an important tool for bringing about moral progress. See Appiah, *The Honor Code: How Moral Revolutions Happen* (New York: W. W. Norton, 2010).

36. While Benedict distinguishes between guilt and shame cultures, she acknowledges that guilt is on the wane and shame is on the rise in American culture: "The early Puritans who settled in the United States tried to base their whole morality on guilt and all psychiatrists know what trouble contemporary Americans have with their consciences. But shame is an increasingly heavy burden in the United States and guilt is less extremely felt than in earlier generations. In the United States this is interpreted as a relaxation of morals. There is much truth in this, but that is because we do not expect shame to do the heavy work of morality. We do not harness the acute personal chagrin which accompanies shame to our fundamental system of morality." *The Chrysanthemum and the Sword*, 223–224.) I agree with Benedict's observations about the decline of guilt and rise of shame in American culture, but I disagree with her interpretation of what this means. As I see it, even moral systems that emphasize guilt, rule following, and wrongdoing, must also make room for emotions that sanction bad attitudes and vice.

characteristically hold that persons are blameworthy only for their voluntary actions, and this has led to the debates about blameworthiness and its metaphysical underpinnings mentioned earlier. An ethics of contempt need not take a stand on these metaphysical issues; contempt makes no claims about the target's freedom or whether the truth of determinism is incompatible with this freedom. Contempt involves an evaluation of the *person* rather than the person's *culpable actions*. Thus whether contempt is a fitting response does not turn on whether free will is compatible with the truth of determinism.[37]

Fourth, contempt's neglect may be due to a general feature of emotions: contempt, like other emotions, is not under the subject's immediate voluntary control. But if our emotions are not under persons' direct control, some may wonder whether they are amenable to moral assessment at all. If we cannot control whether we feel (or do not feel) a particular emotion at a particular time, then it may be argued that we cannot be responsible for our emotions. But if we cannot be responsible for our emotions, then in what sense can they be said to have, or lack, moral value?

It is true that that our emotions are not under our immediate and direct voluntary control: I cannot will myself to experience (or not experience) contempt at this very moment. But acknowledging that emotions are not amenable to this type of control is not to concede that an ethics of contempt is misguided or incoherent. As several philosophers have argued, direct control may not be necessary for responsibility; we may assess a person for her attitudes whether or not they are under her direct control.[38] Moreover, while

---

37. I do think that persons must have certain, minimal, capacities in order to be *aptly* held in contempt. I discuss this issue in chap. 4.

38. See, for example, Robert Merrihew Adams, "Involuntary Sins," *Philosophical Review* 94, no. 1 (1985): 3–31; and Angela Smith, "Responsibility for Attitudes: Activity and Passivity in Mental Life," *Ethics* 115, no. 2 (2005): 236–271.

we lack direct control over our emotions, we do exercise some indirect control over them; whether a person feels contempt at a particular moment is not under her immediate control, yet she did have some control over becoming the sort of person who either does or does not experience contempt or experiences it one way rather than another. Further, no matter what sort of person one now is, one may, indirectly, cultivate one's emotions, thereby exercising some control over one's future emotions. Some may tamp down their feelings of contempt because contempt is often dismissed as a nasty or immoral emotion. In this case, a defense of an ethic of contempt may remove a barrier to an emotional response that is more common than we realize.

My aim in this book is to rectify what I see as the unfortunate lack of attention paid to contempt, and I hope to show that contempt has an important role to play in our contemporary moral lives: despite its bad reputation, contempt is the best response to a range of vices and is an emotion that we ought to cultivate rather than avoid altogether. In chapter 1, I offer an account of the nature of contempt. In offering my characterization of contempt, I review previous philosophical discussions of its central features and canvass the relevant psychological literature. In chapter 2 I consider a common objection that some see as fatal to an ethic of contempt: contempt is a "globalist" emotion that presents its target as all of one piece; some critics insist that contempt's globalism renders it always unfitting—because of its globalism it is thought that contempt *never* correctly presents its target. Against this, I argue that contempt's globalism gives us no reason to dismiss all tokens of contempt as unfitting. Contempt's fittingness conditions are contoured by the relationship between the contemnor and contemned, and I explore the implications of this claim for meta-ethical debates about "fitting attitude" theories of value. In chapter 3, I offer an account of the faults that most clearly merit contempt: the vices of superiority. These vices impair our moral relations, and contempt offers a uniquely apt way of responding to this damage. I continue my defense of the moral value of contempt in chapter 4 by showing how contempt answers the vices of superiority and in so doing realizes several distinct values. In making my case for contempt, I consider and respond to a number of objections that have been raised against it. In chapter 5, I consider contempt's ugly side and explore its role in anti-black racism: I argue that the best response to being a target of race-based contempt is to marshal a robust counter-contempt. I go on to consider the implications of this argument for debates about civility and its limits; while many are quick to insist upon the value of civility in striving to reach a progressive moral consensus on difficult social issues, I argue that civility's value is limited. Contemptuous criticism can help us achieve progressive moral consensus and does not always betray a lack of respect for the person criticized. Despite contempt's value, we sometimes have reason to overcome apt contempt through a process of forgiveness. In chapter 6, I give an account of the reasons to overcome contempt through forgiveness. This account of forgiveness has important implications for debates about social reconciliation and reparations. Using the example of coming to terms with the history of slavery at the University of North Carolina, I sketch an account of the sorts of reparative activities that give persons reasons to overcome their apt contempt for institutions and the persons associated with them.

The conclusions I draw about the moral value of contempt will strike some as counterintuitive, perhaps even offensive. We live in time where many of our everyday, legal, and philosophical discussions about contentious moral issues are couched in the language of respect for persons. That all persons have a basic dignity and are owed respect on that basis is now a truism, and many people presume that this respect is incompatible with contempt. Given this starting point and the strong anti-contempt intuitions that characterize much contemporary moral thought, a great deal of the book will be devoted to considering and responding to objections that have been raised, or could be raised, against contempt. There is, I think, no way to fully defend an ethic of contempt other than by systematically considering (and ultimately disarming) the objections that may be raised against it.

While I defend contempt as a "moral emotion," I hope to do so without first articulating and defending a specific moral theory; this will not be a Kantian, Aristotelian, or utilitarian defense of contempt. In part, my decision to proceed in this way is practical: given the scope of this book, it would be difficult to first defend a particular moral theory, and then go on to defend contempt's moral value from within that theory. But my method is primarily motivated by a basic theoretical commitment: I believe that there is far too much attention paid to issues that divide us as moral theorists, and as a result, ethicists tend to downplay the many areas of agreement that exist even between those that defend very different normative outlooks.

I will consider what role contempt ought to play in the lives of persons who subscribe to a *minimally acceptable morality*.[39] A minimally acceptable morality will provide resources for evaluating our attitudes toward other persons as well as our actions. It will acknowledge our value as persons and stress the importance of respect as a response to this value, and it will recognize

---

39. Although our overarching projects are different, my strategy for defending an ethic of contempt is similar to the methodology Martha Nussbaum employs in her book, *Upheavals of Thought: The Intelligence of Emotions* (Cambridge: Cambridge University Press, 2001). Nussbaum articulates what she calls an "adequate normative view" and uses this thin conception of morality to assess the moral import of the emotions. Linda Radzik adopts a similar methodology in *Making Amends: Atonement in Morality, Law, and Politics* (New York: Oxford University Press, 2009).

the significance of our relationships with others. On a minimally acceptable morality, we have good reasons to hold at least some persons responsible for their actions and attitudes, and forgiveness is considered an important achievement. Despite the many differences between various normative theories, any defensible normative view will include these basic commitments, or so I shall assume in what follows.

Chapter 1

What Is Contempt?

The dictionary tells us that contempt is "[t]he action of contemning or despising; the holding or treating as of little account, or as vile and worthless; the mental attitude in which such a thing is so considered."[1] The activity of *contemning*, to reclaim a rather old-fashioned word, is closely related to deriding (to "laugh at in contempt or scorn"[2]), despising (to "look down upon; to view with contempt; to think scornfully or slightingly of"[3]), disdaining (to "think unworthy of oneself, or of one's notice; to regard or treat with contempt."[4]), and scorning (to "speak or behave contemptuously; to use derisive language; jeer"[5]). Some have argued that "scorn" may be derived from *scornare*, "to deprive of the horns;"[6] contempt and its cognates present their targets as cut down or brought low.[7]

---

1. While the terms "contempt" and "contemn" are superficially similar to "condemnation" and "condemn," the two are actually etymologically independent: contempt derives from the Latin *contemptus* whereas condemn comes from *condemnare*. "Contempt, n." and "Condemn, v." *OED Online*, http://www.oed.com, Oxford University Press, accessed April 2010. For more on the etymology of contempt, see Michelle Mason, "Contempt as a Moral Attitude," *Ethics* 113, no 2 (2003): 234–272.

2. "Deride, v." *OED Online*, http://www.oed.com, Oxford University Press, accessed April 2010. I am listing the senses of "deride" that seem most central; I do the same for subsequent terms.

3. Ibid., "Despise, v."

4. Ibid., "Disdain, v."

5. Ibid., "Scorn, v."

6. Ibid., "Scorn, n."

7. As we will see in later chapters, this image of depriving of horns is an especially good metaphor for understanding what apt contempt accomplishes. The vices of superiority can be symbolized as horns that have the potential to damage the target's relationships and others' self-esteem. In contemning, the subject seeks to remove these horns in order to prevent further damage.

There is, of course, a limit to how much we can learn about emotions from their dictionary definitions. In order to fully understand contempt we need to delve deeper and explore its unique characteristics.

1.1 CONTEMPT AND FEELING THEORIES OF EMOTION

People often describe emotions as "feelings," and according to one influential line of argument, emotions are simply feelings caused by somatic changes. On this view, emotions can be individuated by the distinct physiological changes characteristic of each response. René Descartes was, arguably, an early defender of this type of theory, and William James and Carl Lange independently developed influential somatic theories.[8] Today, a number of theorists defend feeling theories of emotions.[9]

As others have noted, we often use somatic descriptions and metaphors to talk about emotion: we might describe our blood boiling in anger or our stomach knotted in fear.[10] The specific metaphors we use to talk about contempt are also connected to the body; we *look down our noses* at hypocrites and *sneer* at the arrogant. It is commonly thought that our emotions give rise to characteristic somatic states; our stomach turns *because* we are

---

8. William James, "What is an Emotion?" *Mind* (1884): 188–205; and Carl Lange, "The Emotions," in *The Emotions*, ed. K. Dunlap (Baltimore: Williams & Wilkins, 1922, originally published 1885).

9. See, for example, Antonio Damasio, *The Feeling of What Happens: Body and Emotion in the Making of Consciousness* (New York: Harcourt Brace and Co., 1999).

10. See Jesse Prinz, "Embodied Emotions," in *Thinking about Feeling: Contemporary Philosophers on Emotions*, ed. Robert Solomon (New York: Oxford University Press 2004).

scared, or we cry *because* we are sad. James famously rejects this commonplace:

> Common sense says, we lose our fortune, are sorry and weep; we meet a bear, are frightened and run; we are insulted by a rival, are angry and strike. The hypothesis here to be defended says that this order of sequence is incorrect, that the one mental state is not immediately induced by the other, that the bodily manifestations must first be interposed between, and that the more rational statement is that we feel sorry because we cry, angry because we strike, afraid because we tremble, and not that we cry, strike, or tremble because we are sorry, angry, or fearful, as the case may be.[11]

For James, we perceive some exciting fact, and this perception causes physiological changes. Our awareness of these bodily changes *is* the emotion. Emotions, on a somatic account, are individuated by bodily changes, and our feelings of these changes.

Unlike some emotions (e.g., anger or disgust), contempt seems to lack a characteristic feeling. In fact, one distinctive feature of contempt is that it readily combines with a wide variety of affects and can be experienced as a strong aversion similar to disgust, cool disregard, or amused dismissiveness.[12] If there is no single affective characteristic that all tokens of contempt share, then we would seem to have no reason, according to feeling theories, to classify contempt as a distinct emotion. Yet we do, in everyday life, consider contempt to be a unique emotion distinct from other hostile emotions such as anger or hate. In the case of contempt, feeling theories seem unable to account for a recognizably distinct

---

11. James, "What is an Emotion?" 190.
12. See Miller, *Anatomy of Disgust*, 214.

emotional response. This is a specific instance of a more general problem with feeling theories: while these theories can distinguish between general emotion types, they lack the resources to make fine-grain distinctions between emotions.

James was, in fact, dismissive of the project of distinguishing between particular emotions within the same family.[13] As he saw it, making fine-grained distinctions between specific emotions is both tiresome and pointless: "[T]he merely descriptive literature of the emotions is one of the most tedious parts of psychology. And not only is it tedious, but you feel that its subdivisions are to a great extent either fictitious or unimportant, and that its pretences to accuracy are a sham."[14] Instead of distinguishing between emotions, James thought that psychologists ought to focus on the general causes of emotion types.

James was wrong to think that providing detailed accounts of specific emotions is pointless. While there is much that emotions have in common, an adequate moral psychology will take seriously the differences between emotions. We have good reason to reject a theory of emotion that cannot recognize contempt as a unique emotion distinct from its neighbors. Different emotions within the same general family *do* very different things, and an adequate moral psychology ought to be more, not less, fine-grained.

Some might object that I've been too quick to conclude that feeling theorists can't recognize contempt as a distinct emotion. While contempt does not seem to have a characteristic phenomenology, there is reason to believe that it has a distinct facial expression. If this is the case, then sophisticated feeling theorists

---

13. See James, *The Principles of Psychology*, vol 2 (New York: Dover, 1950), 448. This issue is discussed in John Deigh, "Cognitivism in the Theory of Emotions," *Ethics* 104, no.4 (1994): 824–854.

14. James, *Principles of Psychology*, 448. Also quoted in Deigh, "Cognitivism in the Theory of Emotions," 832.

may have reason to recognize contempt as a distinct emotion: a unique contempt expression indicates that contempt involves specific physiological changes that persons could, at least in principle, eventually come to feel.

As part of his grand catalog of the emotions, Charles Darwin was one of the first to discuss contempt's facial expression. He groups contempt together with scorn and distain, and argues that there are several movements of the mouth, nose, and eyes that typically express this affective triad (I refer to this as the "contempt expression" in what follows). The most distinctive feature of the contempt expression is the uncovering of the canine tooth on one side of the face. In the contemporary literature, this movement is referred to as the "unilateral lip curl."[15] As Darwin points out, the unilateral lip curl can morph into an outright snarl or an ironic half-smile:

> I suspect that we see a trace of this same expression in what is called a derisive or sardonic smile. The lips are then kept joined or almost joined, but one corner of the mouth is retracted on the side towards the derided person; and this drawing back of the corner is part of a true sneer.[16]

On the one hand, contempt can merge with amused detachment and be expressed in a half-smile;[17] on the other the other hand,

---

15. See, for example, Hugh L. Wagner, "The Accessibility of the Term 'Contempt' and the Meaning of the Unilateral Lip Curl," *Cognition and Emotion* 14, no. 5 (2000): 689–710.

16. Charles Darwin, *The Expression of The Emotions in Man and Animals* (New York: D. Appleton and Company, 1873), 251.

17. It is interesting to note that the smile associated with contempt is almost never a full-on, toothy grin but is instead a knowing, half-smile. This half-smile emphasizes the ambiguity of contempt, and, as I see it, the self-awareness of the contemnor. The half-smile is expressive of contempt's *slyness*. William Ian Miller points out that contempt expressions have a *one-sidedness* to them that belies a close connection between contempt and the ironic. See Miller, *Anatomy of Disgust*, 219.

contempt can come together with intense hatred and be expressed with a grimace.

Although the unilateral lip curl is the facial movement most clearly characteristic of contempt, the nose and eyes also play a distinctive role in its expression. Sometimes, the contemnor's nose is simply raised toward the sky; other times, the nose is violently wrinkled. It is, Darwin suggests, as if the contemnor smells something offensive and is trying to stop the odor from creeping in. This wrinkling of the nose is quite similar to the characteristic expression of disgust, and, as Darwin notes, certain intense forms of contempt may be indistinguishable from disgust.[18] Contempt's characteristic eye movements also manifest a desire to withdraw from the target; eye rolling and the half-closing of eyelids are common expressions of contempt.

Building on Darwin's observations, contemporary evolutionary psychologists have taken up the question of whether contempt is a basic emotion. The term "basic emotion" is used in a number of different ways in the literature: it may refer to elementary emotions that combine to form more complex emotions, emotions that are presumed to have a biological basis, or emotions that are found cross-culturally.[19] For many years contempt was not considered a basic emotion—on any characterization of what makes an emotion basic—because it was thought to lack a unique facial expression.[20] Some argued that contempt should be understood as

---

18. Charles Darwin, *The Expression of the Emotions in Man and Animals* (New York: D. Appleton and Company, 1873), 253. See also Miller, *Anatomy of Disgust*, 218.

19. For an overview of various accounts of what makes an emotion basic, see Andrew Ortony and Terence Turner, "What's Basic About Basic Emotions?" *Psychological Review* 97, no. 3 (1990): 315–331.

20. As Ekman and Friesen note, contempt also differs from other basic emotions in that it has not been found in other primates, it is one of the last emotions to develop in children, and it involves unilateral facial movement. See "A New Pan-Cultural Facial Expression of Emotion," *Motivation and Emotion* 10, no. 2 (1986): 159–168.

a blending of anger and disgust.[21] Others characterized contempt as a form of anger.[22] Ekman and Friesen originally conjectured that contempt was simply a type of disgust, but they eventually concluded that contempt is actually a basic emotion in its own right.[23] In their later research, Ekman and Friesen found that the unilateral lip curl is recognized across cultures, and the contempt expression is distinguishable from both anger and disgust.

In one study, photographs of the contempt expression were shown to subjects in ten countries. Using a forced-choice method, subjects were given response terms (happiness, surprise, fear, sadness, anger, disgust, and contempt) in the local language and were asked to indicate which term applied to a series of facial expressions. The contempt expression was labeled accurately by 75 percent of subjects.[24] This result was similar to the levels of agreement recorded for recognized basic emotions (74 percent for anger and disgust and 90 percent for happiness).[25] From cross-cultural studies of this kind, Ekman and Friesen concluded that contempt should join happiness, surprise, fear, sadness, anger, and disgust as the seventh basic emotion.

These results have not gone unchallenged: in several studies, respondents have categorized the contempt expression as disgust.[26] Moreover, the forced-choice method employed in Ekman's experiments has drawn fire from some critics.[27] Subjects

---

21. Robert Plutchik, *Emotion: A Psychoevolutionary Synthesis* (New York: Harper & Row, 1980).
22. Richard Lazarus, *Emotion and Adaptation* (New York: Oxford University Press, 1991).
23. Paul Ekman and Wallace Friesen, *Unmasking the Face* (Englewood Cliffs, NJ: Prentice-Hall, 1975).
24. Ekman and Friesen, "A New Pan-Cultural Facial Expression of Emotion."
25. Ibid.
26. James A. Russell, "Negative Results on a Reported Facial Expression of Contempt," *Motivation and Emotion* 15, no. 4 (1991): 281–291.
27. Wagner, "The Accessibility of the Term 'Contempt.'"

may choose to label expressions involving the unilateral lip curl as contempt simply because none of the other labels apply, or because the other terms have already been used for different facial expressions. Some have suggested that the conflicting findings regarding contempt are simply the result of the fact that many American test subjects do not know the meaning of the word "contempt." Studies conducted outside the United States find high rates of categorizing the contempt expression as contempt.[28] Other researchers have moved beyond the simple word-picture matching tests. In more recent experiments subjects have been asked to match the contempt expression to a story or to create their own potential elicitor of contempt, and in these tests contempt performs as well as other basic emotions.[29] While the data is certainly mixed, many now think that we have reason to characterize contempt as a basic emotion: contempt is, arguably, a unique affective response, found cross-culturally, which has a distinct facial expression. If this is right, then feeling theories should be able to acknowledge the existence of contempt, even if subjects are unable, through introspection, to identify a distinct feeling characteristic of contempt. The bodily changes characteristic of contempt may, through education, eventually come to be felt.

But even if feeling theories do have the resources to classify contempt as a unique emotion, these theories face two well-known, seemingly intractable, problems. First, feeling theories have trouble accounting for the *intentionality* of emotions. Second, these

---

28. Jonathan Haidt and Dacher Keltner, "Culture and Facial Expression: Open-ended Methods Find More Faces and a Gradient of Recognition," *Cognition and Emotion* 13, no. 3, (1999): 225–266; and David Matsumoto, "More Evidence for the Universality of a Contempt Expression," *Motivation and Emotion* 16, no. 4 (1992): 363–368.

29. Rosenberg and Ekman, "Conceptual and Methodological Issues in the Judgment of Facial Expressions of Emotion"; Haidt and Keltner, "Social Functions of Emotions at Four Levels of Analysis," *Cognition and Emotion* 13, no. 5 (1999): 505–521.

theories cannot explain how emotions can be *rational*. A brief consideration of these two familiar objections will help highlight several important features of contempt that will be difficult to capture on even the most sophisticated of feeling theories.

1.2 INTENTIONALITY, RATIONALITY, AND COGNITIVE THEORIES OF EMOTION

Contempt, like other emotions, is intentional: it is directed toward its object. When one is jealous or angry, for example, one is jealous *of* one's rival or angry *at* a slight; contempt is directed toward a person that the contemnor sees as failing to meet an important standard. Many have pointed out that feeling theories of emotion seem unable to capture emotions' intentionality, and this gives rise to a well-known argument against feeling theories: sensations of bodily changes lack intentionality; emotions have intentionality; therefore, emotions cannot be identified with sensations of bodily changes.[30]

Not only are emotions intentional, they can also be assessed as rational or irrational, fitting or unfitting.[31] I may, for instance, be called on to justify my anger in a way that I would never be called on to justify my headache; we can give reasons for our emotions

---

30. Many people make this objection to feeling theories. See, for example, Robert Solomon, "The Philosophy of Emotions," in *Handbook of Emotions*, ed. Michael Lewis, Jeannette M. Haviland-Jones, and Lisa Feldman Barrett (New York: Guildford Press, 2008); and Martha Nussbaum, *Upheavals of Thought*. For a defense of feeling theories against this charge, see Demian Whiting, "The Feeling Theory of Emotion and the Object-Directed Emotions," *European Journal of Philosophy* 19, no.2 (2011): 281–303. Some philosophers argue that pain (a sensation of bodily change) is actually a form of perception and thus intentional after all.

31. For a discussion of this claim, see Robert Solomon, *The Passions: Emotions and the Meaning of Life* (Indianapolis: Hackett Publishing Company, 1976); and Prinz, "Emotions Embodied."

in a way that we cannot give reasons for a neck spasm. But feeling theories cannot easily account for the fact that emotions may be assessed in terms of their rationality or reasonableness.

For some, the intentionality and rationality of emotions militate in favor of a cognitivist theory of emotion. There are, at this point, several distinct flavors of cognitivism, and no attempt will be made here to sort through all its different permutations. Most generally, cognitivists maintain that emotions are directly connected to propositional attitudes. According to the most robust versions of cognitivism, emotions are identified with judgments. To be afraid, for example, is to judge that the object of one's fear is dangerous. Other cognitivists offer more nuanced accounts according to which emotions are constituted by belief/desire complexes or affect-laden judgments.[32]

Cognitivism's attractions are clear: if emotions are constituted by judgments, then we can easily account for their intentionality and rationality. Judgments are widely recognized as being intentional, and emotions would, on this account, straightforwardly inherit their intentionality from the judgments that constitute them. So too, it is easy for a cognitivist to explain how emotions admit of rationality. Our judgments may fit or fail to fit the world, and we may have good and bad reasons for judging as we do. Since our judgments can be assessed in terms of their rationality, so too can our emotions.

But despite its theoretical virtues, we have good reasons to reject cognitivism (or at least the strongest versions of cognitivism in which emotions are identified with judgments or beliefs). The problems with cognitivist theories are well known: cognitivism cannot easily explain the *grip* that emotions have on us or

---

32. For an overview of the different kinds of cognitivism, see Ronald De Sousa, "Emotion," in the *Stanford Encyclopedia of Philosophy,* http://plato.stanford.edu/entries/emotion.

capture their distinctive phenomenology.[33] Nor can they account for emotions in most non-human animals.[34] But the most basic problem with cognitivism is that neither judgments nor beliefs seem to be necessary or sufficient for emotions. You may, for example, correctly judge that triangulate spiders (a benign house spider) are harmless, yet respond with fear when you encounter one in your home. But if emotions are identified with judgments, then how could you judge that a triangulate spider is harmless and, at the very same time, fear it? Fear just is, according to robust forms of cognitivism, the judgment that the target is dangerous.[35] Examples like this suggest that judgments are not necessary for emotions. In addition, a person may correctly judge that a brown recluse (a poisonous spider) he finds in his closet is fearsome yet not feel afraid; he may, for example, be a spider enthusiast and experience only curiosity at this rare sighting. Examples like this show that judgments are not sufficient for emotions.

Feeling theories and strict cognitivist theories of emotion face such serious objections, that we should look elsewhere for an adequate account of emotion. I favor accounts that characterize emotions as ways of "seeing-as." According to this kind of approach, emotions are or are similar to perceptions; for example, to fear a spider is, in part, to *see it as* dangerous.[36] While there is a tension within such a stance, it is possible to experience unsupported emotions on this kind of account: one may believe or judge that

---

33. See, for example, William Alston, "Emotion and Feeling," *Encyclopedia of Philosophy*, vol. 2, ed. Paul Edwards (New York: Macmillan, 1967).
34. See Deigh, "Cognitivism in the Theory of Emotions."
35. See Cheshire Calhoun, "Cognitive Emotions?" in *What is an Emotion? Classic and Contemporary Readings*, ed. Robert Solomon, 2nd ed. (New York: Oxford University Press, 2003). These accounts may be characterized as a subtype of cognitivism, but they are far removed from the strict versions of cognitivism discussed above. Calhoun describes emotions as "cognitive sets, interpretive frameworks, patterns of attention."
36. "Cognitive Emotions?" 340. Robert C. Roberts characterizes emotions as "serious concern-based construals." "What an Emotion is: A Sketch" *Philosophical Review*

a spider is harmless, but nevertheless *see* it as dangerous. So too, one could judge a spider to be dangerous without construing it as such. These quasi-perceptual accounts of emotion are able to account for the problem cases that strict versions of cognitivism seem ill equipped to explain or explain away.

To assert that emotions are quasi-perceptual is not to claim that they are completely analogous to sense perceptions. As many have pointed out, emotions, unlike sense perceptions, are "quick-and-dirty" responses.[37] As a result, they are more likely to mis-present the world; as cases of recalcitrant emotion show, emotions can continue to mis-present the world even when subjects acknowledge their unfittingness: one's fear of a triangulate spider may persist even when one knows that these spiders are not fearsome. Of course, sense perceptions can also mislead (think, for example of optical illusions like Müller-Lyer lines), but emotional perception is, given its quick-and-dirty nature, generally less reliable than sense perception.[38]

Rejecting robust forms of cognitivism need not involve denying that emotions can be assessed in terms of their rationality nor must one deny a connection between emotions and beliefs. According to quasi-perceptual accounts, emotions are partially constituted by "evaluative presentations."[39] To be afraid is to see

---

97, no. 2 (1988): 184. See also Ronald de Sousa, *The Rationality of Emotion* (Cambridge, MA: MIT Press, 1987), and Amélie Rorty, "Explaining Emotions," in *Explaining Emotions*, ed. Amélie Rorty (Los Angeles: University of California Press, 1980).

37. See, for example, Jenefer Robinson, *Deeper Than Reason: Emotion and its Role in Literature, Music and Art* (Oxford: Clarendon Press; New York: Oxford University Press, 2005).

38. For an argument against perceptual models of emotion based on the asymmetries between sense perception and emotion, see Michael S. Brady, "Emotions, Perceptions, and Reasons," in *Morality and the Emotions*, ed. Carla Bagnoli (Oxford: Oxford University Press, 2011).

39. Justin D'Arms and Daniel Jacobson use the term "evaluative presentation" in "The Moralistic Fallacy."

the target of one's fear as dangerous, while to be angry is to see the target as having harmed one in some way, and so on. These evaluative presentations are intentional and may fit or fail to fit the world, and may be supported by good reasons or lack such support. Responding to a triangulate spider with terror is an unfitting response, and if the fear is based on weak evidence, the person may be criticized as unreasonable. We can acknowledge that a person who is afraid of triangulate spiders will make a wide range of judgments about spiders and their fearsomeness without identifying his fear with any particular judgment or set of judgments. In short, we can acknowledge that emotions have distinctive ways of presenting the world and very often give rise to cognitions without maintaining that emotions should be identified with some belief or judgment.

Let's turn now to a consideration of contempt's evaluative presentation.

1.3 CONTEMPT'S EVALUATIVE PRESENTATION

There are, as I argue in section 1.4, two distinct kinds of contempt, and the way contempt is experienced will vary with the subject's culture and circumstance. Nevertheless, it is possible to isolate four central features of contempt's evaluative presentation. These are necessary and sufficient conditions for the contempt I'm concerned with in this book, although there are other forms of contempt that will fail to satisfy all four conditions. I discuss these derivative forms of contempt in section 1.6.

First, contempt is partially constituted by an appraisal of the *status* of the object of contempt. Due to a perceived failing or defect, contempt presents its target as having compromised her status vis-à-vis a standard that the contemnor endorses. In a society completely lacking status distinctions, contempt could not exist. But it is important to emphasize that contempt does not presuppose one single, fixed, determiner of status; contempt is a possible response even in societies with competing conceptions of status. Competing accounts of status make possible what William Ian Miller calls "upward contempt": the contempt that those of conventionally low status may come to feel for the high.[40] While the contemnor looks down upon the target of her contempt and sees him as her inferior, she can, at the same time, acknowledge that the target enjoys a higher status along some other dimension. Thus a lowly assistant may, for example, coherently harbor contempt for her famous and well-respected mentor; the assistant may acknowledge that her mentor enjoys a higher social status yet still see him as low vis-à-vis some standard she cares about, for example, humility.

In many instances, targets of contempt may not have *done* anything to open themselves up to being contemned; instead, they are simply seen as low. A racist may hold people of color in contempt, not because of anything the targets have done or anything he thinks they have done, but simply in virtue of their race. Contemnors may see targets as utterly worthless as human beings,[41] or as not fully meeting some standard.[42] This helps to explain the difference between contempt and resentment: resentment is a response to a perceived wrong done, and contempt is a response to a perceived failure to meet some standard. Contempt

---

40. See Miller, "Mutual Contempt and Democracy," in *Anatomy of Disgust*. I say more about upward contempt later in this chapter.

41. While contempt may sometimes present its target as utterly worthless as a human being, this is not a central feature of contempt. For a discussion of this point, see Mason, "Contempt as a Moral Attitude."

42. What it means to fail to meet a standard will vary. In some cases, simply having a certain trait will be sufficient to count as failing to meet a standard.

is *person-focused* as while resentment is *act-focused*.[43] As Michelle Mason points out, contempt's person-focus is reflected in our language:

> One typically *resents that* ___, is *indignant at* ___, or *expresses moral indignation* at ___, where what fills the blank is some propositional content referring to an act as performed by an agent or a state of affairs as brought about by an agent.... In contrast, one typically *holds* ___ *in contempt, regards* ___ *with contempt*, or *expresses contempt for* ___, where what fills the blanks are particular persons or groups of persons.[44]

In short, contempt is a response to perceived *badbeing* whereas hard feelings like resentment and guilt are responses to perceived *wrongdoing*.[45]

A few words need to be said about the standards at the heart of contempt. These standards are typically part of the subject's *personal baseline*.[46] The subject's personal baseline is her framework of values and attitudes that constitute her value system. One's personal baseline demarcates who one would not stoop to be. The baseline itself may not be co-extensive with one's current

---

43. I have borrowed the term "person-focus" from Mason, "Contempt as a Moral Attitude," 246.

44. Ibid.

45. Of course, badbeing and wrongdoing are related in various ways. Sometimes, a person's badbeing is revealed through his wrongdoing (i.e., some wrong done may reveal something about the person's character more generally).

46. I take the term "personal baseline" from Ben-Ze'ev: "The personal baseline, which actually expresses our values and attitudes, depends on many biological, social, personal, and contextual features; it is not a rigid entity, but a flexible framework enabling us to match it with our experiences. Such flexibility, however, is limited since our ability to change our values and attitudes is limited. The possibility of varying baselines is one reason why the same event occurring at different times may be associated with different emotional reactions." Aaron Ben-Ze'ev, *The Subtlety of Emotions* (Cambridge, MA: MIT Press, 2001), 19.

traits, qualities, and circumstances. Often, one expresses one's baseline in hypotheticals: "If I won the lottery, I would stay grounded" or "If I worked in sales, I would always treat customers with respect." Contempt is typically a response to someone who has failed to meet a standard that is part of the contemnor's personal baseline. The subject must care about the standard in order to contemn those who fail to meet it; she must regard the perceived failing as important to her in some way.

Second, contempt is what we might call a *globalist* response toward persons. Like shame and disgust, contempt takes *whole persons* as its object. To describe an emotion as globalist is to claim that it is a totalizing response. The distinction between globalist attitudes and non-globalist attitudes is most clearly seen in the distinction between shame and guilt. When one is ashamed, one's whole self seems compromised. Guilt, on the other hand, does not involve this global sense of diminishment; instead, one feels remorse for what one has done.[47] When we respond to someone with contempt, we see him as low as a person and not merely as a person who has done wrong.

Some will dispute my claim that contempt is a globalist emotion. Aaron Ben-Ze'ev, for example, explicitly denies contempt's globalism: "the inferiority associated with contempt does not have to be global: it can merely refer to a few aspects of the other person's characteristics. I can feel contempt for another person's accent or looks but still realize her general superior status."[48] While

---

47. June Price Tangney and Ronda L. Dearing note that when a person feels shame for some failing, "he views the causes of this transgression as likely to affect many aspects of his life as a characteristic of the type of person he is—disloyal, untrustworthy, immoral, even reprehensible! In short, he makes attributions to quite fundamental features of himself that have much broader implications beyond the specific transgression at hand (global attributions)." *Shame and Guilt* (New York: The Guilford Press, 2002), 54.

48. Ben-Ze'ev, *Subtlety of the Emotion*, 309.

it is possible to have contempt for someone who enjoys a conventionally higher status, I reject the claim that contempt can be compartmentalized in the way Ben-Ze'ev suggests. What is especially distinctive about contempt—at least the form of contempt that is the focus of this book—is its globalism. When Ben-Ze'ev says that we can have contempt for someone for his or her accent but still acknowledge the person's general superior status, what he means is that we can harbor contempt for someone yet still recognize that the target enjoys a high social status. But there are multiple grounds of status in this society, and our evaluations of persons can come apart from their generally recognized social status. Just as one can experience deep shame while acknowledging one's privileged social position, one can have contempt for another while recognizing the target's high social status. Thus the sorts of arguments that Ben-Ze'ev gives do not show that contempt is not a globalist emotion; absent further arguments to the contrary, we have no reason to deny contempt's globalism. This globalism does, however, pose potential problems for my limited defense of contempt: if contempt presents its object as all of one piece, then some will object that it can never be a fitting or morally apt response. (I consider the objection concerning contempt's fittingness in chapter 2 and the moral unsoundness objection in chapter 4).

Third, contempt has an important *comparative* or *reflexive* element. The contemnor makes a comparison between herself and the object of her contempt, and sees the contemned as inferior to her along some axis of comparison. This aspect of contempt is well described by David Hume.[49] On Hume's account, when we contemn someone, we regard the qualities of the target as they "really are in themselves," while at the same time making

---

49. While I think we have reason to reject Hume's general theory of emotion, he offers some important insights into contempt's evaluative presentation.

a comparison between our own qualities and the qualities of the target:

> In considering the qualities and circumstances of others, we may either regard them as they really are in themselves; or make a comparison betwixt them and our own qualities and circumstances; or may join these two methods of consideration. The good qualities of others, from the first point of view, produce love; from the second, humility; and from the third, respect; which is a mixture of these two passions. Their bad qualities, after the same manner, cause either hatred, or pride, or contempt, according to the light in which we survey them.[50]

For Hume, feeling contempt is a way of regarding the qualities of another and, at the very same time, a way of regarding one's own qualities and circumstances. Like a few other emotions (e.g., envy), contempt is *reflexive*, that is, the contemnor always "puts herself into" her feeling of contempt for another. Contempt's reflexivity distinguishes it from mere dislike or disapproval. While disapproval presents its object as having failed to meet some standard that the disapprover endorses, contempt involves the contemnor comparing herself to the target of her contempt. This comparative element is so central to contempt that one commentator claims that "[w]hat is common to all [contempt experiences] is one's relation to someone over whom one is claiming some superiority, the very assertion of the claim being identical with the manifestation of contempt. Contempt is itself the claim to relative superiority."[51]

---

50. David Hume, *A Treatise of Human Nature*, ed. David Norton and Mary Norton (Oxford: Oxford University Press, 2007), 250–251.
51. Miller, *Anatomy of Disgust*, 214.

Although contempt is clearly comparative, we should reject the suggestion that contempt can be *reduced* to a claim of relative superiority. As I hope to show in this chapter, contempt is a complex emotional response that resists this kind of reduction.

Some have argued that *all* emotions are comparative.[52] Perhaps this is true, but what is distinctive about contempt, envy, and other reflexive emotions is that they involve status comparisons between the target and subject. So, while gratitude is comparative because we feel grateful when we receive goods that exceed our expectations (i.e., we make a comparison between our expectations and what we actually receive), emotions like contempt and envy are comparative in a distinct sense: reflexive emotions involve status comparisons between subject and target using some standard drawn from the subject's personal baseline.

Every instance of contempt is reflexive, but not every token of contempt involves seeing oneself as superior to the target. Imagine someone who has utterly failed to meet his own personal baseline, such as an unwilling alcoholic who has lost his close friends and family members to his disease. Such a person may harbor contempt for alcoholics, including himself, but he need not take himself to be *superior* to other alcoholics. In this sort of case, the contemnor may have contempt for himself *and* for others who fail to meet his personal baseline; such a person sees these others as his inferior equals. It should be stressed, however, that these sorts of cases are relatively rare. In most instances, contempt involves the subject seeing herself as superior to the target, and this characteristic of contempt is part of what makes it an especially apt response to the vices of superiority.

Contempt's reflexivity may explain why some have dismissed contempt as a distorting emotion. Insofar as we are vulnerable to

---

52. Ben-Ze'ev, *Subtlety of Emotions*, 18–21.

self-deception, our intersubjective comparisons will likely become distorted. If, for example, the contemnor has an inflated sense of her own status, then any comparisons she makes between herself and the target will inherit these distortions. Those with an inflated sense of self-worth may be more liable to feelings of contempt than those who don't think so highly of themselves.

Finally, the subject of contempt characteristically *withdraws from*, and sees herself as having good reason to withdraw from, the target. This is reflected in the metaphors and gestures we use to express contempt. These metaphors are often spatial: the contemptuous look down their noses at the objects of their contempt and pour scorn over them.[53] And the gestures and facial expressions indicative of contempt often involve the creation or maintenance of distance between the contemnor and the contemned, for example, turning one's back on the target, plugging one's ears, refusing to shake hands, and the like.

Although contempt typically presents its target as someone to be kept at arms length, this need not entail that the contemnor forgo all forms of engagement with the contemned. Consider, for example, the contempt some Americans feel for former president George W. Bush. If you feel contempt for Bush, your contempt may preclude you from *identifying with* him in a robust sense or listening to his criticisms of the new administration with an open mind. The types of engagement precluded by contempt will vary depending upon the exact nature of the relationship between contemnor and contemned. So while contempt for a politician might

---

53. Miller points out that the metaphors used to describe contempt differ markedly from the metaphors used to describe disgust: "Disgust is bound to metaphors of sensation or it is not disgust; it needs images of bad taste, foul smells, creepy touchings, ugly sights, bodily secretions and excretions to articulate the judgments it asserts; contempt, in contrast, usually makes do with images of space and rank-order or various styles of ridicule and derision: looking down upon or looking askance at, or simply smiling or laughing at." *Anatomy of Disgust*, 218.

involve failing to listen to his policy positions with an open mind, contempt for someone who was once a good friend may involve things like refusing to return her calls or deciding not to invite her to important celebrations.

Contempt's disengagement helps to explain certain asymmetries in our emotional responses that arise when we are in the position of observers rather than participants. Consider, for example, what Michael Stocker says about how our emotional responses to a given situation shift dramatically depending upon our perspective:

> Or consider another case: parking a car well out from the side of the road, rather than puling close to the curb. We know many people who react with amused contempt to any driver who parks this way delaying others. But when they, themselves, suffer such delays, they typically react with annoyance, even anger, rarely with contempt. And still more rarely—and then in only somewhat special frames of mind, such as some forms of detachment and ruefulness—do they react with amused contempt.[54]

The reason why we tend to feel anger in some cases and contempt in others has to do with contempt's characteristic withdrawal: when we see ourselves as *wronged* by someone's actions, we often seek to engage the wrongdoer, demanding an explanation or apology; contempt, on the other hand, motivates withdrawal rather than engagement.[55] Anger and contempt are not incompatible with

---

54. Michael Stocker and Elizabeth Hegeman, *Valuing Emotions* (Cambridge: Cambridge University Press, 1996), 317.
55. For a discussion of the role that closeness and identification plays in Aristotle's conception of the angry man, see ibid., 307–320.

one another, but their motivational tendencies do create a tension between them. In fact, there is a fundamental tension between any emotion that stresses closeness or intimacy and contempt. For example, love and contempt are in tension with one another in this sense.[56]

To summarize, contempt is a way of negatively and comparatively regarding or attending to someone who is presented as falling below the contemnor's personal baseline. This form of regard constitutes a withdrawal from the target and may motivate further withdrawal.

Those who harbor contempt will also be disposed to *act* in certain ways and to form additional attitudes on the basis of their contempt. Contempt's behavioral and attitudinal dispositions are varied and culturally dependent, but many of these dispositions will manifest the disengagement and reflexivity at contempt's core.

---

56. Niko Kolodny describes the tension between love and contempt in the following case: "one may fall out of love with someone because one loses respect for him: because his behavior, for example, attracts one's contempt or indignation. Imagine the wife of a once reputable historian, who has since devoted himself to denying the holocaust. He does this, she comes to realize, because the acclaim he receives from neo-Nazi organizations serves what is now revealed as his boundless intellectual vanity. As far as his work is concerned, this is all that matters to him; he gives no thought to its integrity, much less to the harm it causes. Although she does not see this shift as a betrayal of her, and although he continues to have and express deep concern for her, she finds that she cannot respect what he as become, and so cannot love him." "Love as Valuing a Relationship," *Philosophical Review* 112, no. 2 (2003): 164. While there is a tension between love and contempt, I would offer a different description of this tension. As Kolodny sees it, the love that characterizes friendship and romantic relationships is incompatible with contempt because this kind of love is *egalitarian*: both parties view the other as someone with equal status. Insofar as contempt presents its object as low or base, it interferes with the lover's ability to see her beloved as her status equal. I'm not sure that love is quite as egalitarian as Kolodny seems to assume. As I see it, what contempt threatens is not the equal status that is supposedly essential to love and friendship, but the kind of *intimacy* or *closeness* that characterizes these relationships. Contempt's characteristic withdrawal is in tension with love's characteristic approach. As I note in the text, I don't think that contempt is incompatible with love—one may love and harbor contempt for the same person without being irrational or unreasonable; but there is a motivational tension between these attitudes.

WHAT IS CONTEMPT?

Refusing to invite someone to a gathering or declining to shake someone's hand are two common behavioral dispositions associated with, and expressive of, contempt. Refusing a handshake is such a paradigmatic expression of contempt that when someone *does* shake the hand of a person generally regarded as contemptible, there is often an outpouring of condemnation. For example, in 2005 Prince Charles ignited a controversy in the international press when he shook the hand of Zimbabwean president Robert Mugabe.[57] Critics insisted that Prince Charles should have kept his distance and refused Mugabe this gesture of respect.

Whether a particular action expresses contempt will depend upon a variety of social and cultural background conditions. While touching someone on the head may express scorn in some cultures, it is not expressive of contempt in others. In addition, the particular circumstances within a given culture will help to determine whether some behavior counts as an expression of contempt. Consider, for example, the following case of a potential juror charged with contempt of court for yawning while awaiting voir dire:[58]

> "You yawned rather audibly there. As a matter of fact, it was to the point that it was contemptuous," said Superior Court Judge Craig Veals, who was presiding over jury selection for an attempted murder trial.
> "I'm sorry, but I'm really bored," the juror replied.
> "I'm sorry?" the judge responded, and the juror repeated his statement.

---

57. "Prince's Mugabe handshake gaffe," *BBC News*, April 8, 2005, http://news.bbc.co.uk/2/hi/uk_news/4425385.stm. As we will see in later chapters, contempt may be compatible with the basic respect we owe all persons, but it is incompatible with certain *signs* of respect or honorifics.

58. Caitlin Liu, "Sleepy Juror Gets Rude Awakening," *Los Angeles Times*, April 20, 2005. http://articles.latimes.com/2005/apr/20/local/me-yawn20.

The judge called his attitude "lousy."

"Your boredom just cost you $1,000... I'm finding you in contempt," Veals said... "Are you quite so bored now?"

In many contexts, a yawn would simply be interpreted as a sign of fatigue, but within the context of a tightly controlled American courtroom it may be interpreted as an expression of contempt.[59]

1.4 ACTIVE AND PASSIVE CONTEMPT

So far, I've treated contempt as a single emotion and in so doing, I've glossed over an important distinction between two distinct forms of contempt. To begin thinking about these two kinds of contempt, consider Thomas Hobbes's rather surprising definition of contempt:

> Those things which we neither desire nor hate we are said to *contemn*, CONTEMPT being nothing else but an immobility or contumacy of the heart in resisting the action of certain

---

59. What interests me about this example is that the judge found the potential juror's yawning contemptuous, not that he charged him with contempt of court. But let me say a few words about contempt of court: Contempt of court is usually defined as any willful disobedience to or disrespect of the court, and it is punishable by fine or imprisonment. There are both civil and criminal contempt charges. Criminal contempt occurs when the person held in contempt actually interferes with the proper functioning of the court. For example, someone who directs obscenities at the presiding judge during a trial could reasonably be charged with criminal contempt, whereas willfully disobeying a court order may reasonably ground a charge of civil contempt. The latter charge is sometimes referred to as indirect contempt because it takes place away from the courtroom and evidence must be presented to the judge to establish the contempt. In offering this summary of contempt of court, I have relied on *Lectric Law Library's Legal Lexicon* "Contempt of Court," http://www.lectlaw.com/def/c118.htm: http://www.lectlaw.com/def/c118.htm.

things, and proceeding from that the heart is already moved otherwise, by other more potent objects, or from want of experience of them.[60]

For Hobbes, contempt is a kind of *inaction* or *lack of attention*. When we contemn something, we are neither inclined toward the thing or away from it; instead, we fail to pay it any mind. Let's call this "passive contempt." It might seem that passive contempt should be considered simply a *lack of interest* in the target. Nevertheless, Hobbes insists that passive contempt ought to be considered a passion in its own right.[61] His definition of contempt strikes many as odd since it seems quite removed from paradigmatic cases of contempt. Consider, for example, those who greeted Hosni Mubarak with the soles of their shoes after the president's speech in 2011. We would be hard pressed to describe the protesters' contempt for Mubarak as a kind of contumacy of the heart. Passive contempt involves being aware of the existence of the contemned in a very limited way, and to experience this sort of contempt is to notice and attend to a person just enough to ascertain that he is of no importance, but those who contemptuously protested Mubarak can't be said to be aware of him in a limited way. Instead, the protesters expressed what I call "active contempt." Their contempt for Mubarak was

---

60. Hobbes, *Leviathan*, pt. 1, chap. 6. Part of this passage is also quoted in Miller, *Anatomy of Disgust*, 213. I take the term "active contempt" from Miller. What he calls "Hobbesian contempt," I call "passive contempt."

61. See Miller, *Anatomy of Disgust*, 214. The idea that contempt involves treating the object of contempt as of little importance is not unique to Hobbes. Aristotle gives a similar account: in the *Rhetoric* he writes "Contempt is one kind of slighting: you feel contempt for what you consider unimportant, and it is just such things that you slight" (93). Slighting is defined as "the actively entertained opinion of something as obviously of no importance" (92). Aristotle, *Rhetoric*, in *The Rhetoric and the Poetics of Aristotle*, trans. Rhys Roberts and Ingram Bywater (New York: McGraw-Hill Companies, 1984).

characterized by hostility and active non-identification rather than indifference.⁶²

William Ian Miller argues that passive contempt is available only if certain background conditions are in place. Specifically, the contemnor must feel completely secure in his relative superiority vis-à-vis the person he scorns. This sense of security depends upon a society that keeps the lower orders "disattendable": "[passive contempt] depends upon a precise knowledge of where you stand relative to the other and of a corresponding confidence in the disattendability of the other."⁶³

Active and passive contempt are structurally, if not phenomenologically, quite similar. Both involve negatively and comparatively regarding someone who falls below the subject's personal baseline, and both forms of contempt involve withdrawal or disengagement from the target. What sets active contempt apart from its passive counterpart is that the former presents its target as *threatening* while the latter does not.⁶⁴ Passive and active contempt differ in their secondary appraisals: they both present their targets as comparatively low, but active contempt also

---

62. Margaret Urban Walker characterizes the difference between active and passive contempt as follows:
> Contempt is an attitude of distain that comes in two linked kinds. Contempt can be aggressive disrespect, hostility, and rejection to the point of violent and degrading treatment. Yet there is also a contempt that is complacency, lack of concern, and a lack of felt connection to what doesn't feel important or deserve attention. (*Moral Repair: Reconstructing Moral Relationships after Wrongdoing* [New York: Cambridge University Press, 2006], 226)

63. Miller, *Anatomy of Disgust*, 215. Miller notes that the term "disattendable" originates in the work of Erving Goffman.

64. Some will disagree with this assertion. Miller, for example, claims that what distinguishes contempt from disgust is that the former does not involve seeing the target as threatening: "contempt denies being threatened or operates by pretending that no threat exists; disgust necessarily admits the existence of danger and threat." *Anatomy of Disgust*, 251. I think Miller is mistaken. I say more about the kinds of threats to which contempt is an apt response in chap. 3.

presents its target as threatening.⁶⁵ Because of this, active contempt involves patterns of attention that are not found in passive contempt. However, should the social structures that render the target of passive contempt non-threatening break down, then passive contempt often will quickly morph into its active cousin.⁶⁶

In what follows, I explore the moral value and disvalue of *active* contempt, and unless I specify otherwise, I use "contempt" to refer to this form of the emotion. The political and social structures required for passive contempt necessarily undermine its moral value. We have independent reasons to prefer egalitarian societies in which persons compete for status to hierarchical societies with rigid status demarcations, but it is only within the latter societies that passive contempt is available as a response. Moreover, only active contempt can *answer* a certain range of vices.

1.5 CONTEMPT, HATRED, AND DISGUST

We've seen the ways in which contempt differs from resentment: resentment is focused on the target's *actions* and is characterized by *active engagement* whereas contempt is person-focused and

---

65. I take the term "secondary appraisal" from Robinson, *Deeper Than Reason*, 202. As she points out, many emotions (such as anger and fear) share primary appraisals but differ in terms of their secondary appraisals.

66. As Walker notes, passive contempt can quickly turn into active contempt: "The contempt of indifference and the contempt of hostility are linked: what we are comfortable complacently ignoring often becomes the focus of active hostility when it makes itself uncomfortably difficult to ignore, when it insists on our attention and connection. When we have blandly indifferent contempt for other people in their unjustly disadvantaged situations, we can become defensive, irritated, hostile or aggressive when these people seek to involve us in something that we are unwilling to see as our problem. We can become exceptionally resistant to exploring any connection to their disadvantage that might imply our responsibility for it, or for its repair." *Moral Repair*, 226.

motivates withdrawal. To further highlight contempt's distinct characteristics, consider how contempt compares to two other so-called "negative emotions": disgust and hatred.

1.5.1 Contempt and Disgust

Disgust is contempt's closest neighbor, and some have claimed that extreme contempt is almost indistinguishable from disgust.[67] At one time disgust was thought to be a knee-jerk response lacking any cognitive content, but this view has largely fallen into disfavor. The psychologist Paul Rozin and his colleagues have posited that disgust actually has a highly complex structure.[68] According to Rozin's analysis, disgust is a kind of revulsion at the idea of the (usually oral) incorporation of a contaminant. Objects of disgust are seen as contaminants rather than merely inappropriate objects of incorporation; for example, marigolds, paper, and sand are regarded as unfit to ingest, but they are not considered disgusting.[69]

Rozin distinguishes disgust from both distaste (a negative reaction motivated purely by sensory factors) and a sense of danger (a reaction based on the target's potential for harmful consequences). If subjects are asked to sniff a decay odor from two different vials that actually contain the same substance and are

---

67. Darwin, *Expression of the Emotions in Man and Animals*, 253.
68. While Rozin's account of disgust is dominant in the psychological literature, not everyone accepts his analysis. For an alternative account, see Daniel Kelly, *Yuck!: The Nature and Moral Significance of Disgust* (Cambridge, MA: MIT Press, 2011). Since my primary interest is in contempt, I will not attempt adjudicate debates within the disgust literature here.
69. Paul Rozin, Jonathan Haidt, and Clark McCauley, "Disgust," in *Handbook of Emotions*, ed. Michael Lewis and Jeannette Haviland-Jones, 2nd ed. (New York: Guilford Press, 2000). Also cited in Martha Nussbaum, *Hiding from Humanity: Disgust, Shame, and the Law* (Princeton, NJ: Princeton University Press, 2004). I've relied upon Nussbaum's helpful discussion of disgust in what follows.

then told that one vial contains feces while the other contains strong-smelling cheese, those who think they are smelling cheese are likely to find the odor pleasant, while those who think they are smelling feces are likely to describe the odor disgusting and repellant.[70] The conclusion that Rozin draws from many experiments of this kind is that it's the subject's *construal* of the target that contributes most to a disgust response.

Just as disgust is distinct from distaste, it is also distinct from a sense of danger. If assured of our safety, we will tolerate being in close proximity to many dangerous items, but this is not true of things that disgust us. For example, while most people would not be troubled by, and may even enjoy, looking at a collection of poisonous mushrooms displayed under glass in a museum exhibition, many could not tolerate looking at a piece of maggot-infested meat under the same conditions. Further, when the noxious element of a dangerous item is eliminated (e.g., a toxin is removed from food through cooking), subjects may be coaxed to ingest the item, but the same cannot be said for things subjects find disgusting. When presented with sterilized cockroaches, test subjects would not consume them, even if they reported believing that the roaches could not harm them.[71]

Contempt and disgust are similar in several respects. Both disgust and contempt present their objects as threatening, and both motivate withdrawal.[72] Disgust tends to motivate physical withdrawal, and contempt tends to motivate psychological withdrawal. That is, contempt is characterized by active, non-identification with the object of contempt. Despite the

---

70. Rozin and Fallon, "A Perspective on Disgust," *Psychological Review* 94, no. 1 (1987): 23–41.
71. Ibid., 25.
72. As I indicated earlier, this is only true of active contempt. When someone experiences passive contempt for another, the target is seen as harmless or not really "seen" at all.

similarities between the two attitudes, there are several important differences. First, and perhaps most obviously, disgust has a distinctive phenomenology and is often marked by strong somatic reactions like feelings of nausea. While some tokens of contempt may be quite visceral, it is usually not experienced in these ways.[73]

Second, contempt involves both hierarchical and comparative elements that are not present in disgust. Disgust is not reflexive: maggots crawling through a piece of rotting meat elicits disgust without the subject comparing herself to the meat. Even tokens of person-directed disgust lack this feature. One *recoils* from persons that disgust; comparative evaluations seem quite beside the point.

Third, the possible targets of disgust, while numerous, are more circumscribed than the possible targets of contempt. According to Rozin's analysis, the primary objects of disgust are things (or people) that are closely connected to animals, waste products, and decay. If someone were to feel disgusted by marigolds, we would dismiss their disgust as unfitting. But fitting objects of contempt are not constrained in this way; we may, for example, fittingly contemn hypocrites or arrogant blowhards even if we don't see any connection between these vices and contaminants.

This brings us to the most important difference between disgust and contempt: they are responses to very different kinds of threats. If we accept Rozin's analysis, disgust is a response to a contaminant. Martha Nussbaum has argued that in its moralized forms, disgust is a response to persons that engage in activities that remind us of our animal natures, as in those that violate sexual norms.[74] Apt contempt is a response to a very different kind of

---

73. For a discussion of the visceral nature of disgust and the more cerebral nature of contempt, see Miller, *Anatomy of Disgust*, 218.
74. Nussbaum *Hiding from Humanity*.

threat: superbia and the vices of superiority (see chap. 3). There is a story to be told about what makes the vices of superiority contemptible, but this story has nothing to do with waste products, decay, or failures that remind us of our animal nature. Instead, superbia threatens a social system under which we esteem and disesteem persons according to their merits.

1.5.2 Contempt and Hatred

"*Hatred* is a thing of the heart, *contempt* a thing of the head," declares Arthur Schopenhauer.[75] He goes on to argue that contempt and hatred are "decidedly antagonistic" toward one another and mutually exclusive because contempt precludes a certain basic respect for the target that hatred presupposes.[76] Schopenhauer is right to insist that contempt should be distinguished from hatred, and he is right to point out the tension between the two emotions, but he is wrong to claim that contempt and hatred are mutually exclusive.

There are many different kinds of hatred, and Jean Hampton's well-known analysis of hatred will serve as a helpful starting point for thinking about the similarities and differences between contempt and hatred. Hampton individuates four kinds of hatred: simple hatred, spite, malice, and moral hatred.[77] What Hampton refers to as *simple hatred* is "an intense dislike for or

---

75. Arthur Schopenhauer, *Essays and Aphorisms*, trans. Reginald John Hollingdale (London: Penguin Books, 1970), 170. Friedrich Nietzsche also compares hatred and contempt: "One does not hate as long as one still despises, but only those whom one esteems equal or higher." "Epigrams and Interludes," in *Beyond Good and Evil: Prelude to a Philosophy of the Future*, trans. Walter Kaufmann (New York: Vintage Books, 1966), 92.

76. Schopenhauer, *Essays and Aphorisms*, 170. In chap. 4 I argue that contempt and some forms of respect may not be incompatible after all.

77. Jeffrie Murphy and Jean Hampton, *Forgiveness and Mercy* (Cambridge: Cambridge University Press, 1988), 35–87.

a strong aversion to an object perceived as profoundly unpleasant, accompanied by the wish to see the odious thing removed or eliminated."[78] There is one important similarity between simple hatred and contempt: both attitudes present their targets as to be avoided. But simple hatred lacks the complex cognitive structure of contempt. The contemnor does not simply have an aversion to the target of her contempt. Instead, she withdraws from the target because she thinks he fails to meet some standard that she considers important. Moreover, contempt is always comparative, yet this reflexive element is missing from simple hatred.

Simple hatred can be distinguished from malice and spite. The malicious hater sees the object of his hate as "low" or "base" and is prompted to "get even" by diminishing the target in some way (e.g., vilifying the target or seeking his public censure).[79] If you maliciously hate someone, "you desire to see this hated person decrease, either by losing self-esteem or by literally losing value."[80] Spite is closely related to malicious hatred: "Whereas a malicious hater wants to achieve mastery over the hated one in order to be elevated above (or relative to) him, the spiteful hater wants 'company' at the bottom, and so desires to bring the hated one down to her level."[81] Like contempt, malicious and spiteful hatred are comparative: those who hate in these ways see their targets as comparatively low and seek to diminish the target's status. Yet malice and spite are both partially constituted by a desire to *harm* the target, and this is not an essential feature of contempt. Unlike the malicious and spiteful person, the contemptuous person is not necessarily motivated to strike out at the object of her contempt; instead, contempt motivates the non-identification discussed earlier.

78. Ibid., 60–61.
79. Ibid., 65.
80. Ibid.
81. Ibid., 76.

Hampton goes on to distinguish a final kind of hatred, which she terms "moral hatred":

> Much less simple is the kind of hatred towards human beings which is experienced in many moral contexts; for example, I may speak of hating the Nazis for what they did to the Jews, or hating the South African whites for their violence against blacks. I will call this *moral hatred:* it is an aversion to someone who has identified himself with an immoral cause or practice, prompted by moral indignation and accompanied by the wish to triumph over him and his cause or practice in the name of some fundamental moral principle or objective, most notably justice.[82]

Unlike the simple hater who feels a groundless aversion for the object of her hate, the moral hater can articulate reasons why she hates. Moral hatred "involves believing, by virtue of the insulter's association with the evil cause, that she has 'rotted' or 'gone bad' so that she now lacks some measure of goodness or moral health."[83]

Of the four kinds of hatred we've considered, moral hatred is the most similar to contempt; they are both structurally complex emotions based upon reasons that can be publicly articulated. Moreover, they are reflexive responses to persons who fail to meet subjects' personal baselines. But there are still important differences between moral hatred and contempt: most importantly, moral hatred, like anger, is characterized by the subject's active engagement with the target. Contempt, on the other hand, is characterized by disengagement and is partially constituted by the desire to withdraw from the target.

82. Ibid., 61.
83. Ibid., 80.

Is Schopenhauer right to insist that hatred is a thing of the heart while contempt is a thing of the head? As we have seen, there are many different kinds of hatred, and this makes the issue less straightforward than Schopenhauer appreciated. Nevertheless, there are some fundamental differences between contempt and hatred that Schopenhauer seems to be gesturing toward: hatred is more visceral than contempt and doesn't always presuppose a comparative evaluation of the target in the way that contempt does. In these respects, it is indeed fair to characterize contempt as a thing of the head and hatred a thing of the heart. But we should reject Schopenhauer's claim that contempt is always incompatible with hatred. Contempt can, and does, combine with a large and heterogeneous group of attitudes and emotions, including attitudes as diverse as hatred, disgust, pity, and amusement. There is, admittedly, a tension between hatred and contempt insofar as the former involves active engagement and the latter withdrawal; but such tensions are common features of our affective lives. Emotional, ambivalence is not uncommon, and this ambivalence can be quite entrenched before it reaches the level of irrationality or incoherence.[84] This ambivalence may take several forms: we may toggle between hatred and contempt; we may sometimes see the target as someone to be avoided and at other times desire active engagement. Alternatively, we may experience both emotions at the very same time and desire the engagement of moral hatred yet this desire may be trumped by contempt's characteristic withdrawal or vice versa. Thus while Schopenhauer was right to point to the tension between contempt and hatred, he is wrong to insist that they are fundamentally incompatible with one another.

---

84. For a discussion of emotional ambivalence and its implications for theories of emotion, see Patricia Greenspan "A Case of Mixed Feelings: Ambivalence and the Logic of Emotion," in *Philosophy and the Emotions: A Reader*, ed. Stephen Leighton (New York: Broadview Press, 2003).

1.6 POTENTIAL PROBLEM CASES

Some may object that it is impossible to make sense of contempt for non-persons or self-contempt on the characterization of contempt offered in this chapter. I will complete my account by considering these two objections.

1.6.1 Contempt for Non-Persons

If contempt is reflexive and involves seeing oneself as superior to the target of contempt, then this seems to rule out the very possibility of contempt for non-persons. However, even a cursory look at our practices reveals that we regularly use the language of contempt in response to non-persons; people are often described as harboring contempt for science, democracy, the world, laws and justice, and so on. Given that we seem to feel, harbor, and attribute to others contempt for non-persons, my characterization of contempt as person-focused and reflexive looks vulnerable to objection: either our everyday references to contempt for non-persons are confused and always unfitting, or my account should be rejected for its mischaracterization of contempt.

I have two responses to this objection: first, we can easily modify the account articulated in this chapter to make conceptual space for contempt for non-persons. Second, even though people do harbor contempt for non-persons, contempt for persons always enjoys a certain priority.

Contempt for persons and non-persons are each partially constituted by negative evaluations of the target and a desire to withdraw. Moreover, if one feels contempt for a non-person, one takes oneself to be justified in refusing to defer to certain conventions concerning how that thing ought to be treated. If, for example, one feels contempt for white zinfandel, one might take oneself to be justified in not observing proper wine pouring etiquette if one is forced to serve it at a dinner party. Contempt for a non-person depends upon the availability of certain background conditions that specify how the target (or objects like it) *ought* to be treated, and one cannot have contempt for white zinfandel absent some background understanding of how wine ought to be treated. Thus contempt for non-persons involves seeing the target as having failed to meet some standard and treating it accordingly. Contempt for non-persons is not reflexive in the way that person-directed contempt is, but it is comparative: one could only come to feel contempt for white zinfandel by comparing it to other wines and seeing it as coming up short in comparison. Since contempt for non-persons shares many characteristics of contempt for persons, my account can, without much difficulty, be extended to include contempt for non-persons.

Although contempt of court is officially a charge that can be brought against anyone who disrespects the court, in practice, people are held in contempt when they show contempt for the presiding judge who is taken to represent the court.[85] This points to an important aspect of contempt for non-persons: contempt for non-persons is parasitic upon contempt for persons. To see this, try to imagine a case of contempt for a non-person that is in no way associated with a person or persons. When it comes to disgust, this task is easy; we readily can feel disgust for a piece of rotting meat even if the meat is in no way associated with a person. But it is difficult to come up with an example of contempt for a non-person that is not, at bottom, directed toward persons who are in some way associated with the non-person. If *no one* enjoyed

---

85. *Lectric Law Library's Legal Lexicon*, "Contempt of Court," http://www.lectlaw.com/def/c118.htm.

white zinfandel or served it at their parties, then harboring contempt for it would be incoherent. This suggests that contempt is fundamentally person-directed even though a derivative form can be extended to non-persons.

While people can harbor contempt for non-persons, contempt is fundamentally a person-directed emotion. Contempt, like resentment but unlike fear, has a *moral shape*, that is, its evaluative presentation includes moral concepts, and moral features of the target or situation may be assessed in determining whether the emotion fits its target.[86] Resentment presents its target has having *done wrong*, and wrongdoing is a moral concept. To say that resentment has a moral shape is not to deny that that we can resent things like alarm clocks and other artifacts that cannot coherently be said to have done wrong. But when we resent alarm clocks we see them as if they have done wrong. That is, we imagine them as persons. Contempt presents its target as "low as a person," and this too is a fundamental moral concept. When we harbor contempt for non-persons we either see the objects of our contempt as persons or we harbor contempt for those persons associated in some way with the non-person.

1.6.2 Self-Contempt

I've argued that contempt is partially constituted by reflexivity and withdrawal. Given these two features, my account may be thought to render self-contempt impossible or incoherent. Self-contempt seems impossible unless we are willing to allow that each person has a plurality of "selves" such that one "self" can

---

86. I take the term "moral shape" and its gloss from D'Arms and Jacobson, "The Moralistic Fallacy," 87–88. While they don't discuss contempt, I think they would agree that it has at least a partially moral shape.

look down upon and withdraw from another in contempt. This characterization of the self would, at minimum, require some defense. If we reject this metaphysical picture, it may seem as though we cannot make sense of self-contempt on my account.

However, self-contempt can be rendered intelligible without invoking multiple selves in any sort of problematic way. Self-contempt involves the switching of perspectives, not multiple selves. In many cases, self-contempt is temporally bounded: we live our lives without any feelings of negative self-evaluation and are suddenly struck by self-contempt. In other cases, the self-contempt lingers, and we constantly see ourselves as low.

Self-contempt always involves taking up a different perspective on oneself. Namely, one takes up the perspective of the person one aspires to be as is reflected in one's personal baseline. In cases of being struck by self-contempt, we suddenly take up this perspective, whereas in cases of long-standing self-contempt, this is a perspective from which we regularly engage in self-evaluation. Given that we undergo this switch in perspectives, the reflexive element of contempt does not render self-contempt incoherent. Our actual self is seen to be inferior in comparison to the person we would like to be.

Does contempt's characteristic withdrawal render self-contempt incoherent? I don't think so. Recall that contempt's withdrawal is best understood as psychological withdrawal or active non-identification; the withdrawal that partially constitutes contempt may, but need not, involve physically withdrawing from the target. Since there is nothing puzzling about persons withdrawing from themselves in the ways that are characteristic of contempt (i.e., active non-identification), there is no reason to think that contempt's withdrawal renders self-contempt incoherent.

In short, we can make sense of self-contempt without invoking any metaphysically dubious entities such as multiple selves. Self-contempt (like self-love, self-acceptance, and self-hatred) does require a switching of perspectives and active non-identification, but this should not pose any ineliminable obstacles to its coherence.

* * *

Armed with an account of the nature of contempt, we are now in a position to begin exploring its role in a minimally acceptable morality. But before considering the positive contribution that contempt may make to our moral lives, we must first deal with an objection to contempt that some consider decisive. One distinguishing characteristic of contempt is its globalism: contempt presents its target as low as a person, and takes the *whole person* as its object. Some critics insist that this globalism renders *all* tokens of contempt unfitting; since even the worst scoundrel is not completely despicable, an emotion that presents persons as all of one piece will always mis-present its target. If this were right, then defenders of an anti-contempt ethic would be able to claim an important victory. For if contempt never correctly presents its target, then it is difficult to see how it could ever have a positive role to play in our moral lives.

Chapter 2

Contempt as a Fitting Globalist Emotion

In assessing our emotions, we often appeal to the notion of *fittingness*: to criticize an emotion as unfitting is to claim that it fails to accurately present the world in some respect. This is a deep and serious criticism to level against an affective response. In this chapter, I consider the charge that contempt is *always* unfitting in virtue of its globalism. Contempt focuses on persons as such and not simply persons' actions or particular traits; more specifically, contempt takes *whole persons* as its object, and this is what makes it a globalist emotion. Shame and admiration are also globalist in this sense, as are many tokens of love and hate. Some globalist emotions are thought to have an especially important role to play in the psychological life of the mature moral agent. But insofar as these emotions are partially constituted by global assessments of character, they are also viewed with suspicion. Objectors complain that these emotions (henceforth "globalist emotions") can never *fit* their targets and thus can never be all-things-considered appropriate.[1] This conclusion, if true, would have important

---

1. Some, like Justin D'Arms and Daniel Jacobson argue that fittingness is not a necessary or sufficient condition for all-things-considered appropriateness. See "The Moralistic Fallacy." But others, like John Doris, assume that fittingness *is* a necessary condition for all-things-considered appropriateness. See Doris, *Lack of Character*. One way to avoid the conclusion that we ought to give up our globalist emotions would be to defend the claim that fittingness is not a necessary condition for an emotion being all-things-considered appropriate. This will not be the tack I take. While I am

implications for moral psychology; these critics suggest that we ought to rid ourselves of the very emotions that others have argued are of central importance in the moral life.

Those who dismiss contempt and other globalist emotions as unfitting are making a mistake. This objection depends on a flawed characterization of the person-assessments at the heart of globalist emotions. Once we understand the nature of globalist emotions and we recognize that we may legitimately treat some traits as more important than others in our assessment of persons, then we ought to conclude that our globalist emotions can, at least in some cases, *fit* their targets and should not be summarily dismissed as unfitting.

My primary aim in this chapter is to defend contempt against the Fittingness Objection, but in taking on this task I also pose a more general challenge to philosophers who defend "fitting attitude" theories of value (see sec. 2.4). If my arguments succeed, appeals to fittingness will not be able to perform the heavy lifting that many meta-ethical theories demand.[2]

2.1 CAN CONTEMPT EVER FIT ITS TARGET?

To contemn is to negatively and comparatively regard or attend to someone who has fallen below some standard that is part of the subject's personal baseline; this form of regard constitutes a withdrawal from the target of contempt. Given this characterization

---

generally sympathetic to D'Arms and Jacobson's line of argument, I will not defend globalist emotions by insisting on the distinction between considerations of fit and all-things-considered appropriateness. Instead, I argue that globalist emotions can, in some cases, fit their targets.

2. The following discussion is drawn from my paper, "Globalist Attitudes and the Fittingness Objection," *Philosophical Quarterly* 61, no. 244 (2011): 449–472.

of its evaluative presentation, contempt will accurately present its target when the following four conditions are met:

1. The target of contempt has failed to meet some standard.
2. The failure to meet the standard implicates the whole person.
3. In light of the failure, the target of contempt has been rendered "low."
4. The failing is a reason to withdraw from the target of contempt.

Let's call these contempt's *fittingness conditions*. If a token of contempt satisfies every condition, it is *fitting*. In other words, it accurately or correctly presents its object. If a token of contempt fails to meet any of the above conditions, it is *unfitting* and therefore open to criticism on the grounds that it mis-presents its target. As should be clear, fittingness is distinct from moral propriety and reasonableness, and just because an emotion is fitting doesn't mean that it is all-things-considered appropriate.[3] Nevertheless, we do regularly appeal to fittingness as part of our evaluations of emotions.

The second fittingness condition is the most controversial; as it indicates, contempt is a *totalizing* attitude. This feature is what distinguishes globalist emotions from other emotional responses. It is this totalizing or global aspect of shame that Bernard Williams alludes to when he remarks that "in the experience of shame one's *whole being* seems diminished or lessened."[4]

---

3. I discuss contempt's moral appropriateness in subsequent chapters.
4. Bernard Williams, *Shame and Necessity* (Los Angeles: University of California Press, 1993), 89, emphasis added. Also quoted in Doris, *Lack of Character*, 155. Williams goes on to write: "In my experience of shame, the other sees all of me and all through me, even if the occasion of the shame is on my surface—for instance, in my appearance."

Williams argues that shame has an ineliminable role to play in our moral lives. In contrasting the roles of guilt and shame he writes:

> [Guilt] can direct one towards those who have been wronged or damaged, and demand reparation in the name, simply, of what has happened to them. But it cannot by itself help one to understand one's relations to those happenings, or to rebuild the self that has done these things and the world in which that self has to live. Only shame can do that, because it embodies conceptions of what one is and of how one is related to others.[5]

Thus, for Williams, it is shame's person-focus, as compared to guilt's act-focus, that gives shame a crucial role to play in an adequate moral psychology; it is only when we come to see and care about our failings and deficits of character, and appreciate how they affect who we are as persons, that we can begin to put our moral houses in order.

Despite the seeming significance of globalist emotions, critics have objected that these emotions can never *fit* their targets and for this reason ought to be eschewed. According to this line of thought, contempt's second fittingness condition can never be satisfied, and it will always mis-present its target.

Over the past decade, several philosophers have argued that empirical findings in social psychology pose serious threats to our traditional ideas about character and personality. This body of research is often referred to as "situationism" in order to emphasize the contribution that situational differences, as opposed to personal or characterological qualities, make to the explanation of human

---

5. Williams, *Shame and Necessity*, 94.

behavior. Situationists take themselves to have established that minor situational variations can radically alter human behavior, and they argue that these results undermine traditional understandings of moral character and personality. (Thanks to John Doris and Gilbert Harman this literature from social psychology is now well known, and I will not offer a summary of this research here.)[6]

According to Doris's interpretation, the evidence from social psychology suggests that we ought to reject *globalist conceptions of character*. Globalist conceptions of character present character as coherent, integrated, and having strong situation-resistant implications for behavior.[7] As he describes it, globalism about character involves a commitment to the following three theses:

(1.) *Consistency.* Character and personality traits are reliably manifested in trait-relevant behavior across a diversity of trait-relevant eliciting conditions that may vary widely in their conduciveness to the manifestation of the trait in question.

(2.) *Stability.* Character and personality traits are reliably manifested in trait-relevant behaviors over iterated trials of similar trait-relevant eliciting conditions.

(3.) *Evaluative integration.* In a given character or personality the occurrence of a trait with a particular evaluative valence is probabilistically related to the occurrence of other traits with similar evaluative valences.[8]

Doris's central claim is that globalist conceptions of character are empirically inadequate.[9] He rejects globalism and argues that we

---

6. See Doris, *Lack of Character;* and Gilbert Harman, "Moral Philosophy Meets Social Psychology: Virtue Ethics and the Fundamental Attribution Error," *Proceedings of The Aristotelian Society* 99 (1999): 315–331.
7. Doris, *Lack of Character*, 22–23.
8. Ibid., 22.
9. Ibid., 23.

should instead conceive of personality and character as *fragmented*, "an evaluatively disintegrated association of situation-specific local traits."[10]

According to Doris, accepting that our characters are fragmented will have important implications for the fittingness conditions of the globalist emotions. He writes: "[T]here is little assurance that the objects of disdain and its kin [i.e., other negative globalist emotions] will merit such an unfavorable response in all ethically relevant regards. Given the pervasive fragmentation of character, emotions like disdain will often fail to "fit" the person we've sized up for them."[11] Let's call this the Fittingness Objection:

Fittingness Objection: Globalist emotions present their objects as manifesting globalist character and personality traits. The evidence from social psychology demonstrates that persons' behavior displays cross-situational inconsistency. Therefore, globalist emotions fail to correctly present their targets.

For Doris, to say that S merits the globalist emotion of contempt, for instance, is to say that S has certain contempt-meriting traits, for example, haughtiness, and that these traits are *globalist*:

1. S has some mental features relevant to haughtiness.
2. S would engage in haughty behavior across a broad range of situations.

---

10. Ibid., 64. By "local traits" Doris means dispositions that are temporally stable yet sensitive to situational factors. I use the term "trait" in a rather loose sense in what follows. As I'm using the term, emotions, dispositions, values, commitments all count as traits of persons. At times I use the terms "characteristics" and "aspects" to refer to traits in this sense.
11. Ibid., 167.

3. S's *other* traits cohere with her haughtiness. S's other traits are either contempt-meriting or at least do not directly conflict with her contempt-meriting traits (e.g., she has no admirable traits).

But, according to the Fittingness Objection, the evidence from social psychology gives us reason to think that the vast majority of persons do not satisfy these three conditions. If this is right, then contempt and other globalist emotions will fail to fit their targets in all circumstances.

The Fittingness Objection calls into question the *accuracy* or *correctness* of globalist emotions. We may, and frequently do, evaluate emotions on other grounds, such as their moral or prudential value.[12] Nevertheless, we often explicitly appeal to considerations of *fit* when assessing emotions. For example, when we counsel someone "not to judge a book by its cover" or that remind him that "the grass is always greener on the other side of the fence," we are implicitly appealing to fittingness considerations.[13]

It is worth emphasizing that the Fittingness Objection does not depend upon an acceptance of Doris's overarching argument or a particular interpretation of the research from social psychology. Globalist emotions seem vulnerable to the Fittingness

---

12. Doris also argues that globalist emotions ought to be rejected on ethical grounds since they are "inimical to community, charity, and forgiveness." *Lack of Character*, 168. This chapter is focused on the Fittingness Objection, and I do not consider these other objections here. I return to the moral objections to contempt, including the objection that qua globalist attitude, contempt can never be morally appropriate, in chap. 4. While Doris offers these other arguments against globalist emotions, he clearly thinks that fittingness is a necessary, if not sufficient, condition for an emotion to be all-things-considered appropriate. This is evidenced by the fact that Doris cites the Fittingness Objection as a reason why we should eschew globalist attitudes altogether.

13. The grass-is-always-greener homily is discussed in D'Arms and Jacobson "The Moralistic Fallacy," 72.

Objection as soon as we acknowledge that most persons' behavior is inconsistent across situations and our characters are not monolithic. Consider, for example, what Michel de Montaigne writes about the inconstancy of persons: "Those who make a practice of comparing human actions are never so much at a loss as to put them together and in the same light; for they commonly contradict each other so strangely that it seems impossible that they have come from the same shop."[14] Given what we know about the inconstancy of persons, it is natural to worry that globalist emotions cannot fit their targets. We all contain multitudes, and it is difficult to understand how any particular globalist emotion token could be said to fit anything as complex as a human being. Although I focus on Doris's version of the objection in what follows, I hope it is clear that the Fittingness Objection is a serious and persistent objection to globalist emotions, and it does not depend upon a commitment to situationism.

The Fittingness Objection, as Doris presents it, is strikingly ambitious insofar as it calls on us to eschew *all* globalist emotions

---

14. Montaigne, "Of the Inconsistency of Our Actions," in *Selected Essays*, trans. Donald M. Frame (Roslyn, NY: Walter J. Black Inc., 1943), 117. He also writes: "There is some justification for basing a judgment of a man on the most ordinary acts of his life; but in view of the natural instability of our conduct and opinions, it has often seemed to me that even good authors are wrong to insist on weaving a consistent and solid fabric out of us. They choose one general characteristic, and go and arrange and interpret all a man's actions to fit their picture; and if they cannot twist them enough, they go and set them down to dissimulation" (118); "Not only does the wind of accident move me at will, but, besides, I move and disturb myself by the instability of my position; and anyone who observes carefully can hardly find himself twice in the same state. I give my soul now one face, now another, according to the direction in which I turn it. If I speak of myself in different ways, that is because I look at myself in different ways. All contradictions may be found in me by some twist and in some fashion. Bashful, insolent; chaste, lascivious; talkative, taciturn; tough, delicate; clever, stupid; surly, affable; lying, truthful; learned, ignorant; and liberal and miserly and prodigal: all this I see in myself to some extent according to how I turn; and whoever studies himself really attentively finds in himself, yes, even in his judgment, this gyration and discord" (122–123).

on the grounds of their supposed lack of fit. Let's call the claim that we should rid ourselves of our globalist emotions the Eliminativist Conclusion. The Fittingness Objection is notable because it purports to give us reasons for the Eliminativist Conclusion without delving into the messy business of considering the moral and prudential reasons for and against each globalist emotion. Thus the Fittingness Objection may seem especially compelling due to its apparent efficiency; in one quick move, the Fittingness Objection claims to give us decisive reason to reject as unfitting the very emotions that others have claimed are of central importance in our moral lives.

Doris says little about what it means for an emotion to fit, or fail to fit, its target, so it may be worth pausing here to consider what is involved in criticizing an emotion as unfitting. We are often concerned with the fittingness of particular emotion *tokens*. We might, for example, think that anger is sometimes justified but wonder if George's fury at the student who hands in an unstapled paper really fits what might be described as a minor slight or inconvenience. We may also assess emotion *types* as fitting or unfitting. A given emotion type may be assessed as fitting or unfitting depending upon whether its evaluative presentation accurately or correctly presents the world.[15] Phobias are often taken as paradigmatic examples of unfitting emotions. If someone suffers from catoptrophobia (fear of mirrors), he sees mirrors, and their reflections, as dangerous. Since mirrors are not dangerous, the catoptrophobic's fear offers a distorted presentation of the world.

Fittingness, as it is usually understood, describes a relation between an emotion and a target, and whether a given emotion fits a particular target depends on the properties of both the emotion

---

15. This is the position of D'Arms and Jacobson, "The Moralistic Fallacy," 68–69. As they see it, the fittingness of an emotion's evaluative presentation is analogous to the relation between a true belief and the world.

and the target. Those who press the Fittingness Objection insist that the evidence from social psychology provides us with a new understanding of persons, which undermines the fittingness of contempt and other globalist emotions. Globalist emotions take *whole persons* as their objects, and it is claimed that the evidence from social psychology shows that these emotions always mispresent their targets. If persons' behavior is largely determined by contingent situational factors, then an emotion that presents its object as all of one piece is, according to these critics, always unfitting.

2.2 DEFENDING CONTEMPT AGAINST THE FITTINGNESS OBJECTION

How devastating is the Fittingness Objection? Does it give us good reason to accept the Eliminativist Conclusion? In what follows, I will argue that the Fittingness Objection does not give us good reason to dismiss contempt and other globalist emotions as always unfitting. But before giving my argument for this claim, let me consider two alternative strategies for avoiding the Eliminativist Conclusion.

One might attempt to avoid the Eliminativist Conclusion by insisting that globalist emotions actually involve evaluations of *local traits*. As Doris repeatedly points out, the evidence from social psychology does not tell against the existence of local traits.[16] Given this, someone sympathetic to Doris's general line

---

16. Consider, for example, the following passage: "I allow for the possibility of temporally stable, situation-particular, 'local' traits that are associated with important individual differences in behavior. As I understand things, these local traits are likely to be extremely fine-grained; a person might be repeatedly helpful in iterated trials of the same situation and repeatedly unhelpful in trials of another, surprisingly similar, situation." Doris, *Lack of Character*, 25.

of argument might claim that globalist emotions can fit their objects after all. Since Doris will allow that we can make character judgments of the form "Jon is honest in conditions, a, b, and c," he would presumably concede that globalist emotions could fit their targets so long as they involve evaluations of local traits.[17] Thus someone sympathetic to the concerns behind the Fittingness Objection might try and avoid the Eliminativist Conclusion by arguing that localized versions of the globalist emotions could be fitting, for example, shame-as-a-ballroom-dancer, or contempt-for-someone's-taste-in-shoes, and so on.

If globalist emotions referenced only local traits, then they would not be vulnerable to the Fittingness Objection. On this interpretation, globalist emotions would not take as their intentional objects whole persons but only narrowly defined local traits or a collection of such traits. However, this is not a compelling strategy for defending the fittingness of globalist emotions. What is distinctive about these emotions is that they resist compartmentalization. Globalist emotions have what has been described as a "permeating quality," and this quality is what individuates these emotions from their neighbors.[18] For example, shame that tracked only local traits would be difficult to distinguish from guilt. Thus it is not possible to avoid the Fittingness Objection by claiming that these emotions *really* track, or really should track, local traits. To do so is to deny that globalist emotions, qua globalist emotions, can be fitting.

A second way one might attempt to avoid the Eliminativist Conclusion would be to insist that we interpret discourse concerning globalist emotions as a kind of shorthand to refer to

---

17. See ibid., 115, for an apparent endorsement of the suggestion that globalist attitudes should track local traits. Kate Abramson claims that there is no good reason to construe contempt as globalist. See "A Sentimentalist's Defense of Contempt, Shame, and Distain," 198.

18. Mason, "Contempt as a Moral Attitude," 274, n. 30.

the balance of past actions a person has performed.[19] On this interpretation, to admire X is to be committed to the view that X has performed more admirable acts than despicable acts, and to have contempt for X is to judge that X committed more contemptible than admirable acts. If our globalist emotions are simply shorthand for these sorts of judgments, then the Fittingness Objection will not give us reason to reject all globalist emotions as unfitting.

While this understanding of globalist emotions may help us avoid the Eliminativist Conclusion, it fails to capture the important sense in which globalist emotions are *person-focused* as opposed to *act-focused*. In taking up a globalist emotion, one is responding to the target in a way that cannot be reduced to shorthand about the balance of past actions performed. While these past actions may reveal a fault or provide evidence about the person, it is the person, not simply the person's past actions, that globalist emotions take as their objects. Were we to give up on the person-focus of our globalist emotions, then these emotions could not play the special and distinctive role that Williams and others have claimed for them.

For the reasons outlined, we cannot avoid the Eliminativist Conclusion by arguing that globalist emotions ought to track local traits or that globalist emotions are merely shorthand for the balance of past actions performed. Globalist emotions do take *whole persons* as their objects. However, the general strategy these responses share is on the right track: we can avoid the Eliminativist Conclusion by carefully considering globalist emotions' evaluative presentations.

---

19. Doris allows that we may retain "trait-talk" so long as it is understood in a particular way: "We may employ character terms as 'shorthand' for claims about the balance of actions performed—for example, 'bad person' for 'more often behaves deplorably than admirably'—without adverting to globalist personality structures." *Lack of Character*, 115.

Doris seems to assume that the globalism of globalist emotions entails that each and every trait of the target is evaluated under the guise of the globalist emotion, or at the very least, that the globalism entails that it is impossible for the target to have traits that run counter to the evaluative valence of the attitude.[20] If, for example, one feels contempt for a neighbor, one evaluates each and every one of the neighbor's traits as contemptible or one must deny that one's neighbor has any traits that run counter to the evaluative presentation of one's contempt, meaning that one must deny that the neighbor has any admirable traits. On this understanding of globalism, persons' purported lack of cross-situational consistency would provide us with a reason to reject globalist emotions as unfitting. But this is a mistaken characterization of the globalism at the heart of globalist emotions.

Globalist emotions are globalist not in the sense that each and every trait of the target is evaluated under the guise of the globalist emotion or in the sense that it is impossible for the target to have traits that run counter to the emotion's evaluative presentation. Instead, globalist emotions are globalist in the sense that they present some traits as *more important* than others in an overall assessment of the target. Globalist emotions do take whole persons as their objects, but the globalism of globalist emotions is compatible with the recognition of traits that are incompatible with the emotion's evaluative presentation. These traits are simply seen as *less important* to the overall evaluation

---

20. Immediately after claiming that the globalist emotions will often fail to fit their targets, Doris writes: "I have a tendency, inherited from my mother, to respond quite viscerally to the ethically cretinous segment of the nondisabled population that parks in spots reserved for the disabled. 'A jerk like that,' I often think in disgust, 'must be a dead loss.' But if what I've been saying is right, in this I'm very likely wrong: Being ethically handicapped with regard to parking spaces need not prevent one from being an understanding friend, a loving parent, or a conscientious co-worker." Ibid., 168. I'm grateful to Michelle Mason for helpful discussion concerning this point.

of the target.[21] The essential feature of globalist emotions is what we might call a kind of *evaluative prioritization* of their target's traits: in responding to some person with a globalist attitude we see some of the person's traits as more important than others. In shame, for example, shameful characteristics are presented as more important to the overall evaluation of the person than her admirable characteristics.

This account of globalism is supported by many of our responses to actions or characteristics that are inconsistent with our globalist emotions. Consider one's reaction upon learning that some person one has sized up for a globalist emotion actually manifests traits that run counter to the evaluative presentation of the attitude. If Doris were right, we should expect people to vociferously deny that the target of their globalist emotion could possibly have any traits that run counter to its evaluation. But this is not how we usually respond to such cases. Most of the time, we are not *shocked* to find out that someone we admire has some traits that are generally regarded as worthy of contempt or that someone we scorn has some admirable qualities. Nor do we necessarily feel pressure to give up our globalist emotions upon learning about traits that run counter to the evaluative presentation of our globalist emotions. Instead, we usually consider any traits that conflict with our globalist emotions to be *less important* to the overall evaluation of the person than the traits that cohere with our globalist emotions.

Globalist emotions are comparative: they present their targets as having some traits that are comparatively more important than others. They take whole persons as their objects since they treat prioritized traits as more important than targets' other traits.

---

21. Aaron Ben-Ze'ev makes a similar point in his discussion of the globalism of hate and love. See *Subtlety of Emotions*, 382.

If this characterization of globalism is correct, the Fittingness Objection gives us no reason to give up our globalist emotions. The evidence from social psychology cannot give us a reason to conclude that these emotions are always unfitting. Even if we accept that situational factors are far more predictive of behavior than characterological features, this does not give us reason to stop seeing some traits as more important than others in our overall assessments of persons. Once we appreciate that globalist emotions involve evaluative prioritizations, we ought to conclude that the Fittingness Objection does not show that our globalist emotions fail to fit their targets and gives us no reason to accept the Eliminativist Conclusion.[22]

2.3 FITTING EVALUATIVE PRIORITIZATIONS

A proper understanding of the globalism of globalist emotions gives us the resources to answer the Fittingness Objection and avoid the Eliminativist Conclusion. But under what conditions is it *fitting* to see some traits as more important than others in an overall evaluation of a person? That is, under what circumstances do globalist emotions, qua globalist emotions, *correctly* present their targets? If a given evaluative prioritization involves seeing

---

22. Other situationists might argue that the evidence from social psychology shows that persons do not have *any* traits whatsoever. This is not an objection to globalist emotions in particular but to any emotion that takes as its object traits of persons. Since my arguments in this chapter are directed toward those, like Doris, who think that our globalist emotions are *especially* objectionable, I will not take on this objection here. Very briefly, I think the evidence from social psychology is compatible with attributing *situational traits* to persons. Our relationships with other persons count as situations in the relevant sense. For a defense of situational traits that is compatible with the evidence from social psychology, see Candace L. Upton, *Situational Traits of Character: Dispositional Foundations and Implications for Moral Psychology and Friendship* (Lanham, MD: Lexington Books of Rowman & Littlefield, 2009).

trait *y* as more important than trait *x* in evaluating S, then this prioritization will be fitting if and only if *y* really *is* more important than *x* in an overall evaluation of S. In order to understand when a particular evaluative prioritization is fitting, we need to clarify this sense of "importance."

We normally distinguish between objective importance and subjective importance. Which sense of importance is relevant to the fittingness of globalist emotions? If by importance we mean subjective importance, then considering some trait or cluster of traits as more important than other traits would be to make a claim about the trait's relative significance to the evaluator given the evaluator's desires and preferences. If we were to understand the fittingness conditions of the globalist emotions in this way, then an evaluative prioritization would be fitting if the traits prioritized were more important by the subject's lights. But if this is all fittingness requires, then we couldn't make sense of our practices of using considerations of fit (or lack thereof) to criticize or attempt to change people's globalist emotions. On this interpretation, fittingness ceases to be a tool of criticism or persuasion.

Rather than reflecting what is subjectively important, globalist emotions are properly characterized as presenting some traits as *objectively* more important than others. If the emotion is fitting, the traits presented as important really are more important to the overall assessment of the target (and it is not the case that they *merely seem* important to the subject). But while the fittingness conditions for the globalist emotions are, in this sense, objective, they are also *subject-relative*. Specifically, the conditions under which a globalist emotion fits depends, in at least some cases, upon the relationship between the subject and the target.

In a commentary on his book, Doris makes it clear that he assumes fittingness should be assessed from a third-personal perspective and that the relationship between target and subject is irrelevant to assessing whether an emotion fits its target: "In the main, *Lack of Character* was concerned with *third-personal* ethical regard. The origin of this emphasis...is my preoccupation with the historical, and to a greater extent, social scientific, record. We encounter the subjects of these narratives, by and large, in the third person, engaging these *hes* and *shes* as observers, rather than as enmeshed participants in relationships with them."[23] But once we acknowledge that our globalist emotions are globalist insofar as they are partially constituted by evaluative prioritizations, we will be in a position to appreciate the *positional* or *relational* elements of their fittingness conditions.

What would it mean for fittingness conditions to be both objective and subject-relative? Consider the following example:[24] Suppose Jamal is severely allergic to bees and his friend Lynne is not. Nevertheless, they are both *terrified* of bees and avoid them whenever possible. Fear presents its object as threatening or harmful, and while Jamal, given his allergy, has good reason to see bees as harmful, Lynne has no reason to see bees as anything more than a nuisance. In this example, it seems right to conclude that Jamal's fear of bees is fitting while Lynne's is not. As this case brings out, the fittingness conditions of fear may be subject-relative yet objective. The fittingness of Jamal's fear does not depend upon his *thoughts* about bees but on how harmful a bee sting would, in fact, *be* for him. Nevertheless, the content of fear has an indexical element: Jamal's fear presents bees as dangerous *for him*. Thus the fittingness conditions for fear are both objective and subject-relative.

23. Doris, "Replies: Evidence and Sensibility," *Philosophy and Phenomenological Research* 71, no. 3 (2005): 669. Emphasis in original.
24. I owe this example to an anonymous referee.

What I would like to suggest is that *our relationships* with persons (and not simply *our thoughts* about these relationships) can, like Jamal's allergy, contour the fittingness conditions of our globalist emotions.[25]

Let's begin thinking about the subject-relativity of the fittingness conditions of the globalist emotions by turning to some examples:

> **Steven's Shame**:[26] Steven is an artist who, for many years, created complex and challenging abstract oil paintings. In recent years, however, Steven has begun to churn out watercolors of landscapes and dogs because he finds that these paintings sell better than his earlier works. When an old friend from art school drops by Steven's gallery one afternoon, Steven is suddenly struck by a feeling of shame. He realizes that by painting kitschy scenes to satisfy the masses he has compromised his artistic vision. Not being a masochist, Steven attempts to convince himself that his shame is unfitting: "I'm kind to animals," he thinks, "And I always send thank-you cards to my grandmother." Despite reflecting on his many admirable characteristics, Steven's feeling of shame will not abate.

---

25. My arguments here develop and extend a line of thought originally articulated by Mason in "Contempt as a Moral Attitude." As part of her defense of contempt, Mason pauses to consider a version of the Fittingness Objection. In response, she suggests that while our characters are not monolithic, we can be justified in giving greater or lesser weight to particular character traits when evaluating someone's character. Specifically, she suggests that standing in a special relation to someone may justify the subject in "granting greater weight" to the target's negative character traits. She argues for this claim by considering an example of a man who contemptibly attempts to prostitute his wife while also admirably volunteering in a soup kitchen. Mason's line of thought is promising, but since this is not the main focus of her essay, her views are not fully developed.

26. The case of Steven's Shame is inspired by Thomas Hill's example in "Self-Respect Reconsidered," in *Autonomy and Self-Respect* (Cambridge: Cambridge University Press, 1991).

Steven's shame is fitting if it is the case that his lack of artistic integrity is objectively more important than his kindness to animals, gratitude toward his grandmother, and his many other fine traits. But we can't determine whether Steven's shame is fitting by ranking artistic integrity, kindness, and gratitude in terms of overall importance from some third-person perspective. Whether or not Steven's shame is fitting turns on whether Steven values artistic excellence and what role this value plays in his life. If artistic excellence is something that Steven has, for most of his life, prized highly, then his shame upon realizing how he has failed to meet the basic standards of artistic excellence may be fitting. However, I don't think this is to claim that the sense of importance at the heart of our evaluative prioritizations is merely subjective. Steven's *occurent thoughts* about artistic excellence are not directly relevant to whether his shame is fitting. We can, for example, imagine a version of the case in which Steven professes not to care about artistic excellence yet is struck by shame when his old friend visits, and we can sensibly ask whether his shame is fitting. In order to determine if Steven's shame is fitting, we must figure out what role valuing artistic excellence plays in Steven's life; we need to take up his perspective and evaluate whether his shame correctly presents him and the value he places on artistic integrity.[27]

We can give a similar characterization of the globalism of contempt:

Claude's Contempt: Claude is Steven's old friend from art school. As students, Steven and Claude formed a collective devoted to

---

27. Of course, if Steven professes not to care about artistic excellence and never acts in ways characteristic of someone who values artistic excellence, then we would have good reason to wonder if he ever did value artistic excellence at all. My point here is that what it is to value x does not depend exclusively on one's occurent thoughts about x.

abstract expressionism, and their friendship has always been based on their shared commitment to artistic excellence. When Claude visits Steven's studio he is momentarily confused by Steven's watercolors of golden retrievers. When Claude asks, Steven explains that he has stopped making abstract oil paintings altogether and spends all his time producing watercolors because he's discovered that they sell very well and win him the esteem of the members of the local arts community. When Claude learns that Steven has betrayed his artistic integrity, he can't help responding to Steven with contempt. Claude reminds himself of Steven's many admirable characteristics but cannot shake his scorn.

In this case, the importance Claude places on certain standards (e.g., a shared commitment to artistic excellence) gives him reason to bracket potentially conflicting information about Steven's positive characteristics as less important and take up a negative globalist emotion toward him. We can imagine that Steven's utter failure to meet certain "bottom line" standards, which partially constitute their relationship, makes it the case that Claude can correctly treat Steven's lack of artistic integrity as more important than his other good traits.[28]

Our relationships with others are partially constituted by certain standards and norms. In his book *Moral Dimensions*, T. M. Scanlon distinguishes between the "normative ideal of a relationship" and particular relationships of that kind.[29] The normative ideals are what differentiate relationship types, and they set the norms concerning how persons within a given relationship

---

28. There is, of course, a further question about the *moral propriety* of this sort of contempt. Here I am only concerned with the fittingness of contempt and other globalist attitudes. I take up the issue of contempt's moral appropriateness in subsequent chapters.

29. T. M. Scanlon, *Moral Dimensions: Permissibility, Meaning, Blame* (Cambridge, MA: Belknap Press of Harvard University Press, 2008), 133.

type should relate to one another. In addition, relations jointly work out the norms that will regulate their particular relationship. Many of our interactions with others occur within the context of ongoing relationships, and we see these persons as subject to the norms that partially constitute our relationships with them.[30] If it is true that our relationships with others are partially constituted by these normative expectations, then we have reasons to evaluate our relations in light of whether they have met, exceeded, or utterly failed to meet these expectations. From this perspective, what makes a given emotion fitting depends, to a large degree, on our relationship with the target. The norms and standards that partially constitute our relationships will shape the fittingness conditions of our emotions.

If our relationships with others contour the fittingness conditions of globalist emotions, though, an emotion directed at a particular target may be fitting from the perspective of one relationship yet fail to fit the very same target from the perspective of another relationship. Consider, for example, the case of Andrew's Admiration:

> **Andrew's Admiration**: Andrew runs Best Friends Animal Shelter where Steven volunteers every weekend. He has known Steven for the past ten years and has a great deal of admiration for him. The two are now quite close. In Andrew's time at the shelter, he has never seen a more dedicated volunteer. Not only is Steven completely dependable but he also goes out of his way to be of service. When Andrew hears Claude making disparaging remarks about Steven, Andrew is a bit taken aback, but his admiration of Steven is not shaken. Although Andrew recognizes that Claude may have reason to despise Steven, Andrew admires him greatly for being such a committed volunteer.

---

30. While we encounter many persons from within a structured web of robust relationships, we also have more attenuated moral relationships with all members of the moral community. I say more about these relationships in chap. 3.

While Steven is the target of two conflicting globalist emotions—contempt and admiration—both emotions may accurately present him given Claude and Andrew's distinct relationships with Steven. In the case of Claude and Steven, Steven has failed to meet the standard of artistic integrity. Given the nature of their relationship, Claude is in a position to demand that Steven meet this standard, and he expected him to do so. Steven has utterly failed to meet this standard and so Claude's contempt is, arguably, a fitting response from the perspective of their relationship. Given his relationship with Steven, Claude has reason to see this failing as especially important in his appraisal of his old friend. From the description of Andrew's admiration for Steven, it is clear that Steven has not violated any of the standards partially constitutive of his relationship with Andrew: Steven has not for example, been short-tempered with the animals or failed to show up for his shifts. From the perspective of his relationship with Steven, Andrew's admiration fits its target. Finally, given the unique relationship we have with ourselves, we can be justified in holding ourselves to a wide variety of standards. One explanation and defense of Steven's continued shame in the face of seemingly exculpatory evidence is that that the standard of being a person of artistic integrity is partially constitutive of his self-image. Hence, from the perspective of Steve's relationship with himself, he has good reason to see his failings here as more important than his praiseworthy qualities. In short, I am suggesting that the fittingness conditions for our globalist emotions are *contoured* by the relationship between the subject and target of the emotion.

In saying that the fittingness conditions for our globalist emotions are contoured by our relationships, I do not mean to deny that moral standards are sometimes relevant to their fittingness conditions. In determining whether some token of contempt, say, fits its target we may need to ask ourselves whether the traits treated as important are especially important from the moral point of view. Many of the norms that partially constitute our personal relationships are *moral* norms. Moreover, moral norms may constrain what sorts of standards we can hold our relations to. But, as the case of Claude's Contempt is supposed to illustrate, there is a subject-relativity inherent in the content of our globalist emotions. These emotions present certain traits as especially important given the relationship between the subject and the target of the emotion and the norms that partially constitute these relationships.

This is not to suggest that the norms which partially constitute our relationships are entirely provincial and cannot be used by those outside the relationship to evaluative the target. Suppose Steven were to act with an utter lack of artistic integrity and pass off the work of some other artist as his own and sell it in his gallery. Andrew might, under these conditions, have reason to respond to Steven with contempt, and his contempt might be fitting. But I wish to stress that subjects are sometimes in a position to make evaluative prioritizations that those outside the relationship are not in a position to make.

Some will object to my claim that Claude's contempt and Andrew's admiration can both be fitting. According to my proposal, whether a globalist emotion fits its target depends upon whether the traits prioritized are *objectively* more important than the target's other traits. How then can I claim that Claude's contempt and Andrew's admiration can both be fitting? How can I claim that two incompatible emotions are both objectively correct responses to Steven? Haven't I simply returned to the subjective sense of importance that I set aside at the beginning of this section?

I don't believe that I am invoking a subjective sense of importance here. We *are* sisters, and mothers, and friends, and colleagues; and insofar as we are parties to relationships, we are bound by the norms that partially constitute our relationships. While it's true that some relationships are more attitude-dependent than others, the norms that partially constitute these relationships are not themselves attitude-dependent. Whether we are bound by these norms is not simply a question of how we feel or how things subjectively appear to us.

It is worth pointing out that we do recognize other cases where the subject's position vis-à-vis the target changes the fittingness conditions of the subject's attitude. Consider, for example, how Brand Blanshard describes the way in which temporal distance between subject and target can contour the fittingness conditions of aversion:

> We read in the morning paper about a train wreck three miles off, in which many lost their lives. We note that no friends of ours were involved, and there is nothing we can do about it, yet we are much stirred. We then go into our study and read about certain "old unhappy far-off things and battles long ago" which involved, we know, much more misery than the wreck yesterday. About these gigantic far-off ills we feel only a gentle melancholy, and we are not, in our own eyes, guilty of impropriety in so feeling. Here the amounts of evil assigned to the events are the reverse of what they ought to be if the degrees of aversion accepted as fitting in our emotions were the measure of badness.[31]

If we are temporally close to a tragedy, it would be fitting to feel a great deal of aversion, yet if we are removed by many centuries, it would not be fitting to feel this same level of disapprobation.

---

31. Brand Blanshard, *Reason and Goodness* (New York: Macmillan, 1961), 288.

Here there is nothing about the content of "aversion" that makes it fitting to feel in the first case and not fitting to feel in the second. Instead, it is our temporal position vis-à-vis the target that makes our strong aversion fitting in the first case but not the second.

Whether a globalist emotion token is fitting depends upon: (1) the nature of the attitude, (2) the traits of the target, and (3) the relationship between the subject and target. The same emotion directed toward the same target may be fitting from the perspective of one relationship and fail to be fitting from the perspective of another relationship. While those who press the Fittingness Objection argue that we ought to dismiss globalist emotions *tout court*, whether an emotion fits its target can only be determined on a case-by-case basis. In order to assess the fittingness of some globalist emotion we must gain knowledge of the relationship between the target and subject and the norms that constitute this relationship. Given the wide variety of relationships in the world and the many different norms that partially constitute these relationships, it will be difficult to say, in a particular case, whether or not some emotion fits its target. Determining whether a particular globalist emotion is fitting is a more complicated task than those who press the Fittingness Objection appreciate.

Doris seems to understand the question "Is this globalist emotion fitting?" as simply a way of asking "from a third-person perspective, do I have enough evidence about this person to believe that for any globalist emotion Y, all of the person's traits are Y-able (or, at the very least, that none of the person's other traits conflict with Y)?" Doris thinks that the answer to this question is almost always no, and he argues that our globalist emotions are generally vulnerable to the Fittingness Objection. But this argument misconstrues the globalism of our globalist emotions and, as it stands, does not give us reason to reject all globalist emotions as unfitting. According to my alternative account, the fittingness conditions of globalist emotions will vary depending on the relationship between the subject and target. Given this, we can acknowledge that our characters are, in some sense, fragmented, yet we can still insist that many globalist emotion tokens fit their targets. The globalism of contempt gives us no reason to suppose that it will always be unfitting.

2.4 RELATIONSHIPS, FITTINGNESS, AND FITTING ATTITUDE ACCOUNTS OF VALUE

If my arguments are sound, one might wonder whether we ought to hold on to the idea of attitudinal "fittingness" at all. Some will object that there is a tension between the concept of fittingness and my suggestion that the fittingness conditions of globalist emotions are contoured by the relationship between the subject and target of these emotions. Fittingness, an objector might argue, must be insensitive to these sorts of background conditions.

I've tried to counter this objection in section 2.3, but I will say a bit more in response to this worry here. It is worth stressing that fittingness is thought to be analogous to correctness, and there is nothing odd about the claim that the correctness conditions for some judgment are relative to one's position. For example, different listeners, in different locations along a platform, will each hear an incoming train's whistle at a different pitch depending upon their location vis-à-vis the train. We can ask these listeners to report the whistle's pitch, and these listeners may be correct or incorrect about the pitch without it being the case that there is one, position-independent, correct answer to report concerning the whistle's pitch.[32] So too, subjects of the globalist emotions may, given their relationships, prioritize different traits when responding to a relation with a globalist attitude. They may be correct or mistaken about these prioritizations without there being a single, relationship-independent fact about which prioritizations are correct.

Philosophers who write about the fittingness of our emotions often assume or stipulate without argument that we must assess fittingness from an impartial, third-person perspective. Perhaps this assumption is so prevalent because those writing about fittingness are usually either defending or critiquing Fitting Attitude (FA) accounts of value. According to these accounts, value is analyzed in terms of what emotion would be a *fitting* response: the admirable is whatever would be fitting to admire, the contemptible is whatever would be fitting to contemn, and so on. Since proponents of FA accounts of value usually want to give an account of objective and non-relativized value, they are concerned only with whether an emotion fits its target from a non-relational perspective. While the debates about whether we should accept an FA account of value are obviously important, a full account of what makes an emotion fitting should not be hostage to this particular research program. Fittingness is significant for reasons that have nothing to do with FA accounts of value. As pointed out in the first section of this chapter, we often appeal to fittingness in criticizing or justifying our emotions, and the notion of fittingness that is relevant to these critical activities is, very often, fittingness given a particular relationship-dependent perspective. Moreover, FA accounts of value should not, if they are to be useful forms of

---

32. I have borrowed this example from Christopher Kutz, *Complicity: Ethics and Law for a Collective Age* (Cambridge: Cambridge University Press, 2000), 24. Kutz uses this example in his defense of the positionality of moral and legal accountability.

conceptual analysis, *simply stipulate* that fittingness is not to be assessed from a relationship-dependent perspective.[33]

If I'm right and the fittingness conditions of our globalist emotions may be contoured by our personal relationships, then this will pose a serious problem for FA accounts of value. When it comes to globalist emotions, the question we ought to ask is not "does emotion a fit target t?" but "does emotion a fit target t given relationship r?" As we have seen, this approach may lead us to conclude that a particular emotion may fit—and fail to fit—the very same target depending upon the relationship between the subject and target. If this is right, then it looks like defenders of FA accounts of value face a dilemma: on the one hand, they could allow that two incompatible emotions could both fit the same target. For example, Steven could be both contemptible and admirable. On the other hand, they could insist that we assess fittingness from a non-relational perspective. If they choose this second option, then they must give an account of this non-relational perspective. Presumably, this non-relational perspective *just is* the moral perspective. But a defender of a FA account of value risks circularity if she stipulates that the appropriate perspective for assessing the fittingness of our emotions is the moral perspective since FA accounts of value are supposed to be giving an account of morality itself.

To claim that the fittingness conditions of the globalist emotions vary depending upon the relationship between the subject and target is to acknowledge that there will be irresolvable disputes about whether a particular attitude fits its target. Suppose Claude and Andrew were debating whether Steven is contemptible; that is, they were trying to figure out whether Steven merits contempt. Claude and Andrew both encounter Steven as enmeshed

---

33. I am grateful to an anonymous referee for helping me sharpen this point.

participants in distinct relationships with him. From Claude's perspective Steven is contemptible and from Andrew's perspective Steven is admirable, and there is no way for Claude and Andrew to adjudicate this dispute since there is no common subject matter. They could, of course, agree to change the question and consider whether, from the moral perspective, Steven is indeed contemptible, but it must be noted that this is *not* the question they originally asked. To ask this new question is to ask whether, from the moral point of view, the contemptible characteristics of Steven are more important than his admirable characteristics. This is a perfectly sensible question to ask, but it is not identical to the question of whether contempt for Steven would be fitting.[34]

Some might object that my argument ignores that our evaluative prioritizations can legitimately be criticized. For example, a racist is someone who sees race as especially important in his overall assessment of persons. Yet most people think we can criticize the racist for just this prioritization; the racist gets something about the world wrong when he prioritizes racial categorizations. But if the fittingness conditions of our evaluative prioritizations are contoured by our personal relationships, couldn't the racist appeal to his relationship with people of other races to support the fittingness of his racial hatred? If, for instance, the racist is a slave master and the person he despises is his slave, couldn't the master appeal to the master/slave relationship in order to justify his racist contempt as fitting?

I don't think the racist can claim that his emotion is fitting by appealing to some standard that is partially constitutive of his relationships with the members of the despised racial group. I have argued that our relationships contour the fittingness conditions of

---

34. In chap. 3, I give an account of which faults, from the point of view of a minimally acceptable morality, most clearly merit contempt.

our globalist emotions, but not *every* relationship will contour the fittingness conditions in this way. Those who defend special obligations must distinguish between those relationships that give rise to special obligations and those relationships that do not. Defenders of special obligations don't want to maintain, for example, that John's special relationships with his fellow Vice Lords give him reason to shoot a member of the Bloods or provide reasons to aid a fellow Vice Lord and withhold aid from someone else. Philosophers have put forward a number of solutions to the problem of which relationships give rise to special obligations, but I won't go through these solutions here.[35] Just as some relationships may give rise to special obligations and others do not, only some relationships contour the fittingness conditions of our attitudes. A relationship may contour the fittingness conditions of our globalist emotions if and only if the relationship meets certain standards of morality or justice. Unfortunately, providing a full account of which relationships meet these standards is beyond the scope of this chapter.

But even without a full specification of which relationships contour the fittingness conditions of our globalist emotions, we can explain why the relationship between the slave and the slave master does not: this relationship is not an *interpersonal* relationship in the relevant sense because the slave master utterly fails to treat the slave as a *person*. Instead, the slave master treats the slave as property. Thus, while the slave and the slave master may be said to enjoy a relationship, it is not the kind of relationship that contours the fittingness conditions of globalist emotions.

Still, there might be a more serious worry about some globalist emotions implicit in this objection. The trouble with the racist

---

35. For a discussion of which relationships give rise to special obligations see Niko Kolodny, "Which Relationships Justify Partiality? General Considerations and Problem Cases," in *Partiality and Impartiality: Morality, Special Relationships and the Wider World*, ed. Brian Feltham and John Cottingham (Oxford: Oxford University Press, 2010).

is not simply that he sees race as important in the evaluation of other persons but that the emotions he harbors for members of despised racial groups are impervious to certain forms of critical engagement. If we point out members of the despised race who are esteemed and well-respected members of the community, chances are that the racist will not take this as a reason to give up his racist attitudes. I don't think it is an accident that negatively valenced globalist attitudes, such as those evinced by racists, are resistant to critical engagement. We tend to withdraw from those we evaluate negatively and globally (while we are drawn to engage those we evaluate positively and globally). Because of this, there is a tendency for negative globalist emotions to become hyper-resistant to revision.[36] The very structure of these emotions makes it difficult to assess reasons for revision. If this is right, then we do have reason to be cautious when taking up contempt and other negative globalist emotions; these emotions have some tendency to become utterly unmoored from their purported targets and are often constituted by inaccurate evaluative presentations. But while we ought to be cautious about harboring these emotions, we shouldn't dismiss all negatively valenced globalist emotions as unfitting. Instead, we should be aware of their tendency to distort our perceptions of their targets and engage in compensatory measures. Even as we withdraw from the targets of our negative globalist emotions, we ought to do our best to remain open to signs that targets do not merit our response.

* * *

The Fittingness Objection does not give us reason to accept the Eliminativist Conclusion. Globalist emotions involve seeing some

---

36. Ben-Ze'ev makes a similar point about hate. See *Subtlety of Emotions*, 401.

traits as more important than others in coming to an overall evaluation of the target, and this makes the fittingness conditions of globalist emotions fundamentally *relational*. Whether or not some token of contempt fits its object depends, in part, upon the relationship between the contemnor and the contemned.

Having shown that the Fittingness Objection does not give us reason to dismiss all tokens of contempt as unfitting, we are now in a position to consider contempt's positive contribution to our moral lives. In the next two chapters I will argue that contempt is, in at least some cases, the best response to what I call the "vices of superiority"; contempt may be both fitting and morally valuable. Although the fittingness conditions of contempt are relational, it does not follow that we must dismiss the concept of the "contemptible" altogether. Whether a *particular* token of contempt fits its target depends on the relationship between the contemnor and the contemned, but there are some failings that, on a minimally acceptable morality, call for contempt as a response. What makes some failing merit contempt as opposed to resentment or disgust? An adequate answer to this question will reveal a further relational aspect of contempt: contempt is apt in cases where the failing of the target has damaged the relationship between the target and subject. While all serious immorality brings relational harms, the vices of superiority damage relationships in a unique way. Contempt answers these vices in such a way as to ward off further damage.

Chapter 3

Contempt and the Vices of Superiority

In chapter 2 we saw that contempt is not rendered unfitting simply in virtue of its globalism. But even those who accept my arguments and are willing to acknowledge that contempt can sometimes fit its target may still insist upon an anti-contempt ethic. We have reasons, according to these critics, to object to contempt on *moral* grounds even if it is fitting. Contempt is a dismissive emotion that fails to respect the dignity of persons, and for this reason has no role to play in a minimally acceptable morality. Against this, I hope to show that contempt is the best response to the attitude at the core of what I will call the "vices of superiority."[1] Contempt *answers* these vices and mitigates their damage. Those who evince vices of superiority see themselves as having comparatively high status, desire that their status be recognized, and often attempt to exact esteem and deference on this basis. Contempt is, in many cases, the best way of responding to those who evince these vices, and it is both instrumentally and non-instrumentally valuable.

This is, no doubt, a surprising—perhaps even disturbing—claim; contempt is normally dismissed as an antisocial emotion

---

1. In what follows, the terms "merit" and "apt" refer to the moral appropriateness of an attitude, and "fittingness" refers to its correctness or accuracy. While we shouldn't conflate considerations of fit and moral appropriateness, an emotion is only morally appropriate if it is also fitting; fittingness is a necessary, but not sufficient, condition of the moral appropriateness of contempt. For a discussion of the different senses of affective "appropriateness," see D'Arms and Jacobson, "The Moralistic Fallacy."

that impairs human relationships rather than one that aptly answers vice. Against this, I argue that the withdrawal and disengagement characteristic of contempt can be morally salubrious. Moreover, a liability to contempt is partially constitutive of relationships that we have reason to value, and it plays a vital role in holding people responsible for their badbeing. In this chapter, I offer an overview of the vices of superiority and argue that these vices are especially contemptible on a minimally acceptable morality. In chapter 4, I argue that contempt has unappreciated moral value, both instrumental and non-instrumental. Since contempt is, in some cases, the best response to the damage wrought by the vices of superiority, we ought to strive to cultivate contempt in responding to those who evince these vices.

3.1 SUPERBIA AND VICES OF SUPERIORITY

The category of "the contemptible" is fundamentally relational. But acknowledging this does not preclude us from asking what sort of faults, in general, merit contempt on a minimally acceptable morality.

For each of the following vices, I invite the reader to consider whether contempt would, in general, be a fitting and apt response:[2]

1. Overweening ambition
2. Arrogance
3. Hypocrisy
4. Impatience
5. Cowardice

---

2. Some may wonder if these faults should all be considered *vices*. Since a complete discussion of this issue would take us too far afield, I will put it to one side.

6. Disloyalty
7. Apathy
8. Cruelty
9. Racism
10. Greed
11. Gullibility
12. Miserliness
13. Jealousy
14. Slothfulness
15. Recklessness
16. Bitterness
17. Envy
18. Gluttony
19. Lust
20. Wrath

Ambition, arrogance, hypocrisy, racism, and cowardice strike me as particularly contemptible while bitterness, envy, gluttony, lust, and wrath do not. Others may come up with somewhat different lists, but I imagine that most readers will report that arrogance and hypocrisy seem to call for contempt, while vices, such as gluttony, do not seem particularly contemptible. Recent work in social psychology provides indirect support for my classifications: researchers have shown that several of the faults I list as especially contemptible are the same faults that the majority of subjects predict will be met with contempt when given a questionnaire listing a variety of norm violations. Psychological studies of this sort obviously cannot settle the issue of which vices are contemptible—subjects may predict that others will respond with contempt when contempt would not be a fitting or merited response—but these studies do provide a helpful starting point for thinking about which faults, if any, are especially contemptible.

Why do people predict that faults like arrogance will be met with contempt and other faults will not? And if some faults are especially contemptible, what do these faults have in common?

My hypothesis is that the vices of superiority are especially contemptible.[3] Those who evince these vices see themselves as having a comparatively high status, desire that this high status be recognized, and, in paradigmatic cases, attempt to exact esteem and deference on this basis.[4] This hypothesis explains why some faults are intuitively contemptible while others are not. For example, the envious person doesn't, through his envy, presume a high status or attempt to exact esteem and deference, and this is why envy does not seem especially contemptible. The hypocrite, on the other hand, sees himself as enjoying a comparatively high status, desires that this status be recognized, and attempts to exact esteem and deference on this basis.

Status is a ground of esteem or deference. One's status, and the kind of esteem and deference that it is thought to merit, clearly depends on one's culture. At one time, being born into a titled family accorded one an elevated status that brought with it, and was thought to merit, esteem and deference; in modern democratic societies this is less likely to be the case. But even as its grounds change and evolve over time, status is still very much a part of our social lives. Judging by how little is written on the topic, it seems that most contemporary ethicists think that status, esteem, and deference are of little moral importance.[5] Against

---

3. I do not claim that the vices of superiority are the *only* faults that merit contempt. Instead, I hope to show that contempt is an especially apt response to these vices.

4. This claim will be refined in the following paragraphs. I am grateful to Akeel Bilgrami and Achille Varzi for a helpful discussion of these issues.

5. One notable exception is Kwame Anthony Appiah. Appiah has recently argued that what he calls "honor" has an important role to play in motivating moral revolutions. See *The Honor Code*.

this, I think ethicists should take status much more seriously that they currently do.

First, there is such a thing as moral status. Moral *status*, as I'm using the term here, is distinct from moral *standing*: one's moral status depends upon one's actions and character traits whereas one's moral standing is typically thought to derive from whatever features are sufficient for one to count as a member of the moral community.[6] According to many moral theories, one either has or lacks moral standing, but moral status comes in degrees. Mother Teresa, for example, is more worthy of moral esteem and deference than Kim Kardashian, and therefore has higher moral status. To say that a person is worthy of moral esteem and deference means that we have good reason to admire her as a moral exemplar, we should carefully consider her opinions about how to resolve moral difficulties, and so on. Of course, Kim Kardashian and Mother Teresa are both persons, and on a minimally acceptable morality each is owed equal recognition as such. We should, for example, give equal consideration to the rights of each when deciding what to do. But we can acknowledge this point without absurdly claiming that both women merit the same level of moral esteem and deference.[7] We can acknowledge that the women have equal moral standing while insisting that they have unequal moral status.

Second, ethicists have reasons to critically evaluate society's conception of what merits esteem and deference. There are multiple (and often competing) bases of status within a given society: celebrity, athletic prowess, wealth, good looks, and the like. One

---

6. Compare this use of "standing" and "status" to Linda Radzik, *Making Amends*, 143.

7. Stephen Darwall has distinguished two kinds of respect—appraisal respect and recognition respect—that track the distinction between standing and status that I've made here. Standing is the ground of recognition respect, whereas status grounds appraisal respect. See "Two Kinds of Respect," *Ethics* 88, no. 1(1977): 36–49. I return to this issue in chap. 4.

question we might ask is what sorts of characteristics, if any, offer *apt* bases for esteem and deference. Is it, for example, ever morally appropriate to esteem someone because of his celebrity or good looks, or are such evaluations always morally pernicious? We may offer critiques of societies or subcultures when they have accounts of status that we think we have reason to reject.

Finally, seeing oneself as having a higher status than others and desiring that this status be recognized may constitute a serious moral fault, especially when this involves dishonoring other persons or attempting to *exact* esteem and deference.[8] In this chapter, I focus my attention on the latter issue and aim to show that this attitude is at the heart of the vices of superiority and is best answered by contempt.

Let's consider some examples. The psychologist Paul Rozin has investigated persons' emotional reactions to norm violations. In one study, Rozin and his colleagues asked Japanese and American test subjects to read a list of moral violations and then determine an onlooker's facial expression or the most appropriate word to describe the onlooker's feelings. Below are three examples of the kinds of moral violations that subjects were asked to evaluate:

1. A PERSON is seeing someone steal a purse from a blind person.
2. A PERSON is watching a company executive refuse to sit next to a laborer on a train.
3. A PERSON is hearing about a 70-year-old male who has sex with a 17-year-old female.[9]

---

8. This claim will be explained and refined in the following paragraphs.
9. Paul Rozin, Laura Lowery, Sumio Imada, Jonathan Haidt, "The CAD Triad Hypothesis: A Mapping Between Three Moral Emotions (Contempt, Anger, Disgust) and Three Moral Codes (Community, Autonomy, Divinity)," *Journal of Personality and Social Psychology* 76, no. 4 (1999): 578.

When subjects were asked what emotion "the Person" in each scenario would experience, Rozin found that the onlooker was judged to harbor contempt for the business executive, anger for the thief, and disgust for the seventy-year-old.[10] Why do test subjects think observers would respond to the executive with contempt? While Rozin and his colleagues offer their own explanation of these results,[11] I think the imagined executive expresses a certain attitude through his actions: he seems to consider it *beneath* him to sit next to a common laborer. He takes himself to have a high status qua executive and he thinks this status entitles him to have a certain class of persons as seatmates. He is described in the prompt as "refusing" to sit next to the laborer, and the language of refusal suggests that he

---

10. Seventy percent of respondents indicated that the person in the first scenario would most likely experience anger; 60 percent of respondents indicated that the person in the second scenario would most likely experience contempt; and 80 percent of respondents indicated that the person in the third scenario would most likely experience disgust, "The CAD Triad Hypothesis," 580. It is worth stressing (again) that Rozin and his colleagues asked what the imagined observer *would* feel while I am interested in which responses are fitting and apt.

11. Rozin et al. argue that the results of this experiment lend support to Richard Shweder's taxonomy of ethical codes. I think we have reasons to reject this claim. Very briefly, even if we concede that Shweder's taxonomy is coherent (and it is not at all clear that it is), I don't think we should accept Rozin's claim that contempt tracks violations of Shweder's "Ethics of Community." First, it is easy to imagine violations of this code that would not seem to give rise to contempt. For example, burning the American flag in protest is surely a violation of a community norm, but Rozin's own research shows that the majority of subjects consider anger a more likely response to the flag-burner than contempt. Second, we can imagine failures that would likely give rise to contempt but which are not clear violations of the Ethics of Community (Rozin and his colleagues summarize the ethics of community as follows: "Community/hierarchy violations. In these cases an action is wrong because a person fails to carry out his or her duties within a community, or to the social hierarchy within the community. To decide if an action is wrong, you think about things like duty, role obligation, respect for authority, loyalty, group honor, interdependence, and the preservation of the community," 575–576.) Hypocrisy, for example, is often met with contempt, but it is not clear that it is best characterized as a violation of the Ethics of Community. Finally, it remains unclear under Shweder's taxonomy why contempt is an especially *apt* response to violations of the Ethics of Community.

has openly rejected, without good reason, an invitation or suggestion to sit. In refusing to take the seat the executive does not violate anyone's rights, and, if asked, he may well acknowledge the fundamental moral equality of all persons. But by refusing to sit next to the laborer, he *deprecates* or *dishonors* the man and others on the train. To dishonor someone, as I'm using the term, means to withhold the esteem and deference the person merits (i.e., to fail to show proper appreciation for the person's status); in this case, the executive doesn't simply withhold the esteem that the laborer merits, but instead he expresses disesteem for him without cause. By treating the laborer as someone too lowly to serve as a seatmate, the executive displays ill will for his fellow passenger. At the same time, by refusing to sit, he expresses his own sense of superiority and may be interpreted as attempting to exact an appreciation of what he regards as his high status in comparison to the laborer. The attitude expressed by this imagined executive is at the heart of the vices of superiority.[12]

What is most clearly objectionable about the executive's attitude is his belief that his position as an executive provides an *apt* ground for his high status: while I do not attempt to defend the claim here, many would acknowledge that executives do have high status in this society but would balk at the claim that business executives, as business executives, *merit* this status. And this explains what many find objectionable about this case. But while his false beliefs about what merits esteem and deference is part of

12. Of course, all we can assess is the attitude that the executive appears to express in the prompt. Perhaps the executive refused to sit in the unoccupied seat because he had a backache. If this were the reason for the executive's refusal, then his behavior would not give us evidence that he evinces a vice of superiority. But if the executive refuses to sit next the laborer because he thinks that to do so is beneath him qua business executive, as the description of the case suggests, then this attitude is morally objectionable and contemptible.

what makes the executive contemptible, there is more to the vices of superiority than simply believing you merit esteem and deference when you do not.

Let's consider another example: a woman, Anastasia, is talking on her cell phone while riding a Metro-North train to Connecticut. Her conversation becomes increasingly animated, and she begins to swear loudly and annoy her fellow passengers. Two employees approach her and ask her to lower her voice or move to the vestibule; if she continues to loudly swear in the compartment, they warn, she will be removed and fined. Anastasia does not take kindly to the admonishment and begins arguing with the employees. At one point she shouts, "Excuse me? Do you know what schools I've been to and how well educated I am?" Later, she exclaims, "I'm not a crazy person. I am a very well-educated person," and demands that the employees stop the train so that she can disembark.[13] Anastasia uses her presumed status as a "well-educated person" in an attempt to exact deference from the Metro-North employees whom she clearly regards as her inferiors.

Anastasia's meltdown differs from the case of the executive in several respects. Most importantly, being well educated *is*, arguably, an apt ground of status; we do think that those who are well educated merit a certain amount of esteem and deference, at least in some circumstances.[14] Despite this, there is still something troubling about Anastasia's attitude. A full account of the unsavory attitude evinced by Anastasia and the executive must take into

---

13. The example of Anastasia is inspired by the case of Hermon Raju whose meltdown on Metro-North received a great deal of media coverage. See, for example, Ben Yakas's "Video: 'Very Well-Educated Person' Flips out on Metro-North Train," http://gothamist.com/2011/06/16/video_very_well_educated_person_mak.php. I've fictionalized the example, but the words quoted are Raju's own.

14. I will not attempt to defend this claim here since it is not crucial to my overarching argument. My point is that even when we think a person *does* merit esteem and deference (for whatever reason), we may still think she evinces an objectionable attitude in attempting to exact this merited esteem and deference.

account what *kind* of deference and esteem subjects think their elevated status affords and what they do in response to what they see as a challenge to their status. Even though Anastasia's high status is aptly grounded in her educational accomplishments, she reveals an objectionable attitude regarding what she thinks she is entitled to in virtue of her status and through her attempt to exact deference from the Metro-North employees. As this example illustrates, it is objectionable for very well-educated persons to use their comparatively high status as a justification for rude behavior or as a defense against justified sanctions. In stressing her education, Anastasia demands that the Metro-North employees defer to her and ignore her infraction. And this attempt to *exact* deference on the basis of her status is part of what makes her attitude contemptible.

It is important to stress that those who evince the vices of superiority do not necessarily think that their status entails anything about their or others' rights or moral standing. Those who evince the vices of superiority can, and often do, recognize that other persons are their moral equals and are bearers of the same fundamental moral and political rights that all persons as persons enjoy. Nevertheless, people who evince these vices take themselves to be owed special esteem and deference given what they see as their comparatively high status. The executive may think that he deserves a seat in a VIP compartment, Anastasia may think that her education entitles her to ignore Metro-North employees, and so on, and they may perceive the world in this way while also sincerely believing that all persons have rights that must be respected.

In paradigmatic cases (such as the two examples we have considered so far), those who manifest a vice of superiority attempt to exact esteem and deference from others. But not every person who evinces a vice of superiority will, like our executive and

Anastasia, attempt to exact esteem and deference.[15] Attempting to exact esteem and deference is a common, but not necessary, feature of the vices of superiority. However, there is a clear connection between the beliefs and desires characteristic of these vices and the attempts to exact esteem and deference: if you believe that you have a comparatively high status and desire that this status be recognized, then you will be disposed to seek or attempt to exact this recognition if it is not given to you. If you are *already* being deferred to, then you are less likely to attempt to exact esteem and deference in this way. While it is possible for a person to believe that he merits esteem and deference, desire that others recognize his comparatively high status, yet forgo any attempt to exact esteem and deference from others, it is highly unlikely for a person's attitudes to come apart from these exacting activities unless he is assured of his high status in some other way.

Insofar as there is this deep connection between the vices of superiority and attempts to exact esteem and deference, we might think this explains what is objectionable about these vices. Attempts to exact esteem and deference are likely to backfire, and we might be tempted to conclude that the badness of the vices of superiority can be fully explained by the imprudence of attempting to exact esteem and deference in the first place. As Jon Elster notes, "The general axiom in this domain is that nothing is so unimpressive as behaviour designed to impress."[16] Anastasia's assertion that she is well educated did not impress the Metro-North employees or her fellow passengers, and it is easy enough to come up with other cases that support Elster's axiom: think, for example, of the person who attempts to exact esteem

---

15. I thank Akeel Bilgrami for pressing me to say more about this point.

16. Jon Elster, *Sour Grapes: Studies in the Subversion of Rationality* (Cambridge: Cambridge University Press, 1983), 66. Also quoted in Geoffrey Brennan and Philip Pettit, "The Hidden Economy of Esteem," *Economics and Philosophy* 16 (2000): 82.

by name dropping or bragging about her professional accomplishments. Trying to impress is likely to be counter-productive, and we generally find braggarts and name-droppers disestimable. Given this, we might be tempted to characterize the fault at the heart of the vices of superiority as the fault of *trying* to exact esteem and deference. It is always objectionable, according to this line of thought, to attempt to exact esteem and deference from others. Attempts to do so will backfire and reveal the person to be calculating and manipulative, and they will not receive the esteem they so desperately desire.

While Anastasia's attempt at exacting deference was morally ugly, surely this kind of activity is not always objectionable; people regularly try and impress others without thereby meriting criticism. Suppose I'm hosting my first holiday dinner, and in an attempt to impress my new mother-in-law, I set out to make a first-rate sweet potato casserole. There doesn't seem to be anything objectionable about my attitude or behavior, and if others were to become aware of my attempt to exact esteem, it would not merit criticism. What accounts for the difference between this sort of case and the cases of Anastasia and the executive? In this case, I attempt to impress in order to *strengthen* my relationships with my extended family—I try to impress in order to create a memorable holiday and please my in-laws. Anastasia, on the other hand, attempts to impress in order to deflect criticism of her behavior. More to the point, Anastasia seeks esteem and deference at the *expense of others*: in stressing how well educated she is, she suggests that the Metro-North employees who sanctioned her were not adequately educated and their criticisms of her were therefore misplaced. That is, she attempts to use her high status to dishonor the employees and undermine their valid claims.

We could imagine another iteration of this case where my attempt to impress wouldn't seem quite so innocent. Suppose, for example, that I have an unjustified aversion to my sister-in-law, and I attempt to impress my in-laws with the casserole in order to show up my sister-in-law who arrives to the dinner empty-handed. In this case, my desire to impress impairs my relationships insofar as I seek esteem at *the expense of* another person. This suggests that what distinguishes innocuous esteem seeking from criticizable esteem seeking is whether the esteem seeking strengthens or impairs relationships.[17] In central cases, this will turn on whether the esteem seeking comes at *expense of others* or *for the sake of one's relationships with others*. Those who evince vices of superiority need not set out to damage their relationships. More often, they simply set out to procure some benefit and, in the process, end up damaging a relationship. But I suggest that it is the *relational damage* that sets the attitude at the heart of the vices of superiority apart from innocuous cases of esteem and deference seeking.

This suggestion gains support from considering cases where a person believes that she has a high status, desires that her status be recognized, and attempts to exact esteem and deference on this basis, yet does not manifest a fault. Think, for instance, of the teaching assistant who has a high status vis-à-vis her undergraduates (at least as far as her position and education goes), and who attempts to exact deference on this basis in order to maintain classroom control. She may, for example, set harsh penalties on late papers in order to encourage her students to turn their work in on time. In this case, there is no reason to suppose that the teaching assistant evinces a vice of superiority. That's because

---

17. Several philosophers argue that wrongdoing impairs our relationships with others. See, for example, Anne C. Minas, "God and Forgiveness," *Philosophical Quarterly* 25, no. 99 (1975): 138–150, Linda Radzik, *Making Amends*; and T. M. Scanlon, *Moral Dimensions*. What I wish to stress is that badbeing, as well as wrongdoing, impairs our relationships.

her beliefs concerning her relatively high status and her attempts to exact esteem and deference on this basis don't come at the *expense* of her students or damage the relationship she has with them. The student-teacher relationship always involves some status differential, and the teaching assistant does not impair this relationship when she reminds the students of her comparatively high status.

To better understand how the vices of superiority impair our relationships, consider two specific faults in this category: arrogance and hypocrisy. What arrogance, hypocrisy, and other vices of superiority have in common is an attitude that I call "superbia":

A person evinces superbia when the following conditions are satisfied:

1. The person believes he has a comparatively high status.
2. The person desires that his high status be recognized.
3. Through his beliefs about his status and his desire that it be recognized, the person manifests ill will.

These three conditions are necessary for an attitude to count as superbia and jointly they are sufficient. In central cases, a person who manifests this attitude will also satisfy a fourth condition:

4. The person attempts to exact esteem or deference at the expense of others.

Attempting to exact esteem and deference is characteristic of many cases of superbia, and it is through this attempt that many, like Anastasia and the executive, manifest their ill will. This fourth condition, however, is not necessary for superbia (though it may, when satisfied, render persons especially contemptible).

Superbia is objectionable for several reasons. In some cases, it is unfitting; as we saw in the case of the executive, persons may think they merit esteem and deference when they don't. In other cases, such as in the example involving Anastasia, a person may merit esteem and deference but make a mistake about what sort of esteem and deference can reasonably be expected or they may attempt to exact esteem and deference on the basis of their status. In all cases, superbia damages our personal and moral relations because it manifests ill will, and it is, for this reason, objectionable.

There is much philosophical debate about what makes some trait a virtue or vice, and philosophers have defended various accounts of how virtues are connected to motivation. In this book I aim to show that contempt is the best response to the relational damage brought about by superbia, and to make this case there is no need to first articulate and defend a specific account of the virtues. (If readers object to my referring to arrogance and hypocrisy as "vices" absent an overarching account of what makes some trait a vice, then they should feel free to replace my vice-talk with the language of "moral fault.")

3.2 HYPOCRISY AND ARROGANCE

Perhaps the two clearest examples of vices of superiority are arrogance and hypocrisy. While they differ from one another in many important respects, central to each is superbia: the hypocrite and the arrogant person see themselves as persons of high status, desire that others recognize this status, and in so doing manifest ill will. In this section, I sketch their main features in order to bring out how superbia structures each vice.

Arrogant people think highly of themselves, and we might be tempted to conclude that the defining feature of arrogance is the arrogant person's favorable opinion of herself. According to this understanding, to be arrogant is to believe that one is talented or virtuous or accomplished, and think highly of oneself in light of these praiseworthy characteristics. The corresponding virtue of modesty is, conversely, characterized as a kind of ignorance of one's accomplishments and praiseworthy traits.[18]

This description of arrogance captures some of what we criticize when we condemn someone as arrogant, but it cannot provide a complete account of the fault. Valerie Tiberius and John Walker argue that the common characterization of arrogance as thinking highly of oneself ought to be rejected. First, not all people who think highly of themselves are properly criticized as arrogant. The student who leaves her final exam believing that she did well and pleased with herself for her performance is not necessarily arrogant. Depending on the details of the case, we may instead conclude that she is appropriately self-confident. Self-confidence seems to preclude arrogance—those we describe as self-confident cannot, at the same time, be criticized as arrogant.[19] Moreover, it is difficult to see what could be vicious about having accurate beliefs about one's accomplishments and thinking highly of oneself on the basis of these beliefs. If the student really did do well on her exam, why would believing she did well and feeling pleased about her accomplishment betray a moral fault?[20]

If we recognize a distinction between self-confidence and arrogance, we might think that what differentiates the two is that arrogant people *inaccurately* think highly of themselves while self-confident people *accurately* think highly of themselves.

---

18. Julia Driver develops this sort of account of modesty. See *Uneasy Virtue* (New York: Cambridge University Press, 2001).
19. Valerie Tiberius and John D. Walker, "Arrogance," *American Philosophical Quarterly* 35, no. 4 (1998): 379.
20. Ibid.

That is, the arrogant lack good reasons for thinking highly of themselves while the self-confident have grounds for their positive self-assessments. But while many arrogant people do have an inflated estimation of their talents, the example involving Anastasia illustrates that a person can have accurate beliefs about her praiseworthy characteristics yet still be criticized as arrogant.[21] The badness of arrogance cannot be fully explained in terms of the inaccuracy of the arrogant person's beliefs about her abilities and accomplishments.

Perhaps the problem with arrogance is not that arrogant people have false beliefs about their accomplishments and good qualities but that that they think *highly of themselves* in light of their accomplishments and good qualities.[22] Anastasia, for example, might have accurate beliefs about her high status as a well-educated person, but she may be criticizable for thinking so highly of herself on that basis. But again, this characterization of arrogance does not allow us to distinguish between arrogance and self-confidence.

If the badness of arrogance cannot be fully explained in terms of the arrogant person's beliefs about her accomplishments and talents or her positive evaluation of herself on the basis of these talents and accomplishments, what is the bad-making feature of arrogance? According to Tiberius and Walker, it is the fact that arrogance impairs our interpersonal relationships: "the attitudes that are the essence of arrogance are inimical to the creation of relationships characterized by reciprocity and mutual enrichment."[23] Thus arrogance is a fault because it is an obstacle to forming valuable interpersonal relationships. Later, Tiberius and Walker admit that arrogance does not make such relationships

21. Ibid., 380.
22. Ibid.
23. Ibid., 386.

impossible, but they insist that it makes it very hard for the arrogant person to form and maintain genuine friendships.[24] Arrogant individuals, like Anastasia, think so highly of themselves that it is difficult for them to find persons whom them deem worthy of their friendship. Because of this, arrogance also deprives persons of the self-knowledge that comes from considering how others see them: since the arrogant person thinks so highly of herself in comparison to other people, she is unable to learn anything about herself by paying attention to how she is perceived by others.[25] Unable to give the opinions of others appropriate weight in her deliberations and evaluations, the arrogant person becomes mired in a kind of solipsism. In short, the problem with arrogance is that it makes it difficult to secure the important goods of friendship and self-knowledge.

Tiberius and Walker's relational account of arrogance is an improvement upon accounts that attempt to locate the badness of arrogance in the arrogant person's beliefs about her talents and accomplishments or positive self-evaluations, but it faces its own difficulties. They write as if the only relationships of value, and the only relationships that merit the honorific of "friendship," are relationships of *complete equality and reciprocity* in which each party will think the other worthy of the very same level of esteem and deference. According to this view, only those who see one another as complete status equals can form genuine friendships. The putative reason why the arrogant person cannot easily enjoy reciprocal relationships is that she believes she merits greater esteem than other people, and this belief makes it difficult for her to enter into relationships and impairs any relationships she does manage to form. But this is too quick. Believing that you merit

---

24. Ibid.
25. Ibid., 387.

more esteem and deference than another need not necessarily constitute a barrier to friendship. Suppose Katherine is a brilliant and widely admired neurosurgeon, and Sebastian is her old friend from medical school. Sebastian is bumbling and accident-prone and is not an especially good doctor. Katherine knows she is a talented surgeon, thinks highly of herself in light of her accomplishments, and believes she is more deserving of esteem and deference than Sebastian. Nevertheless, the two bonded at university, share interests in opera and mystery novels, and have many friends in common. Given their shared interests and history, we don't have reason to think that Katherine's self-evaluations will necessarily constitute a barrier to friendship with Sebastian. In fact, if Katherine believed that bumbling Sebastian was just as worthy of praise and esteem, then one might question the basis of their friendship; under these conditions, she would seem to evince a confused paternalism rather than friendly good will. As I've described the case, Katherine's downward-looking comparative evaluations take place within the context of an ongoing relationship of general good will and mutual interest. Under these conditions, there is no reason to think that her beliefs about her status or desire that it be recognized will necessarily impair her relationship with Sebastian or constitute a fault.

Arrogance does impair relationships, but not in the way Tiberius and Walker suggest. In central cases, relationships are impaired by persons who see themselves as meriting greater esteem or deference than their relations, who desire to see their high status recognized, and who *show ill will* either by dishonoring their relations or by attempting to exact esteem and deference at their relation's expense. In short, relationships are damaged by superbia. Suppose Katherine constantly puts Sebastian down in front of their mutual friends or regularly brags to him about her latest professional accomplishment. This sort of behavior expresses a kind of ill will that is incompatible with the norms of friendship, and over time this attitude would likely have a corrosive effect on their relationship. Sebastian could justifiably complain that Katherine was lording her superiority over him. If you care about your friend and his well-being, then you will not attempt to gain esteem and deference at his expense or refuse to give him the esteem and deference that he merits.

So far, I've stressed the way arrogant behavior—verbal put-downs or ribbings for example,—may damage our relationships. But in stressing arrogant acts, I do not intend to suggest that we can give a purely behavioral account of the fault. Even if her arrogance never led her to perform any arrogant acts, simply harboring superbia would impair Katherine's relationship with Sebastian. For through her unacted-upon arrogance she would see Sebastian as someone she could use as a tool to get others to recognize her high status. This attitude would, by itself, damage her relationship with him since in regarding him as a mere tool to gain esteem and deference, Katherine would be evincing ill will toward him. But while Katherine's unspoken and unacted-upon arrogance would impair her relationship with Sebastian, expressing this attitude through arrogant acts damages her relationship in a further way. For it is through the arrogant person's actions that she attempts to exact esteem and deference from others. How an arrogant individual goes about attempting to exact esteem and deference will vary from case to case. Katherine may attempt to exact the esteem of her colleagues by constantly teasing Sebastian and laughing at his clumsiness in such a way as to bring attention to her own dexterity. Conversely, the student who interrupts class discussion and rolls her eyes at others' contributions may not be seeking the esteem of her classmates but merely their deference. By sighing and rolling her eyes when they speak, she may seek to silence the other students in the class.

While those who evince the vices of superiority do not always attempt to exact esteem and deference, when they do, this makes their fault especially damaging.

Like arrogance, hypocrisy is structured by superbia. The word "hypocrisy" derives from the Greek Ὑπόκρισις meaning "the acting of a part on the stage,"[26] and central to many forms of hypocrisy is *pretense*: the hypocrite is someone who pretends to be someone he is not.[27] Due to this pretense, there is an inconsistency between the hypocrite's avowed commitments and what he actually believes. The man who publicly rails against homosexuality but is later discovered soliciting a male prostitute may be criticized as hypocritical because there is an obvious tension between what he publicly professes to believe and what he does in private. We might be tempted to characterize the badness of hypocrisy in terms of this inconsistency between what a hypocrite avows and what he does.

However, it isn't clear why this sort of inconsistency should render a person vulnerable to criticism. First, most of us are inconsistent in this way, but the charge of hypocrisy would lose its characteristic force if the vast majority of persons were open to censure on this basis. Second, it is not obvious why others should care about these sorts of inconsistencies.[28] Perhaps the lack of consistency between my avowed attitudes and actions gives *me* a reason to revise my attitudes or change my actions, but why think this inconsistency gives *you* reason to criticize me? Third,

---

26. *Oxford English Dictionary On-Line*, "Hypocrisy," http://www.oed.com.

27. Roger Crisp and Christopher Cowton argue that the hypocrisy of pretense is just one form of hypocrisy, and they criticize philosophers for not acknowledging the hypocrisy of blame, inconsistency, and complacency. See "Hypocrisy and Moral Seriousness," *American Philosophical Quarterly* 31, no. 4 (1994): 343–349. While pretense is not central to all forms of hypocrisy, it does play a role in many paradigmatic examples.

28. For more on this point, see R. Jay Wallace, "Hypocrisy, Moral Address, and the Equal Standing of Persons," *Philosophy & Public Affairs* 38, no. 4 (2010): 307–341.

concealing some aspects of ourselves may be morally important.[29] A certain inconsistency between a person's public persona and what he does privately may actually be expressive of the person's decorum or good manners rather than a fault. For these reasons, there must be more to the moral badness of hypocrisy than just an inconsistency between what a person publicly avows and what he does in private.

Perhaps it is the pretense and deception characteristic of hypocrisy that is morally troubling. Insofar as the hypocrite offends against norms of honesty, we may have reason to criticize hypocrites as vicious. But not all instances of deception are distinctly hypocritical. As Christine McKinnon notes, "We think of the hypocrite as one who dissembles or shams regarding her motives or intentions in regions where we take such things seriously, namely religion and morality, and probably also politics."[30] This is an improvement upon the suggestion that it's deception alone that makes hypocrisy a fault, but surely not just *any* pretense within these realms would count as hypocritical. Suppose someone pretended to be vicious according to the prevailing standards of virtue and vice. Such a person would seem confused—maybe even shameless—but we wouldn't describe the person as hypocritical. What is essential to hypocrisy is that one *pretends* to have virtuous or praiseworthy characteristics (relative to a particular community's conception of virtue or praiseworthiness) in order to gain esteem or deference from others.

The hypocrite sees himself as a person of high status and desires that this status be recognized. In central cases, he will pretend to be especially virtuous in order to exact others' admiration

---

29. See, for example, Thomas Nagel, "Concealment and Exposure," *Philosophy & Public Affairs* 27, no. 1 (1998): 3–30. Wallace also emphasizes this point (and cites Nagel) in "Hypocrisy, Moral Address, and the Equal Standing of Persons."

30. Christine McKinnon, "Hypocrisy, with a Note on Integrity," *American Philosophical Quarterly* 28, no 4 (1991): 321–330.

and deference as well as external goods such as political power or wealth. The hypocrite uses others, and the conventional understandings of virtue and vice, to exact esteem and deference for himself, and in this way he manifests ill will. Like the arrogant, the hypocrite harbors superbia.

The vices of superiority presuppose background norms concerning which traits merit esteem, and these norms will vary from society to society and between communities within societies. Sometimes, the norms concerning which traits merit esteem ought to be rejected as morally objectionable. Despite this, someone who attempts to exact esteem and deference by *pretending* to evince traits that are esteemed in order to secure external goods may evince a vice of superiority. For example, someone who pretended to be a Nazi sympathizer during the Second World War in an attempt to gain esteem and power would manifest superbia even if we categorically denounce Nazi ideology. Elisabeth Schwarzkopf, for instance, is especially contemptible insofar as she pretended to be a Nazi sympathizer in order to further her own career.[31] In fact, Schwarzkopf may be *more* contemptible—though less vicious—than those who were ideologically committed to the Nazi cause.

Like arrogance, hypocrisy impairs relationships. Consider Molière's Tartuffe: Tartuffe clearly thinks highly of himself in comparison to other people, and he uses ostentatious displays of apparent virtue in order to exact deference and esteem at others' expense. Many characters in the play are taken in by Tartuffe's pretense and come to see him as a paragon of virtue. Here's how Orgon describes meeting Tartuffe for the first time:

> I wish you'd seen how it turned out when first we met!
> Like me, you'd have been drawn to him from the outset.

---

31. I'm grateful to Akeel Bilgrami for a probing question about Schwarzkopf that led me to think more about this example.

> He came to church, and every day I saw that he
> Fell on his knees and bowed his head in front of me.
> The congregation as a whole became aware
> Of how much ardour he would pour into his prayer.
> He heaved great heavy sighs, and waved his arms around,
> And often he'd bend very low and kiss the ground.[32]

Throughout the play, Tartuffe makes a show of his apparent piety in order to exact esteem and deference and secure power. His pretense to piety often comes at the expense of other characters. When, for example, the maid Dorine pays him a visit, he theatrically pulls a handkerchief from his pocket and gives it to her with the following instructions:

> Cover your bosom, I don't want to see.
> The soul can be disturbed by such a wanton sight;
> I wouldn't want to have ideas if they're not right.

By making a spectacle of his apparent virtue—and in particular his supposed elevated moral status in comparison to Dorine—Tartuffe attempts to seem better than he is, at Dorine's expense, in order to exact esteem and deference from her and others.

Tartuffe's hypocrisy makes certain relationships impossible. As depicted in his interaction with Dorine, he puts others down in order to make himself look especially worthy of esteem. While friendship does not require equality in status, it does presuppose reciprocated good will, and good will is something Tartuffe utterly lacks. Of course, Tartuffe and Dorine are not friends, but other

---

32. Molière, Tartuffe, *The Misanthrope, Tartuffe, and other Plays*, ed. Maya Slater (New York: Oxford University Press, 2008), 142. The example of Tartuffe is also discussed in Judith Shklar, *Ordinary Vices*, (Cambridge, MA: Belknap Press of Harvard University Press, 1984).

relationships, even our "moral relationships," are characterized by a minimal level of good will (unless a person has given us reason to withhold it), and Tartuffe clearly lacks this good will. He lords his sense of own superiority over others in order to secure power, and the attitude he expresses through his feigned piety dishonors many of those he encounters. By unfairly treating her as a temptress and his moral inferior, he fails to give Dorine the esteem and deference she merits.

Some have argued that the badness of arrogance and hypocrisy comes from the way these vices "corrupt the souls" of those in their grip and that this corruption is what makes the vices of superiority vicious.[33] For example, arrogance has been said to "[subvert] the very qualities that make persons persons."[34] The vices of superiority are corrupting in two general ways; to see this, let's use hypocrisy as an example.

A person who knowingly evinces hypocrisy has cultivated a "public self" distinct from his private self. Given the sharp split between the hypocrite's public and private selves, it is impossible for a knowing hypocrite to wholeheartedly value what he takes himself to value. Suppose, for example, that Tartuffe takes himself to value power, and he knowingly pretends to value piety in an attempt to get the power he values and craves. To value something is to believe that it is valuable, to be vulnerable to a range of emotions concerning it, and to act in ways that respects its perceived value.[35] Due to his elaborate pretence, Tartuffe cannot

---

33. See Robin Dillon, "Arrogance, Self-Respect, and Personhood," *Journal of Consciousness Studies* 14, no 5–6 (2007): 101–126; and Gabriele Taylor, *Pride, Shame, and Guilt: Emotions of Self-Assessment* (Oxford: Clarendon Press; London; New York: Oxford University Press, 1985).

34. Dillon, "Arrogance, Self-Respect, and Personhood," 101.

35. For a full account of what is involved in valuing, see Samuel Scheffler, "Valuing," in *Equality and Tradition: Questions of Value in Moral and Political Theory* (New York: Oxford University Press, 2010).

actually value what he takes himself to value: if Tartuffe really values vice and power, then he would have and express positive attitudes toward gaining power and negative attitudes toward virtues, like piety, that constrain power. But this is not the attitude he expresses. Instead, he publicly cheers on his community's conception of virtue and quite dramatically condemns vice. Tartuffe refuses to publicly stand behind what he privately takes himself to value, and this ruse makes wholehearted valuing impossible. While someone might keep what they wholeheartedly value under wraps for a short period of time, if one *never* publicly stands behind what one takes oneself to value by expressing the relevant value-attitudes, then one doesn't wholeheartedly value it.

Unknowing hypocrites are self-deceived, and this self-deception undermines their capacity to value as well. Suppose, for example, that Tartuffe truly believes that his community's conception of virtue is valuable and also genuinely believes that he is an exemplar of piety. How could someone genuinely value virtue yet be disposed to lie, cheat, and cruelly manipulate others in order to gain wealth and power? Clearly such a person doesn't really value virtue after all. Like the knowing hypocrite, the unknowing hypocrite cannot wholeheartedly value what he takes himself to value. Even if Tartuffe genuinely believed that the conventional understanding of virtue is valuable, his emotions, motivations, and actions would belie a rather different attitude. If he is never distraught by his own lack of virtue or troubled by others' vices, then we should not conclude that he actually values virtue.

In short, the vices of superiority are corrupting insofar as they constitute barriers to valuing: those that evince these vices cannot wholeheartedly value what they take themselves to value. This is an especially serious form of corruption since one of the distinctive characteristics of persons is our capacity to value. In this way, the vices of superiority make it difficult for those who evince these vices to flourish as persons.

If the badness of the vices of superiority could be accounted for solely in terms of the way in which they corrupt their subjects, then it would be unclear why they merit an attitudinal response from others. For instance, your failure to flourish does not seem to give me reason to respond to you with contempt or any other hard feeling. However, I don't think the corrupting qualities of these vices fully accounts for their disvalue and moral badness; these vices also damage our relationships with other persons.

Those who evince vices of superiority will have a difficult time forming friendships, and the relationships they do manage to create will be impaired by their superbia. Friendship involves an expectation of reciprocated good will and those who evince these vices lack this good will. In seeing others as tools they may use to gain esteem and deference, they manifest ill will that damages their relationships. This relational impairment is a central aspect of what makes these vices vicious, and it is what calls for contempt as a response.

It isn't just our personal relationships that are impaired by the vices of superiority. Our *moral relationships*, more generally, are also corrupted by these vices. By "moral relationship" I mean the relationships that we have with all members of our moral community. The suggestion that we participate in moral relationships strikes some critics as implausible or even incoherent.[36] How can we be said to have "relationships" with strangers we will never

---

36. See, for example, Norvin Richards "Forgiveness," *Ethics* 99, no. 1 (1988): 77–97; and Samuel Scheffler "Morality and Reasonable Partiality," in *Equality and Tradition*. Other philosophers have defended the idea that we have moral relationships with all members of the moral community. Margaret Urban Walker describes our moral relationships as follows: "moral relations are those relations in which we reciprocally trust each other and ourselves to honor certain values and to avoid crossing certain boundaries out of a sense of responsibility." *Moral Repair*, 162. T. M. Scanlon

meet? Despite the apparent implausibility of the suggestion, we cannot fully understand the badness of the vices of superiority until we recognize the ways in which they impair our relationships with strangers as well as friends.

We care about the attitudes that others, including strangers, harbor toward us.[37] Many of our actions are motivated by a desire to win the esteem and avoid the disesteem of strangers. Consider a trivial example: psychologists have shown that whether people wash their hands after using a public toilet largely depends on whether they believe they are being observed: 77 percent of college women washed their hands after using a public toilet if they believed that a stranger was watching, but the rate of hand washing fell to 38 percent if the women believed that they were not being observed.[38] Presumably, most people recognize the hand-washing norm, want to avoid being disesteemed for failing to meet the norm, and for these reasons are more likely to wash their hands when they know they that they are being observed by a stranger. Our desires for esteem and the avoidance of disesteem doesn't just affect our bathroom habits; they are also important moral motivations.[39] Of course, these motivations are

---

claims that impairment to our moral relations "occurs when a person governs him- or herself in a way that shows a lack of concern with the justifiability of his or her actions, or an indifference to considerations that justifiable standards of conduct require one to attend to." *Moral Dimensions*, 141.

37. Peter Strawson makes this point in "Freedom and Resentment," 187–211.

38. Kristen Munger and Shelby J Harris, "Effects of an Observer on Handwashing in a Public Restroom," *Perceptual and Motor Skills* 69 (1989): 733–734. This experiment is discussed in Geoffrey Brennan and Philip Pettit, *The Economy of Esteem: An Essay on Civil and Political Society* (New York: Oxford University Press, 2004) 142–143.

39. Even moralists who worry about the perils of heteronomy acknowledge the power of our desire for esteem. Kant, for example, writes that the love of honor is a "constant companion to virtue." Kant, *Anthropology from a Pragmatic Point of View*, trans. V. L. Dowdell (Carbondale: Southern Illinois University Press, 1978), 257. This passage is also quoted in David Sussman, "Shame and Punishment in Kant's *Doctrine of Right*," 301.

easily corrupted; if we live in a community of moral cretins and see ourselves as members of their moral community, then our desire for their esteem will be disastrous. Under these conditions, our desire for others' esteem has the potential to motivate us to do objectionable things and cultivate objectionable traits. But the potential for corruption should not lead us to be unduly suspicious of our desire for esteem and our aversion to disesteem.

Ideally, we would esteem the worthy and disesteem the unworthy, and persons would want and accept the esteem they merit but would not attempt to exact esteem in such a way as to dishonor persons or manifest ill will. A number of virtues and vices can be explained in terms of this ideal. If a person is completely unwilling to accept merited esteem she may be criticized as lacking self-respect, and the person who is completely indifferent to the esteem and deference of others may be condemned as shameless. The appropriately modest person is one who believes that she is accomplished, accepts the esteem and deference that she is due but doesn't dishonor others or attempt to exact esteem in ways that express ill will. When she is unduly praised, the modest person will deprecate herself in order to maintain harmonious relationships with others.[40] People who are falsely modest also deprecate themselves, but unlike the genuinely modest who downplay their accomplishments in order to strengthen their interpersonal relationships, the falsely modest use self-effacing behavior in an attempt to indirectly exact esteem.[41] They seek assurance from others that their self-effacing claims are false or esteem for being self-deprecating. So the falsely modest student who does

---

40. In "A Modest Proposal: Accounting for the Virtuousness of Modesty," *Philosophical Quarterly* 60, no. 241 (2010): 783–807, Irene McMullin argues that modest people recognize that they are more accomplished than others, but they do not seek out esteem and deference on this basis since they believe that this would bring pain to others.

41. Thanks to Jada Strabbing for a helpful discussion concerning false modesty.

well on an exam might complain to her peers that she didn't fully understand the material and just got lucky, and in downplaying her accomplishments seeks assurance from others that her effacing claims are false or admiration for her apparent modesty.

The vices of superiority impair our moral relationships insofar as they undermine a social system in which praiseworthy traits are esteemed and objectionable traits are disesteemed. Worlds where the vices of superiority are evinced but go undetected are worlds where the unworthy are likely to gain esteem and deference from members of the community. In deciding whom to esteem, we take seriously how persons present themselves; very often, a person's self-presentation is the only information we have about his or her status. Since we can't peer into the hearts and minds of all those we encounter or carefully consider their histories, we rely upon the way persons present themselves in determining their status. By presenting himself as a person of piety and upright character, Tartuffe won Orgon's esteem and very nearly won Mariane's hand in marriage. When the vices of superiority go undetected, vice pays.

When those who evince superbia receive unmerited esteem and deference, those who actually deserve esteem and deference are less likely to receive it. For those who manifest the vices of superiority see themselves as entitled to treat others as their inferiors and may attempt to exact esteem and deference at others' expense. As social creatures that seek esteem and struggle to avoid disesteem, we have reason to object to this distribution of esteem and deference; it is unfair for those who do not merit esteem and deference to receive it at the expense of others who do. And this is precisely what tends to happen when the vices of superiority are not answered.

Worlds where the vices of superiority are detected but go unanswered are worlds where people become cynical and are less likely to esteem anyone. If we know that some use their presumed high status to put others down, then there is a danger that we will begin to think that no one ever genuinely merits esteem and deference. This kind of cynicism renders us unable to appreciate the good qualities of persons, and this lack of affective openness is to be lamented.[42] In short, persons care about the opinions of others—we seek others' esteem and seek to avoid their disesteem. We may lament how much stock we put in the opinions of others, but we are social beings who care about the esteem and disesteem of others. Ideally, we would esteem and disesteem persons in accordance with their merit, and aiming for this ideal is the best way of managing persons' desire for esteem. Those who evince the vices of superiority attempt to take advantage of and undermine a system in which persons are esteemed when they show themselves to be worthy of esteem; in so doing, those who manifest these vices damage their relationships with other persons.

3.3 CONTEMPT AS AN ANSWER TO VICES OF SUPERIORITY

Hard feelings are forms of regard that *answer* wrongdoing and badbeing. They draw subjects' attention to lingering damage and, at the same time, are ways for subjects to enact their commitments. These attitudes may highlight and, in a sense, entrench relational damage, but they are not the primary locus of impairment.[43] Instead, they draw our attention to this relational damage and prepare us to engage in reparative activities.

---

42. I will say more about affective openness in chap. 5.
43. Of course, this is not to deny that these emotions may be excessive, and when we experience these hard feelings in unfitting ways, we may damage our relationships in ways that exceed the damage already wrought by wrongdoing or badbeing.

Resentment answers wrongdoing by focusing the subject's attention on the wrong done. Part of the badness of wrongdoing comes from its expressive dimension. As Jeffrie Murphy notes: "[Moral wrongs] are also *messages*—symbolic communications. They are ways a wrongdoer has of saying to us, 'I count but you do not,' 'I can use you for my purposes' or 'I am here up high and you are there down below.'"[44] Resentment is, paradigmatically, a response to a target that has violated the subject's rights and is focused on the target's actions. It is characterized by dispositions to confront the wrongdoer and demand his acknowledgement of the wrong done or an explanation that absolves him from blame. Resentment answers the damage wrought by wrongdoing by focusing the subject's attention on the offender's actions and presents him as someone who has done wrong. It motivates its subjects to demand that the offender explain away or take responsibility for the wrong done.

Contempt answers superbia in a quite different way. Through contempt's characteristic withdrawal, its subjects do not simply seek explanations or apologies; instead, the contemnor seeks the target's *character change*. If the target does not attempt to change his ways, then the contemnor will see him as someone to be avoided altogether. Once Tartuffe's charade is revealed (and it is clear that he will not change his ways), the other characters in the play seek to deny him the esteem and deference he attempted to exact through his hypocrisy. The play ends with Tartuffe being taken away to jail, and this symbolic expulsion is an apt response to his hypocrisy.[45] Responding to Tartuffe with anger or resentment would not have answered his faults—he needed to be

---

44. Murphy, *Forgiveness and Mercy*, 25.
45. I do not mean to suggest that actual incarceration would be a just response to persons who evince the vices of superiority. Rather, Tartuffe's incarceration is symbolic of the social withdrawal that is characteristic of contempt.

removed from the community, at least symbolically. Engaging a hypocrite and demanding that he take responsibility for his actions or explain why he should not be held accountable for his actions is to fail to address the distinct moral trouble created by hypocrisy and other vices of superiority; responding in this way fails to answer the superbia at the heart of these vices.

Contempt is a *demoting emotion* that presents its target as having a comparatively low status. Answering superbia in this way helps to restore the ideal equilibrium between the esteem and deference a person is given and the esteem and deference the person merits. Those who evince vices of superiority disrupt this equilibrium; they see themselves as entitled to more esteem and deference than others, desire to have this comparatively high status recognized, and may attempt to exact the esteem and deference they seek. Contempt demotes the target, thereby negating his sense of entitlement and undermining his attempts at dishonoring or exacting esteem and deference. In short, contempt puts those who manifest vices of superiority in their place by presenting its targets as comparatively low in status in virtue of their superbia. Contempt presents its targets as persons to be looked down upon, not persons to be admired or deferred to.

Some may object that on a minimally acceptable morality we should not disesteem anyone and for this reason we always should prefer an anti-contempt ethic to an ethic of contempt. This critic may concede that arrogance and hypocrisy are vices that have the potential to damage our personal and moral relations but insist that it is morally ugly to respond to someone who evinces these vices with a demoting emotion like contempt. We would do better, according to this line of thought, to respectfully remind the arrogant and the hypocritical that everyone is owed a certain basic level of moral consideration. We should, in other words, answer the unfitting and inapt contempt of the arrogant or hypocritical with respectful engagement, rather then contemptuous dismissal.

I think it is important to challenge the misplaced sense of superiority of those who evince vices of superiority, but we cannot challenge their superbia by simply reminding them that others are equally worthy of respect. For those who evince superbia do not have false beliefs about others' moral *standing*; instead, their main fault is taking themselves to have a comparatively high *status* and lording this presumed status over people in a way that expresses ill will. Given this, reminding the arrogant or hypocritical that others are just as worthy of respect won't answer their vices. Such people may concede the point but continue to harbor superbia and see it as justified. In order to properly challenge the target's perception of his superior status, one must attempt to make his *inferior* status felt. This is why contempt's characteristic demotion is such an apt response to the vices of superiority.

To be clear, I do not claim that contempt merely *causes* the target to feel bad about her fault. While contempt and other emotions have causal powers, they do not simply operate in a hydraulic fashion.[46] Contempt *provides reasons* for the contemned to change her ways.[47]

In the third act of *King Lear*, as he is caught in a brutal storm, Lear begins to pay attention to the feelings of others. Thinking back on how he had neglected the poor during his reign, the now-suffering Lear at last begins to understand their plight:

> Take physic, pomp,
> Expose thyself to feel what wretches feel,

---

46. I will say more about what apt contempt *does* in chap. 4.
47. I am grateful to Akeel Bilgrami for asking a question about this point and for a helpful discussion of the issue.

> That thou mayst shake the superflux to them,
> And show the heavens more just.[48]

As this example illustrates, our sympathy is often engaged by shared experience. When we respond to someone who evinces a vice of superiority with apt contempt, we give the target a small taste of what it feels like to be on the receiving end of superbia. Of course, the target does not get the full experience of what this is like since he is being contemned for *good* reasons; nevertheless, through being the target of a downward-looking comparative assessment and withdrawal, he gets some sense of what it feels like to be at the mercy of another's superbia, and this puts him into a position to better appreciate reasons to change his ways. By responding with contempt, the contemnor does not *give* the target a reason to change, that is, she does not bring into existence a reason to change that would not have existed except for the contempt. Those who manifest the vices of superiority have ample reason to change whether or not they are the targets of anyone's scorn; the vices of superiority are corrupting and impair persons' relationships with others. What apt contempt does is *provide* reasons to change: it puts those who evince the vices of superiority in a position to appreciate their reasons to change; the experience of being put down and disesteemed makes one's reasons to change particularly salient. In this way, being the target of contempt may *inspire* someone who evinces a vice of superiority to change his ways.[49]

---

48. William Shakespeare, *King Lear*, act 3, sc. 2. I am grateful to Akeel Bilgrami for suggesting this example.

49. For a discussion of inspiration and the distinction between giving and providing reasons, see Macalester Bell, "Forgiveness, Inspiration, and the Powers of Reparation," *American Philosophical Quarterly* 49, no. 3 (2012): 205–221.

Some argue that superbia is not a serious fault.[50] If this is right, perhaps we shouldn't respond to superbia with such a corrosive and damaging emotion as contempt. According to this line of thought, those who evince vices of superiority should be considered more pathetic than vicious. Since superbia can't, by itself, bring about a change in anyone's status, we shouldn't be overly concerned about those who manifest vices of superiority.

Against this, I think it is wrong to downplay the moral seriousness of superbia and the vices of superiority. We are social beings who gain knowledge of ourselves and our values through interactions with others, and those who evince the vices of superiority disrupt and corrupt this process.[51] People who are put down through negative comparative evaluations or dishonored as part of a process of esteem and deference seeking may come to believe that they really *do* have a comparatively low status even if this is not the case. If, for example, Tartuffe constantly shudders with horror at the exposed bosoms of the women he encounters, then these women may be shamed by his recoiling and come to believe the messages about them that he expresses through his criticisms.[52] Dorine's contemptuous ridicule of Tartuffe does more than provide comic relief; within the world of the play, her put-downs help shore up her own sense of self-esteem. As long as she holds Tartuffe in contempt, his sly attempts to gain esteem at her expense cannot shake her self-confidence. Contempt inoculates

---

50. This is the position taken by Brennan and Pettit in "The Hidden Economy of Esteem."

51. Béla Szabados and Eldon Soifer argue that self-aware hypocrites may lose an important form of self-knowledge by presenting a persona to the world. See *Hypocrisy: Ethical Investigations* (Peterborough, ON: Broadview Press, 2004), 267. I think those who evince the vices of superiority and those who live among people who evince these vices will find it difficult to attain knowledge of persons' status.

52. So too members of racial minorities may come to feel shame under the weight of others' racist contempt. I discuss this issue in chap. 5.

its subject from being brought low by the target. If you harbor contempt for someone, they cannot shame you.[53]

3.4 COWARDICE, STUPIDITY, AND LIGHTHEARTEDNESS

Some report intuitions about the contemptible that may seem hard to countenance on the account of the vices of superiority offered in this chapter. Cowardice and stupidity are often cited as especially contemptible faults, yet there doesn't seem to be any connection between them and the downward-looking comparative evaluations and esteem-seeking that I've argued is characteristic of superbia. If cowardice and stupidity are paradigmatically contemptible and if my account of the vices of superiority cannot make sense of what makes them contemptible, then there may be reason to reject the arguments offered here. Others acknowledge that the vices of superiority are dangerous but object that contempt is too lighthearted to be a morally apt response to these faults.

I have not claimed that the only faults that ever merit contempt are vices of superiority. Instead, I have shown that contempt is a particularly apt response to those who evince these vices. As argued in chapter 2, our relationships are partially constituted by norms, and whether a token of contempt is fitting will depend upon the norms associated with a particular relationship.

---

53. Some may see this as giving us a reason to avoid contempt. We should, some might argue, always remain open to the possibility of being shamed by others in the moral community. See Cheshire Calhoun, "An Apology for Moral Shame," *Journal of Political Philosophy* 12, no. 2 (2004): 127–146. I disagree; allowing oneself to be shamed by those one has good reason to believe are misguided evinces an objectionable lack of integrity. For a discussion of contempt's role in inoculating persons from race-based shame, see J. David Velleman, "The Genesis of Shame," *Philosophy & Public Affairs* 30, no. 1 (2001): 27–52.

Some relationship-dependent failing may be contemptible without being a vice of superiority—at least I have not attempted to rule out this possibility.

Second, even if the majority of people contemn the stupid or cowardly, that obviously wouldn't settle the matter of whether these faults *merit* contempt. The contemptible cannot be reduced to simply a claim about what the majority of persons do, in fact, contemn. In order for this observation to pose a problem for the characterization of the vices of superiority offered in this chapter, we would need a persuasive explanation of why these faults do indeed *merit* contempt. Moreover, this explanation, if it is to count as a rival to my characterization of the vices of superiority, must be able to account for paradigmatically contemptible faults such as hypocrisy and arrogance.

Finally, I do not think stupidity and cowardice *simpliciter* merit contempt. Instead, the stupid or cowardly person merits contempt only if certain background conditions are in place. For instance, some harbor contempt for George W. Bush and will point to one of the many well-known "Bushisms" in order to justify their scorn. While it is unfair to assess a person's intelligence on the basis of a few off-the-cuff remarks, let's assume for the sake of the argument that these comments do, in fact, reveal a lack of intelligence. Is this lack of intelligence contemptible? Perhaps. But Bush's apparent lack of intelligence merits our contempt (if it does) only because he was president of the United States. Suppose you are on the bus and you overhear a fellow passenger say, "Natural gas is hemispheric. I like to call it hemispheric in nature because it is a product that we can find in our neighborhoods."[54] I think few of us would take this remark as a reason to respond to the passenger with contempt; we

---

54. From *The Complete Bushisms*. http://www.slate.com/articles/news_and_politics/bushisms/2000/03/the_complete_bushisms.html

may be puzzled or amused or annoyed, but it is difficult to see why this comment would be regarded as grounds for contempt under the circumstances. However, when the president of the United States makes such a remark, it may reasonably be thought to reveal a contemptible fault. For one may begin to suspect that the speaker is not worthy of his position as president and is claiming a higher status than he merits in order to exact esteem and deference from others. On this interpretation, it is not lack of intelligence alone that merits contempt; it is lack of intelligence *given one's social position and power* that merits contempt. Similarly, I suspect that it is not cowardice itself that is contemptible but only the cowardice of those whose role or position in society requires that they be especially courageous. Contempt is, for example, a more apt response to the cowardly commanding officer than to the cowardly enlisted soldier. In short, these putative counter-examples do not give us reason to reject my arguments in this chapter.

Others object that contempt is an inappropriate response to the vices of superiority because those who are vicious are dangerous, and contempt is an inapt response to the dangerous. Consider, for example, what Immanuel Kant writes concerning the appropriate objects of contempt:

> What is *dangerous* is no object of contempt, and so neither is a vicious man; and if my superiority to his attacks justifies my saying that I despise him, this means only that I am in no danger from him, even though I have prepared no defense against him, because he shows himself in all his depravity.[55]

Kant is making two claims in this passage. First, he asserts that what is dangerous does not merit contempt. Second, he claims

---

55. Kant, *Metaphysics of Morals*, 463.

that when we are justified in contemning a vicious person this is only because the person is so obviously depraved that he does not pose a threat to anyone.

Let's begin by responding to the second point. Those who make a spectacle of what they take to be their high status and the comparatively low status of others are actually *less* contemptible than those who do a better job keeping their feelings of superiority partially under wraps. Consider, for example, the pop star that thinks he's God's gift to the world. While we may think that his unbridled self-love and low opinion of others leaves him vulnerable to criticism, contempt seems like an inappropriate response to such an overt, in your face, expression of superiority. Those who openly declare their superiority are less likely to damage their personal and moral relations than those who keep such feelings partially under wraps. In part, the vices of superiority are objectionable because of their *subterranean qualities*: people who evince these vices often fool others into thinking that they merit the esteem and deference that they presume they are owed or attempt to exact, and this is what makes them so dangerous. Those who wear their feeling of superiority on their sleeves, as it were, are less likely to fool others into thinking that their comparative evaluations are fitting and apt. This brings us to Kant's first point. What should we think of Kant's claim that the dangerous are inappropriate targets of contempt?

Kant doesn't give an argument for this claim, but he suggests that contempt betrays a lack of moral seriousness. In chapter 4, we see that this criticism is difficult to square with many of Kant's criticisms of contempt, but for now let's focus on this claim. Is there any reason to believe that contempt lacks moral seriousness? Contempt, again, is a dismissive emotion that presents its target as low, but this in itself need not constitute a lack of seriousness. For one can, without incoherence or confusion, be dismissive of serious threats. As noted in chapter 1, some think "scorn" derives from *scornare*, "to deprive of the horns." This is a helpful metaphor for understanding how contempt answers the vices of superiority: by presenting its targets as low, contempt mitigates the dangers of the vices of superiority by cutting off the "horns" (i.e., the superbia) of those who evince these vices. In dismissing the contemptible, we mitigate the damage they may do to our personal and moral relations. While we may dismiss a person's superbia with a smile or a pointed joke, we should not confuse contempt's occasional lack of solemnity with a lack of seriousness. Contempt is a perfectly serious emotion that is well equipped to play an important role in confronting those who evince vices of superiority.

* * *

The vices that most clearly merit contempt are vices of superiority. While it is open to debate whether a particular person evinces superbia or whether a specific fault is structured by it, contempt is, in general, a fitting response to this attitude. Superbia matters to us. It has the potential to impair our relationships and undermine persons' self-esteem; contempt answers the moral damage wrought by the vices of superiority, and for this reason, it has a positive role to play on a minimally acceptable morality. But more needs to be said about the value of responding to superbia with contempt, especially since so many have insisted that contempt is a wholly nasty emotion, which has no positive role to play in our moral lives. What is the moral value of contempt and what moral work does it do?

Chapter 4

The Moral Value of Contempt

Contempt's critics insist that it is a pernicious emotion utterly devoid of moral value. The list of objections commonly raised against it is long: some argue that contempt's globalism gives us reason to dismiss it on moral grounds. Contemporary Kantians often argue that it is incompatible with our duty to respect all persons as persons. Other critics object to the comparisons that structure contempt. Finally, some maintain that contempt is morally objectionable because it is an antisocial emotion characterized by withdrawal from its target. Given the number of objections raised against contempt and their seriousness, it may seem that we have decisive reasons to adopt an anti-contempt ethic. Against this, I argue that contempt has a positive role to play in our moral lives. Contempt is, in at least some cases, the best response to superbia, and we should strive to cultivate contempt so that we may respond appropriately to hypocrisy, arrogance, racism, and other vices of superiority.

This chapter aims to defend an ethic of contempt against those who insist upon an anti-contempt ethic, and in making that case, I respond to the most common objections raised against contempt. Many of these objections have a Kantian tone, and it may seem that Kantian moral theory is incompatible with an ethic of contempt. However, when we carefully consider Kant's writings on contempt and the social virtues, we see that his own assessment of contempt is more nuanced than is often appreciated. While Kant is notoriously suspicious of emotions as moral motives, and while he is clearly concerned about abuses of contempt, he is not the strong critic of contempt that many take him to be.

I begin by describing the role that contempt plays in the moral psychology of Aristotle and Friedrich Nietzsche. Looking back to these philosophers provides an important counterweight to the anti-contempt rhetoric that pervades much contemporary moral discourse. While both Nietzsche and Aristotle think contempt has a central role to play in lives of excellence, their anti-egalitarianism must be rejected and with it their defenses of contempt.

4.1 PASSIVE CONTEMPT IN ARISTOTLE AND NIETZSCHE

While contemporary moral theorists have tended to ignore contempt or dismiss it as a nasty or immoral emotion, both Aristotle and Nietzsche acknowledge that contempt has an important role to play in lives of excellence. Considering their views will help us begin thinking about contempt's moral value.[1] I do not aim to give a scholarly exegesis of Aristotle and Nietzsche but will sketch, in broad strokes, the role contempt occupies in their moral psychologies before raising some concerns about their respective defenses.

In book 4, chapter 3 of the *Nicomachean Ethics*, Aristotle describes the figure of the *megalopsychos* (sometimes translated as the "high-minded" or "magnanimous" man). The *megalopsychos*

---

1. How to characterize Nietzsche's positive views concerning morality is a topic of active debate. Some deny that Nietzsche has anything approaching a theory of ethics, while others classify him as a kind of virtue theorist or perfectionist. In this book, though, I'm interested only in the role contempt plays in Nietzsche's moral psychology however we end up classifying his views.

correctly believes that he is worthy of great things including the important external goods of honor and admiration. He is worthy of these goods because he exemplifies "[g]reatness in each virtue"[2] and he knows that he is great.[3] Aristotle describes this greatness of soul as "a sort of adornment of the virtues; for it makes them greater, and it does not arise without them."[4]

What is most interesting about Aristotle's discussion of the *megalopsychos* is his description of how this person will respond to the failings of others:

> He cannot let anyone else, except a friend, determine his life. For that would be slavish; and this is why all flatterers are servile and inferior people are flatterers. He is not prone to marvel, since he finds nothing great, or to remember evils, since it is proper to a magnanimous person not to nurse memories, especially not of evils, but to overlook them...he does not speak evil even of his enemies, except [when he responds to their] wanton aggression. He especially avoids laments or entreaties about necessities or small matters, since these attitudes are proper to someone who takes these things seriously.[5]

The *megalopsychos* is unconcerned with the wrongdoing or badbeing of his inferiors. Should he be "wronged" by another or forced to suffer an evil at the hands of someone beneath him, he will not hold on to these memories or respond with resentment. Instead,

---

2. Aristotle, *Nicomachean Ethics*, 1123b.
3. Ibid. For a helpful discussion of the *megalopsychos*, see Howard J. Curzer, "Aristotle's Much Maligned *Megalopsychos*," *Australasian Journal of Philosophy* 69, no. 2 (1991): 131–151. My understanding of the moral psychology of the *megalopsychos* owes much to Curzer's analysis.
4. Aristotle, *Nicomachean Ethics*, 1124a.
5. Ibid., 1124b–1125a.

he will simply overlook these apparent slights, and in so doing, show that he does not take the actions or character traits of his inferiors seriously.

Aristotle marks a distinction between the *megalopsychos* and those who have good fortune but lack virtue. The latter tend to *flaunt* their disdain for others. Those who are superior in terms of birth or wealth, but who lack virtue, often strive to make their superiority felt by those around them:

> Those who lack virtue but have these other goods are not justified in thinking themselves worthy of great things, and are not correctly called magnanimous; that is impossible without complete virtue. They become arrogant and wantonly aggressive when they have these other goods. For without virtue it is hard to bear the results of good fortune suitably, and when these people cannot do it, but suppose they are superior to other people, they think less of everyone else, and do whatever they please. They do this because they are imitating the magnanimous person though they are not really like him.[6]

But while the *megalopsychos* does not flaunt his disdain for his inferiors, he does believe that he is superior to non-*megalopsychoi*, and this judgment of superiority manifests itself by the lack of attention he pays to others: not only does the *megalopsychos* not notice slights but he also quickly "forgets" any help he has received: "Magnanimous people seem to remember the good they do, but not what they receive, since the recipient is inferior to the giver, and the magnanimous person wishes to be superior."[7]

---

6. Ibid., 1124a–b.
7. Ibid., 1124b.

THE MORAL VALUE OF CONTEMPT

As Aristotle describes him, the *megalopsychos* is dismissive of and withdraws from those whom he judges to be inferior. Non-*megalopsychoi* are not worthy of his attention—they cannot harm him, and he is emotionally unaffected by harms that befall them. The attitude the *megalopsychos* evinces is one of haughty indifference, and it is reasonable to interpret this indifference as a kind of passive contempt.

Although his moral views differ substantially from the Greeks, Nietzsche also highlights the importance of passive contempt in lives of excellence. Like Aristotle's *megalopsychos*, Nietzsche's noble man is someone prone to passive contempt for those he judges to be low or base. To better understand the role of contempt in Nietzsche's moral psychology, it is helpful to compare his treatment of contempt and *ressentiment* in On the Genealogy of Morals and Beyond Good and Evil.

In the *Genealogy*, Nietzsche purports to offer an account of the value of modern morality; through his genealogy, he hopes to illuminate its (modest) value and (great) disvalue. Morality was born out of *ressentiment*, and *ressentiment* is a product of the people he describes as "slaves." There are, according to Nietzsche, two basic classes of people: masters or nobles and slaves.[8] The former are strong, powerful men who take what they want when they want it, whereas the latter are weak, meek, and constitutionally unable to directly pursue what they desire. And what these men want most keenly is what the noble naturally possess: power. The key difference between masters and slaves is that the latter are *volitionally impotent*; in other words, they are unable to openly pursue what they desire, and this leads to

---

8. Within each class are a variety of subclasses (including priests who have characteristics of both the nobles and the slaves); these subclasses of persons are important for Nietzsche's overarching argument but not for our specific focus on the role of contempt in lives of excellence.

anxiety and frustration. These feelings ultimately come together in *ressentiment*, an impotent anger that the weak direct toward the strong.⁹ Slaves hate noble men and desire vengeance, but being weak, they are unable to launch a direct attack against the strong. Their desire for vengeance is pushed down and inward, changing the way they see themselves in comparison to the strong.

Ressentiment's evaluative presentation is, according to Nietzsche, always deceptive. In reality, the slaves compare themselves to the noble and immediately feel inferior. Since they are weak, they cannot deal with these feelings of inferiority through direct aggression. Instead, they devise a new structure of values according to which strength becomes vicious cruelty and weakness becomes virtuous humility. When the noble act in accordance with their natures as strong and independent beings, this is chastised as wrongdoing; whereas the slaves' weakness is celebrated as virtue. This revaluation of values is driven by *ressentiment*: through their *ressentiment* the weak come to see the strong as low and themselves as high.

Since the noble man is a man of action and power, he will rarely experience *ressentiment*. If he does, he will not allow it to fester:

> *Ressentiment* itself, if it should appear in the noble man, consummates and exhausts itself in an immediate reaction, and therefore does not *poison*: on the other hand, it fails to appear at all on countless occasions on which it inevitably appears in

---

9. As Bernard Reginster points out, Nietzsche sometimes claims that it is the noble priests who harbor *ressentiment*, not the slaves. However, in other passages, Nietzsche clearly suggests that *ressentiment* is the emotion characteristic of the slaves as a group. See Reginster, "Nietzsche on *Ressentiment* and Valuation," *Philosophy and Phenomenological Research* 57, no 2 (1997): 281–305. But whoever experiences *ressentiment*—noble priests or slaves—it is clear that Nietzsche thinks that contempt is a less objectionable response than *ressentiment*.

the weak and impotent. To be incapable of taking one's enemies, one's accidents, even one's misdeeds seriously for very long—that is the sign of strong, full natures in whom there is an excess of the power to form, to mold, to recuperate and to forget (a good example of this in modern times is Mirabeau, who had no memory for insults and vile actions done him and was unable to forgive simply because he—forgot.) Such a man shakes off with a *single* shrug many vermin that eat deep into others.[10]

The noble man does not pay attention to others' activities. He cannot be harmed by others and does not usually respond with *ressentiment*. Instead, he simply *forgets* or *fails to attend* to those around him even when their faults interfere with his own life. In this there is a striking similarity between Nietzsche's description of the noble man and Aristotle's description of the *megalopsychos*. Like the *megalopsychos*, the attitude that the noble will take toward badbeing of others is something very much like passive contempt; secure in his own sense of superiority, he simply fails to notice the low or base individuals he encounters. In fact, Nietzsche compares contempt favorably to *ressentiment* and makes it clear that the noble man will be much more likely to respond to others with contempt rather *ressentiment*.[11]

Nietzsche's main complaint about *ressentiment* is that it is unfitting: its evaluative presentation fails to accurately present the world. Those who harbor *ressentiment* mistakenly see the strong (who are simply acting in accordance with their nature) as vicious wrongdoers, and they see themselves as virtuous. One virtue of contempt is that it is much less likely to distort subjects'

---

10. Friedrich Nietzsche, *On the Genealogy of Morals*, trans. Walter Kauffman and R. J. Hollingdale (New York: Vintage Books, 1989), 39.
11. Ibid., 37.

perceptions of its target. To the extent that contempt's evaluative presentation is distorted, the falsification is more benign:

> ...even supposing that the affect of contempt, of looking down from a superior height, *falsifies* the image of that which it despises, it will at any rate still be a much less serious falsification than that perpetrated on its opponent—*in effigie* of course—by the submerged hatred, the vengefulness of the impotent. There is indeed too much carelessness, too much taking lightly, too much looking away and impatience involved in contempt, even too much joyfulness, for it to be able to transform its object into a real caricature and monster.[12]

Both Aristotle and Nietzsche recognize a role for contempt in lives of excellence and offer helpful correctives to the anti-contempt rhetoric that characterizes contemporary thought. There is much that Nietzsche and Aristotle get right about contempt. They correctly characterize it as a downward-looking, defensive emotion, which has a constructive role to play in lives of excellence. They both recognize that contempt's characteristic withdrawal and disengagement can be constructive. Moreover, Aristotle is right to distinguish what we might call "apt contempt" from the sort of inapt contempt the wealthy feel simply in virtue of their wealth. Even if we have reason to reject the way Aristotle draws the distinction, he is right to stress that not all contempt has a positive role to play in our moral lives. Sometimes contempt presents the world in a false light, and this sort of contempt should be driven out since it has no positive contribution to make to our lives.

There is, however, more that can be said in defense of contempt (and other hostile emotions) than either Aristotle or

12. Ibid.

Nietzsche appreciates. First, neither gives an account of the *value* of contempt. We know that the noble man and the *megalopsychos* will each contemn their inferiors, but we are never provided an account of what reasons people have for responding to another with contempt or why this may be a valuable response. We are left without a clear sense of what contempt does or whether it should be cultivated.

Second, we have reason to reject their accounts of who merits contempt. Aristotle's *megalopsychos* will harbor contempt for *all* non-*megalopsychoi*, and he is just as likely to contemn the person who does him a favor as he is to contemn the person who slights him. Likewise, Nietzsche's noble man harbors contempt for *all* slaves. Neither Aristotle nor Nietzsche take up the question of which faults are especially contemptible or offer an account of when contempt would be an unfitting or inapt response.

Third, the contempt that Nietzsche and Aristotle defend is *passive* contempt, and a defense of this form of contempt raises special concerns.[13] Passive and active contempt are similarly structured: they each present their object as comparatively low and are characterized by withdrawal and other forms of disengagement. The primary difference between active and passive contempt is that the former presents its object as threatening, while the latter does not. As a result, those who harbor passive contempt simply fail to notice the target of their contempt or immediately "forget" any slights they endure. Neither Aristotle's *megalopsychos* nor Nietzsche's noble man sees those they contemn as threats—the weak or base are simply not worthy of the strong's time and attention. Passive contempt is available as a response to other persons only when social and political structures are in place that allow the object of contempt to be safely ignored (see chap. 1).[14] We have independent

---

13. For more on the distinction between passive and active contempt, see chap. 1.
14. For more on this point, see Miller, *Anatomy of Disgust*.

reasons to object to any such social structures, and because of this we have reason to reject the accounts of those who give passive contempt an important role to play in standing against badbeing.

Both Nietzsche and Aristotle reject the egalitarianism that characterizes contemporary moral philosophy. In particular, they reject the now-entrenched idea that all persons qua persons are owed a certain basic form of moral consideration. Nietzsche acknowledges that persons who are similar to one another have reasons to avoid injuring each other without cause, but he denies that this consideration ought to be extended toward those who differ in terms of strength and values:

> Refraining mutually from injury, violence, and exploitation and placing one's will on a par with that of someone else—this may become, in a certain rough sense, good manners among individuals if the appropriate conditions are present (namely, if these men are actually similar in strength and value standards and belong together in *one* body). But as soon as this principle is extended, and possibly even accepted as the *fundamental principle of society*, it immediately proves to be what it really is—a will to the *denial* of life, a principle of disintegration and decay.[15]

It is good manners for the noble to show respect for one another and refrain from direct attack in at least some circumstances. But we shouldn't confuse good manners with a moral principle that makes demands on all of us. There is, for Nietzsche, no reason to show all persons respect or equal consideration.

Aristotle's anti-egalitarianism is well known. Only a few have the traits and background necessary for virtue, and some persons

---

15. "What is Noble," in Nietzsche, *Beyond Good and Evil*, 203.

are natural slaves. While the *megalopsychos* won't lord his superiority over the masses, this is because to do so would be *base* or vulgar; it is not the case that the virtuous *ought* to respect their inferiors or that they would *wrong* them in doing so.

Contemporary ethicists reject the anti-egalitarianism of Nietzsche and Aristotle. Those who accept a minimally acceptable morality recognize that each person is owed a basic form of consideration regardless of the person's strength, values, or other qualities. While there is robust debate and considerable disagreement about what grounds this basic consideration and little consensus concerning its content and scope, there is wide agreement that all persons enjoy a fundamental moral equality. Yet this is precisely what both Aristotle and Nietzsche deny.

If we reject the anti-egalitarianism of Nietzsche and Aristotle, is there still a place for contempt in our moral lives? I believe there is. While it may seem counterintuitive, an ethic of contempt is compatible with a system that recognizes the fundamental moral equality of all persons.

4.2 CONTEMPT'S APTNESS CONDITIONS

No reasonable defender of an ethic of contempt would hold that *all* forms of contempt are valuable. In some cases, responding with contempt is positively disvaluable and is among the *worst* ways of responding to persons. Thus a reasonable ethic of contempt will distinguish between forms of contempt that are prima facie valuable and forms of contempt that are utterly disvaluable. What are the conditions that must be satisfied for a token of contempt to be prima facie valuable?

First, contempt must *fit* its target. As we have seen, contempt is a globalist emotion, which presents an aspect or aspects of its target as especially important to the overall evaluation of the person. More specifically, it presents the person as "low" in virtue of his perceived fault. For contempt to be fitting, the target must really manifest the fault in question. If, for example, I contemn a politician for his arrogance, but it turns out that I misinterpreted his fear of public speaking as arrogance, then my contempt would not be fitting and would, therefore, fail to satisfy this condition.

Second, the contemnor's reasons for contempt must be *morally defensible*. In chapter 3 I argued that the paradigmatically contemptible faults are vices of superiority. Superbia damages our personal and moral relationships, and contempt answers this damage. Persons may harbor contempt for morally indefensible reasons. The racist, for example, harbors contempt for persons simply on account of the target's race. Contemning someone because of his race is morally indefensible.[16] Admittedly, moral theorists will differ with regard to what they think counts as an indefensible reason for contempt. However, there is little debate about which forms of contempt are clearly based on morally indefensible reasons: racist, sexist, or heterosexist contempt are all indefensible on a minimally acceptable morality.

Third, the contempt must be *reasonable*. Not only should the contempt be fitting and based on good reasons, but the contemnor should have some *evidence* that supports these reasons. If I don't have some evidence that the politician I see on TV is arrogant, then my contempt for him is, in this respect, inapt even if it turns out to be fitting and based on morally defensible reasons.

Fourth, the fault that is the focus of contempt must be *serious*. Contempt presents its target as low in virtue of failing to meet

---

16. I will say more about racist contempt and why it is morally indefensible in chap. 5.

some standard that is part of the contemnor's personal baseline. The target's fault must be significant in order for contempt to satisfy this condition. Significant faults are, like the vices of superiority, those that have the potential to seriously impair our relationships with other persons. While some harbor contempt for frat boys who shuffle while walking in flip-flops[17] or teenagers who wear their jeans past their boxer shorts, these "faults" lack the seriousness characteristic of the best forms of contempt. Absent a special story, these faults do not significantly impair our personal and moral relationships in the way that hypocrisy, arrogance, racism, and other vices of superiority do. Subjects who treat these characteristics as especially important in their relationships with targets are prioritizing the wrong things. The shallowness of these tokens of contempt undermines their value or may eliminate it completely.

Fifth, the excellence of contempt is compromised by the *contemnor's hypocrisy*.[18] The hypocrite claims to have contempt for some characteristic, yet his own past actions suggests that he doesn't contemn it after all. In fact, his actions may suggest he values or admires it. The inconsistency that characterizes hypocritical contempt undermines its value because under these conditions, we may have reason to attribute darker motives to the hypocrite. Such a person seems to enjoy feeling superior to the target but does not appear to actually care about the standard or fault in question.

Sixth, contempt's value is undermined if the contemnor is utterly *unresponsive to reasons* that count in favor of overcoming

---

17. I owe this example to graduate students in the Department of Philosophy at the University of Michigan.
18. Michelle Mason argues that contempt that is "morally justifiable" is not hypocritical, but she doesn't fully explain why hypocrisy undermines contempt's value. See "Contempt as a Moral Attitude," 252.

his contempt through a process of forgiveness.[19] This is not to say that we always have reasons to overcome our contempt; in standing against those who evince serious faults and objectionable attitudes, we may well have reason to maintain our contempt. However, one should strive to remain *open* to revising one's contempt in the face of reasons to forgive; that is, the person who contemns excellently should be open to appreciating the good qualities of persons. If someone maintains her contempt in such a way as to be no longer open to reasons to overcome this contempt, the excellence of her contempt has been compromised.

Seventh, there may be cases where contempt would be fitting but where the value of contempt would be *undermined by its unfairness*. If your colleague Zoë is always bragging about her own accomplishments and putting down others, contempt for her may be an apt response to her apparent superbia. If, however, her need to exact esteem at the expense of others is the result of feelings of profound shame and self-contempt instilled in her from a young age by her brutally abusive parents, then responding to her with contempt may be unfair. We may think that Zoë should be excused rather than contemned: due to her unfortunate upbringing she may be more likely than the average person to suffer from feelings of shame and self-contempt, and may also be more likely to deal with these feelings by attempting to build herself up at the expense of others. There is, of course, considerable debate concerning what sorts of conditions, if any, genuinely excuse, and perhaps Zoë's family history and deep feelings of shame do not excuse her superbia. No matter how we ultimately resolve these

---

19. Mason also thinks that morally appropriate contempt must be open to revision in the face of reasons to forgive. Unlike Mason, I don't think that the kinds of considerations that give us reason to overcome resentment through forgiveness will also give us reason to overcome contempt. I return to this issue in chap. 6.

sorts of controversies, the value of contempt that unfairly ignores excusing conditions is undermined.

Unfittingness, harboring contempt for objectionable reasons, unreasonableness, shallowness, hypocrisy, lack of openness to forgiveness, and ignoring excusing or exempting conditions all have the potential to undermine contempt's value. I will call these contempt's aptness conditions. These conditions must be satisfied if a particular token of contempt is appropriate. Apt contempt has both instrumental and non-instrumental moral value, as I argue in the next section.[20]

To be clear, just because a token of contempt is apt, it doesn't follow that it is all-things-considered appropriate or that the would-be contemnor *ought* to feel contempt—there may be overriding reasons against harboring contempt even when it satisfies the aptness conditions. However, apt contempt often has a positive role to play in our moral lives and may sometimes be the best way of responding to superbia. Inapt contempt, on the other hand, usually does not have positive moral value.[21]

4.3 CONTEMPT'S MORAL VALUE

To begin thinking about the moral value of apt contempt, consider the example of Tracy Lord's contempt for her father in *The Philadelphia Story*:[22] Tracy is a smart and headstrong young woman

[20]. The following discussion incorporates, with significant modification, the defense of contempt I offer in "A Woman's Scorn: Toward a Feminist Defense of Contempt as a Moral Emotion," *Hypatia* 20, no.2 (2005): 80–93.

[21]. I say inapt contempt "usually" lacks moral value because it can occasionally contribute to our moral lives (the example of Elizabeth and Darcy in the next section illustrates this point). Nevertheless, inapt contempt is likely to be disvaluable, and we should only strive to cultivate apt contempt in responding to superbia.

[22]. *The Philadelphia Story*, dir. George Cukor, Warner Bros.1940. I am grateful to Susan Wolf and Peter Railton for helpful discussions of this example.

who suffers from a deficit of self-knowledge. Tracy's father, Seth Lord, has run away with a young dancer, devastating Tracy and her mother in the process. While we might expect Seth to be remorseful and contrite, he is not. Instead, he chastises Tracy for being overly critical and laments that an ideal daughter would blindly love her father and have faith in his moral goodness. He even goes so far as to suggest that his philandering was caused by Tracy's judgmental and unloving attitude toward him. Tracy responds to her father, at least initially, with contempt.[23] Her contempt is a fitting response to her father's arrogance and hypocrisy, and it satisfies contempt's other aptness conditions: her concern is serious, she is not hypocritical, she is open to forgiveness, she contemns for good reasons and based on solid evidence, and there is nothing in the film to suggest that Seth's failings are excused. What's the moral value of the sort of contempt that Tracy harbors for her father?

4.3.1 Contempt's Instrumental Value

Many defenders of an ethic of resentment have defended resentment as instrumentally valuable in helping to bring about important ends. Given the concerns that have been raised regarding anger throughout the history of philosophy, getting people to recognize anger's instrumental value has been a considerable accomplishment. But while resentment's instrumental value is now widely acknowledged, contempt's instrumental value has not received much attention. Like resentment, contempt has several modes of instrumental value: it may serve as a form of protest, as a way of gaining knowledge about the world, and as an important moral motivation.

---

23. By the end of the film, Tracy overcomes her contempt for her father (though not, as I see it, for morally good reasons).

Contempt as Protest

Some defend resentment as a form of protest. Those who fail to resent wrongdoing, when resentment is called for, may be guilty of *condoning* the wrong done and failing to respect themselves; resentment is valuable insofar as it protests the wrong done.[24] Like resentment, contempt is a valuable form of protest, but the way contempt protests badbeing is very different from the way resentment protests wrongdoing. As we have seen, contempt is characterized by psychological disengagement, and removing oneself from a perceived threat is often the strongest form of protest that one can make. Many political theorists recognize this, and some argue that residency is a sign of tacit consent to the social contract. Just as leaving one's country of origin can be a kind of protest, psychologically distancing oneself from persons can also serve as a form of protest.[25] Here, the protest is not directed toward other persons in response to a violation of one's rights. Instead, contempt's protest provides the contemptuous a way to express their commitments and remind themselves of their own values in the face of others' failure to meet standards that they care about. Resentment protests the claim made by the wrongdoing.[26] Contempt, on the other hand, protests the *person* who manifests badbeing.

Moreover, the *way* contempt protests badbeing differs from how resentment protests wrongdoing. Resentment is psychologically demanding: it focuses the subject's attention on the wrong done and motivates engagement—albeit hostile

---

24. See, for example, Murphy and Hampton, *Forgiveness and Mercy*, 16–19.

25. In addition, we recognize certain *expressions* of contempt (e.g., turning one's back or refusing to shake hands) as ways of indicating protest.

26. For more on how resentment protests the claim made by wrongdoing, see Murphy and Hampton, *Forgiveness and Mercy*; Pamela Hieronymi, "Articulating an Uncompromising Forgiveness," *Philosophy and Phenomenological Research* 62, no. 3 (2001): 529–555; and Darwall, *Second-Person Standpoint*.

engagement—with the person. Contempt, on the other hand, motivates withdrawal. Because it makes relatively few psychological demands on its subject, contempt is especially valuable in circumstances where resentment is not likely lead to social change.[27] In addition, contemptuous protest is often *jocular* in a way that resentful protest is not; contempt is intimately connected to the comic and often presents its target as an object of amusement. Resentment, on the other hand, presents its target as a formidable opponent; when we resent, we take our target too seriously to scoff or laugh. But contempt's connection to the comic does not undermine its function as a form of protest; dismissing someone with amused contempt is no less a form of protest than responding with indignation or resentment.

The Epistemic Value of Contempt

Some defend resentment by emphasizing its epistemic value. Philosophers who stress resentment's *direct* epistemological value claim that those who harbor resentment gain knowledge that those who do not experience the emotion lack. For example, Uma Narayan has argued that members of oppressed groups may possess a kind of epistemic privilege as compared to the non-oppressed; an important component of this advantage is the knowledge gained through their emotions, especially their resentment.[28] Those who are not oppressed lack full understanding of the emotional costs of oppression, miss the subtler manifestations of it, and are unable to recognize it in new or unfamiliar contexts.[29] These

---

27. Margaret Urban Walker suggests that the resentment of the oppressed may be transformed into contempt if the circumstances that gave rise to their resentment are not ameliorated. See *Moral Repair: Reconstructing Relations After Wrongdoing*, 130, n. 33.

28. Uma Narayan, "Working Together Across Difference: Some Considerations on Emotions and Political Practice," *Hypatia* 3, no. 3 (1988).

29. Ibid.

epistemic failures result from the fact that the non-oppressed do not experience resentment and other hard feelings often felt by the oppressed.

What might one learn from one's feelings of contempt? When contempt is apt, one gains a better understanding of the vices of superiority. Those who evince apt contempt see their target for who he really is, that is, a person who is comparatively low due to his superbia. Those who don't respond with contempt when contempt would be apt do not fully understand the serious threat posed by superbia, and they may, like Orgon, end up believing that contemptible persons actually merit higher esteem and deference than others.

Other defenders of resentment stress its *indirect* epistemic value. For example, Marilyn Frye argues that we can learn a great deal about women's status in this society by investigating the restricted range of circumstances in which women's anger is intelligible *as anger* to others. She relates the story of a woman who angrily confronts a mechanic who takes it upon himself to adjust the woman's well-tuned and well-functioning carburetor. When she angrily confronts the mechanic, he calls her a "crazy bitch," thereby dismissing her anger and utterly failing to give it uptake. For Frye, anger has important epistemic value, but it gives us knowledge indirectly: women gain knowledge by paying attention to how their anger is received and the conditions under which it is not given uptake. In Frye's memorable phrase, "anger can be an instrument of cartography."[30] Through the process of noting, analyzing, and categorizing circumstances in which they can get angry and get uptake, women can map out others' conceptions of who and what they are.

---

30. Marilyn Frye, "A Note on Anger," in *Politics of Reality: Essays in Feminist Theory* (Trumansburg, NY: Crossing Press, 1983), 94. While Frye is discussing anger more generally, her point more clearly applies to resentment in particular.

Like anger, persons' contempt is often dismissed, and through this process one may learn where one stands in the moral community. For example, in Alberto Moravia's novel, *Contempt*, the main character, Ricardo, initially responds to his wife's apt contempt for him with a self-professed desire to rape her. Later in the novel, Moravia describes Ricardo savagely squeezing her hand when she expresses her scorn.[31] Although Seth Lord does not respond to his daughter's contempt with violence, he also fails to give her contempt uptake. Instead, he treats her apt contempt as further evidence of her unloving and judgmental character.

To have your anger or resentment dismissed or not given proper uptake suggests that others fail to see you as *wronged* by the object of your anger. If your contempt is not given proper uptake, it indicates that others think you are unjustified in holding the target to the standard implicit in your attitude. You can learn important things about your status in the moral community by attending to the circumstances in which your contempt is and is not given uptake. Specifically, you can learn whether others see you as justified in holding them to certain standards. Of course, we can gain this knowledge about our status in a number of ways. But given the systematic ways in which some people's contempt is dismissed, investigating how others receive contempt is an especially important way of gaining this knowledge.

The Motivational Value of Contempt
Some defend resentment by stressing its motivational value. Resentment and anger motivate us to confront those whom we believe have wronged us, and this sort of confrontation can motivate positive change. Audre Lorde has emphasized this aspect of

---

31. Alberto Moravia, *Contempt*, trans. Angus Davidson (New York: New York Review Classics, 2004), 109. Mason focuses on Jean-Luc Godard's treatment of Moravia's novel in "Contempt as a Moral Attitude."

the value of resentment in her discussion of the uses and importance of anger for women of color. Expressed anger, while occasionally painful, is ultimately a constructive tool for responding to the injustices of racism and sexism, and can motivate social progress.[32]

But while anger's motivational value is widely acknowledged, most deny contempt's motivational value. For example, the psychologist Jonathan Haidt writes:

> As guardians of the moral order, [contempt, anger and disgust] all... motivate people to change their relationships with moral violators. But only anger motivates direct action to repair the moral order and to make violators mend their ways. Anger thus can be considered the most prototypical moral emotion of the three (at least for Western cultures), followed by disgust, and lastly by contempt.[33]

Haidt's contention that "only anger motivates repair of the moral order" is both widespread and mistaken.[34] Both contempt and

---

32. Audre Lorde, "The Uses of Anger: Women Responding to Racism," in *Sister Outsider* (Trumansburg, NY: Crossing Press, 1984), 131.
33. Jonathan Haidt, "The Moral Emotions," 859.
34. Martha Nussbaum offers a similar argument against disgust: "Second, even when the moralized disgust is not a screen for something else, it is ultimately an unproductive social attitude, since its direction is anti-social. Anger is constructive: Its content is, 'This harm should not have occurred, and the imbalance should be righted.' Most philosophical definitions of anger include the thought that the wrong should be punished or somehow made good. Disgust, by contrast, expresses a wish to separate oneself from a source of pollution; its social reflex is to run away. When I am disgusted by certain American politicians, I fantasize moving away to Finland—a country in which I have worked a little, and which I see as a pure blue and green place of unpolluted lakes, peaceful forests, and pristine social-democratic values. And I don't know it enough to know its faults. To fantasize about moving to Finland is not a constructive response to present American problems." Nussbaum, "Discussing Disgust: On the Folly of Gross-Out Public Policy," an interview with Julian Sanchez, July, 15, 2004 http://reason.com/archives/2004/07/15/discussing-disgust.

resentment can motivate people to respond appropriately to immorality, albeit in very different ways. While anger tends to motivate *direct engagement* with its object, contempt motivates *disengagement*. Some might see this as evidence that contempt cannot be ameliorative, but I disagree. There is a widespread tendency to think that the fundamental moral stance we ought to take toward others is always one of active engagement. But in some situations, disengagement can motivate positive moral change. Disengaging from a person who has failed to meet certain basic standards that are especially important to the contemnor can allow her to maintain her self-esteem. Returning to the example from *The Philadelphia Story*, Tracy's contempt for her father motivated her to cut off all ties with him for several years. Haidt and other critics of contempt suggest that by distancing herself from her father, Tracy was doing nothing to help repair the moral order. But in cases where continued relations may undermine a person's self-esteem, breaking off relations may forestall further damage. Tracy's contempt for her father provided a bulwark against his unfair criticism of her, allowed her to maintain her self-esteem, and helped prevent others, such as her younger sister, from being damaged by her father's superbia.

Moreover, being the target of contempt can have motivational value. Stuck in our own first-person perspectives, we tend to isolate ourselves and to harbor the illusion that we alone can control how others perceive us. Being the object of contempt can shake this certainty, and through this experience we may come to recognize that we have failed to live up to standards that we care about. In *Pride and Prejudice*, Elizabeth Bennett comes to harbor contempt for Fitzwilliam Darcy, a seemingly presumptuous snob.[35] Given her impression of Darcy as pompous and uncaring,

---

35. Given his arrogance, Elizabeth's contempt for Darcy is fitting; it is not, however, completely apt since it is based, at least in part, on a false report of which she

Elizabeth rejects his marriage proposal with more than a little contempt. While he initially dismisses her contempt as misplaced, Darcy eventually comes to feel the fittingness and sting of her contemptuous dismissal of him, and he sets to work on improving his character. Over time, Elizabeth comes to appreciate Darcy; she eventually falls in love with him and accepts his marriage proposal. Toward the end of the novel Darcy describes the effect Elizabeth's contempt had on him:

> Your reproof, so well applied, I shall never forget: "had you behaved in a more gentlemanlike manner." Those were your words. You know not, you can scarcely conceive, how they have tortured me.... As a child I was taught what was right, but I was not taught to correct my temper. I was given good principles, but left to follow them in pride and conceit. Unfortunately an only son (for many years an only child) I was spoiled by my parents...who allowed, encouraged, almost taught me to be selfish and overbearing, to care for none beyond my own family circle, to think meanly of all the rest of the world...such I was, from eight to eight and twenty; and such I might still have been but for you, dearest, loveliest Elizabeth! What do I not owe you! You taught me a lesson, hard indeed at first, but most advantageous. By you, I was properly humbled. I came to you without a doubt of my reception. You showed me how

---

should have been suspicious. As this example illustrates, sometimes even inapt contempt may have moral value. I have, in discussion, encountered a fair bit of resistance to the suggestion that Elizabeth ever felt contempt for anyone, least of all Darcy. I think some of this opposition comes from a lingering worry that contempt is a nasty or base emotion unfit for such a beloved literary character. There is textual support for my reading (including Darcy's reaction to Elizabeth's reproof as quoted below), but I do not intend to offer a definitive interpretation of the novel here. In the end, I am most interested in what we might learn from being a target of contempt, and I think Darcy's reaction to Elizabeth's dismissiveness is instructive whether or not there is wide agreement that Elizabeth can properly be said to have harbored *contempt* for Darcy. I am grateful to Philip Kitcher for comments concerning this example.

insufficient were all my pretensions to please a woman worthy of being pleased.[36]

As this example illustrates, being the target of contempt can provide us with a morally valuable second-personal perspective and can shake us into the realization that we have failed to meet certain basic standards. Darcy says that he was "properly humbled" by Elizabeth's contempt. Had Darcy not felt the sting of Elizabeth's scorn, he would have never reflected on his arrogance and attempted to mend his ways.

Contempt is valuable insofar as it can serve as a form of protest, offer us insights concerning our status within the moral community, and motivate appropriate responses to badbeing. In response, some might insist that *other* attitudes or practices do a better job helping secure the goods described. If this were the case, we could have reason to prefer an anti-contempt ethic to an ethic of contempt after all.

I'm skeptical that these goods could be realized as efficiently through any other attitude, but even if I'm wrong about this, contempt's value is not determined solely by the goods it brings about; contempt also has non-instrumental value.

4.3.2 Contempt's Non-Instrumental Value

There is an old ethical tradition that counsels us to love the good and hate the evil. For example, Romans 12:9 (King James Version) reads: "*Let* love be without dissimulation. Abhor that which is evil; cleave to that which is good." In recent years, Robert Adams and

---

36. Jane Austen, *Pride and Prejudice* (New York: Simon & Schuster, 2004), 411–413. While a "reproof" now (as in Austen's time) primarily refers to a rebuke or censure, it originally referred to "an object of scorn or contempt," OED online "reproof n.1," www.oed.com.

Thomas Hurka have suggested that virtuous agents will love the good and hate the evil (or as Adams puts it, "be for the good and against the evil").[37] In addition, something like this idea shapes many of our intuitions about what is non-instrumentally valuable and disvaluable. The person of integrity is someone who not only does the right thing but also has the right *attitudes* toward her commitments.

There is a conceptual connection between valuing and being disposed to a range of hard feelings when what one values is threatened. If you claim to value something but you aren't disposed to feel any negative emotions when what you claim to value is in jeopardy, there is reason to doubt that you actually value what you claim to value. And part of what it means to be a person of integrity is that one's affective dispositions are in line with what one professes to value; for example, one experiences the relevant valuing-emotions when what one values is threatened. Suppose Frank routinely responds to others' vices with private mirth and joy. While he claims to be committed to the values of truthfulness and beneficence, he is regularly amused by his miserly friend and pleased by his colleague who is a compulsive liar. Assume for the sake of the argument that these positive feelings toward others' vices never cause Frank to violate anyone's legal or moral rights. Despite the fact that his attitudes never lead to wrongdoing, most of us would conclude that there is something seriously amiss with Frank. The problem with Frank is that he lacks integrity: he does not genuinely value what he claims to value.[38] Frank's attitudes are inapt and do not express his purported values.

---

37. See Thomas Hurka, *Virtue, Vice, and Value* (Oxford: Oxford University Press, 2001); and Robert Merrihew Adams, *A Theory of Virtue: Excellence in Being for the Good* (Oxford: Oxford University Press, 2006).
38. There are, of course, competing philosophical accounts of integrity, and I will not attempt to survey all of them here. It seems clear that integrity requires, at minimum, genuinely valuing what one claims to value, and the philosophically interesting

Someone who genuinely and fully values truthfulness and beneficence will not be amused by others' disregard or displays of disrespect for these values. If one values something, one will not be indifferent when what one values is threatened. In this case, if Frank genuinely and fully values truthfulness and beneficence, then he will not be indifferent if these values are threatened by others' disregard and disrespect. Instead, he will seek to defend what he values by answering the threat. Superbia, I have argued, poses a threat to our shared practice of morality. Since contempt is the hard feeling that best answers the threat posed by superbia, then a person of integrity who genuinely values our shared practice of morality, will be disposed to respond to superbia with contempt. Responding with contempt, when apt, is a way for persons to maintain their integrity.

In addition, a liability to hard feelings is part of the activity of holding persons accountable for their actions and faults. When I resent you for your betrayal of our friendship, my resentment addresses a demand to you: you should not have treated me in that way, and I demand that you take responsibility for your wrongdoing and attempt to make amends.[39] When we

---

task is showing what is involved in "genuinely valuing" something. But even if some disagree with this characterization of integrity, the problem with Frank is, I submit, that he doesn't really value what he claims to value. I have suggested that valuing what one claims to value is non-instrumentally valuable. If some object to calling this "integrity," I am happy to adopt some other term to describe this stance.

39. Several philosophers have pointed out the connection between a liability to the negative emotions and systems of accountability. The *locus classicus* is P. F. Strawson, "Freedom and Resentment." R. Jay Wallace in his *Responsibility and the Moral Sentiments* develops a Strawsonian account of responsibility but insists that the emotions involved in holding persons responsible are limited to resentment, indignation, and guilt. I reject Wallace's strategy of narrowing the class of the reactive attitudes involved in holding people responsible; responding with contempt is a way of holding people responsible for their *traits*; resentment, given its action-focus, cannot do this work.

forgo apt resentment, we risk condoning the wrong done.[40] Like resentment, contempt also addresses a demand to its target. While resentment demands that its target take responsibility for the wrong done, contempt demands that its target change her attitudes and overcome her superbia. Responding with apt contempt, then, is the clearest way of holding persons accountable for their superbia. Resentment cannot be marshaled to do contempt's job here, for resentment is characteristically focused on *wrongdoing* as opposed to *badbeing*. Moreover, since it lacks contempt's characteristic downward-looking evaluative presentation, it cannot answer the distinctive threat posed by superbia. To accept an ethic of contempt is to accept that persons are mutually accountable for their status claims. These relationships of mutual accountability for status claims are non-instrumentally valuable.

In short, a liability to contempt is part of two important activities: maintaining one's integrity, and holding persons accountable. If we accept an anti-contempt ethic, we would lose two things of great moral importance: relationships of mutual accountability for our attitudes in which we hold persons to certain standards and are held to certain standards in turn, and one important way of maintaining our integrity. Being liable to feelings of appropriate contempt does not help to *bring about* the contemnor's integrity or *help to realize* relationships of mutual accountability. Instead, responding with apt contempt *partially constitutes* integrity and relationships of mutual accountability. Insofar as we think integrity and relations of mutual

---

40. I do not claim that we must respond with contempt and other hard feelings toward *every* instance of wrongdoing and badbeing that we encounter; we have no obligation to disvalue all that is disvaluable. But under some circumstances (e.g., the offender is a close associate), a failure to respond with apt hard feelings would be to condone the wrongdoing or badbeing.

accountability are non-instrumentally valuable, we ought to conclude that a liability to apt contempt is non-instrumentally valuable as well.

While *other* negative emotions such as disappointment, sadness, or anger might also have a role to play in maintaining a person's integrity and in holding persons accountable, contempt does the best job of (1) *fitting* the fault; and (2) *expressing* the contemnor's respect for herself, the object of her contempt, and the standards in question. Consider, for example, the person who claims to value honesty and is justified in expecting others to be honest, and yet is disposed to feel mere disappointment, and not contempt, when she confronts her co-worker's hypocrisy. Disappointment is a feeling of dissatisfaction when one's expectations are not met. These expectations may be very trivial, for instance, one's expectation that the local bakery will have one's favorite bread available. We may also experience disappointment in response to states of affairs that have no connection to persons, as in the disappointment one feels when one's walk is spoiled by a sudden thunderstorm. Disappointment is not a way of holding persons accountable for their failings, and it isn't a way for persons to stand up for what they value. Nor can another negative emotion, such as resentment, do contempt's job in this case. While resentment may protest the hypocrite's wrongdoing, it cannot protest his badbeing. Contempt is the emotion that best fits the fault and expresses the contemnor's values. While disappointment and anger may be fitting responses to others' failure to meet certain basic standards and they may express one's expectation that the standards should be met, contempt does a *better* job both of fitting the failure and of expressing the contemnor's commitments.

Apt contempt has both instrumental and non-instrumental value. This conclusion may well be met with skepticism; as I noted in the introduction to this chapter, contempt has come in for a great deal of criticism. But, do any of these objections pose an insurmountable objection to an ethic of contempt?

4.4 CHALLENGES TO AN ETHIC OF CONTEMPT

I have argued that we would forgo something that is both instrumentally and non-instrumentally valuable if we were to give up contempt and accept an anti-contempt ethic. However, we are often willing to give up something valuable if we have overriding moral reason to do so. Do we have overriding reasons to forgo contempt? Some object that contempt's globalism renders it always morally pernicious. Others argue that because contempt involves a denial of the respect we owe to all persons qua persons, it cannot have any role to play in our moral lives. Still others object to the comparative element of contempt. Finally, some insist that contempt can never serve as a form of moral address.

4.4.1 Contempt's Globalism and Aptness

In chapter 2, I argued that contempt's globalism does not entail that it is *always* unfitting. Some may accept those arguments but insist that contempt's globalism gives us reason to question its aptness. Kate Abramson, for example, has argued that genuinely globalizing attitudes "preclude *appreciation* of [the target's] redeeming qualities" and for this reason are always morally objectionable.[41] According to Abramson, the morally mature will be able to appreciate persons' admirable qualities. But if contempt is a globalist emotion and presents its target as low, this kind of

---

41. Kate Abramson, "A Sentimentalist's Defense of Contempt, Shame and Distain," 194. Emphasis added.

appreciation will be impossible. Given this concern, she concludes that the only morally defensible forms of contempt are those that are not globalist.

Against this, I think that to give up on contempt's globalism is to give up on contempt. A defensible globalism is one that presents some qualities of persons as more important than others given the relationship between the target and subject (see chap. 2). A person may recognize that someone she contemns has many admirable qualities, but she sees these admirable qualities as less important, overall, than the target's faults. If contempt satisfies the aptness conditions outlined at the beginning of this chapter, the subject will be *open* to appreciating the admirable qualities of the person she contemns (as she will be open to forgiving the target should he change his ways), but she will not *appreciate* these qualities as she contemns. For Abramson, such a person would be making a deep mistake: a morally mature person would not just *believe* that the target has admirable qualities as well as despicable qualities or be *open* to appreciating the target's admirable qualities, but she would *actually appreciate* the target's admirable qualities.[42] And this is something that a person who contemns globally does not do.

It is true that on my account of contempt the contemnor does not, as she withdraws in contempt, appreciate the admirable qualities of the contemned. However, I question why one would think that this kind of appreciation is a mark of moral maturity. In claiming that the morally mature will appreciate all the admirable qualities of persons, Abramson seems to be committed to the thesis that the morally mature will value *all that is valuable*. But

---

42. Abramson writes, "Note that the worry at issue isn't about 'mistakenly *equating* a person with certain traits,' i.e., a worry about making some kind of mistaken judgment. Rather, the worry is that to hold a person in contempt, or to be ashamed of oneself as a person, is to adopt an attitude that precludes appreciation of another's or one's own redeeming qualities." Ibid., 193–194.

we have good reason to reject this thesis. There are many things in life that are valuable—a well-sung fado, teaching a child the alphabet, the complete works of Shakespeare—but it is implausible to insist that the morally mature have reason to *value* all that is valuable or even all that they judge to be valuable.[43] You may judge that *King Lear* is a great play, but it may leave you unmoved. There is nothing incoherent or immature in saying, "Look, I recognize that *King Lear* is a great tragedy, but I've always had a soft spot for *The Tempest*—it's my favorite." Thus there is no reason to accept Abramson's claim that the morally mature will appreciate all the good qualities of persons.

Some might worry that my argument here contradicts my earlier claims about integrity. In the previous section I argued that someone who claims to value ϕ, but who does not respond with the relevant ϕ-valuing attitudes evinced a lack of integrity. Some might think it follows from this that the person who believes ϕ^* is more valuable than ϕ, yet is disposed to ϕ-valuing attitudes and not ϕ^*-valuing attitudes is making a mistake. Such a person, it may be thought, also shows a lack of integrity. But this argument conflates *valuing* something (or claiming to value something) and simply *believing* that something is valuable (or claiming to believe that something is valuable). Someone lacks integrity when they claim to value something yet are not disposed to any of the attitudes that partially constitute valuing; such persons don't really value what they claim to value. We cannot say the same thing about the person who judges something to be valuable but does not value it; this person is not making the same mistake since they don't claim to value the thing in the first place. Of course, such a person may be making another kind of mistake. Perhaps they don't value

---

43. For more on this point, see Samuel Scheffler, "Valuing," in *Equality and Tradition*, 15–40.

something they *ought* to value; in some cases, merely believing something is valuable without actually valuing it is criticizable. I'm happy to accept this. What I do not accept, however, is the claim that we ought to value everything that is valuable.

We shouldn't judge a person to be wholly rotten when he has some redeeming features, but there is nothing in my account of contempt's globalism that would give us reason to respond in this way. The globalism of contempt does not entail that the contemnor see the target as completely despicable with no admirable qualities. Instead, the despicable qualities of the target are seen as more important than the person's admirable qualities given the nature of the relationship between subject and target.[44]

4.4.2 Respect-Based Arguments against Contempt

On a minimally acceptable morality, all persons are owed a basic form of respect. If contempt involves a *denial* of respect, and if all persons are owed respect, then this would seem to give us clear reason to favor an anti-contempt ethic over an ethic of contempt. This Kantian-sounding objection can be answered by first distinguishing between two forms of respect and then turning to Kant's own discussions of contempt. Careful attention to Kant's views concerning *demonstrating* respect and the social virtues suggests that there is no deep tension between Kantian ethics and an ethic of contempt.

---

44. Just as I deny that we have reason to value all that is valuable, I don't think we have reason to disvalue all that is disvaluable. A defender of an ethic of contempt need not hold that the morally mature will seek out all those who evince vices of superiority and contemn them. Given all the badbeing in the world, such a person would have time for little else! A defender of an ethic of contempt insists that responding to persons with contempt is sometimes valuable, and we do have an obligation to cultivate contempt so that we may respond with contempt when it is called for, but it doesn't follow that we have an obligation to contemn all those that merit our contempt. Whether we have overriding reasons to respond with contempt in a particular case will depend on the details of the case including our relationship to the (potential) target.

Two Kinds of Respect

Kant defines contempt as the refusal to grant the target of contempt the respect that is owed to every person within the moral community: "To be *contemptuous* of others (*contemnere*), that is, to deny them the respect owed to human beings in general, is in every case contrary to duty; for they are human beings."[45] Given this definition, it is not surprising that many contemporary Kantians have serious reservations about the moral value of contempt. Contempt has no positive role to play in our moral lives, they argue, for contempt *just is* the denial of the respect we owe to each other as persons. Rather than contemning those who evince the vices of superiority, we should always respond with respectful engagement. Thomas Hill, for example, suggests that the Kantian ideal of respect should motivate our responses toward racists and sexists by "replacing contemptuous dismissal with firm but respectful confrontation."[46]

But those who insist that contempt is incompatible with respect are making a mistake. Michelle Mason points out that there are at least two different kinds of respect, and this objection equivocates between them.[47] The kind of respect that contempt denies its target is not the kind of respect we owe all persons qua persons.

Respect is derived from the Latin "respicere" which means to "to look back at" or "to look again,"[48] and this suggests that respect is importantly connected to attention. Respect involves

---

45. Kant, *Metaphysics of Morals*, 6:463.
46. Thomas Hill, "Must Respect be Earned?" in *Respect, Pluralism, and Justice: Kantian Perspectives* (Oxford: Oxford University Press, 2000), 92.
47. Mason, "Contempt as a Moral Attitude."
48. Robin Dillon and David Velleman make this observation about the etymology of respect. See Dillon, "Respect and Care: Toward Moral Integration," *Canadian Journal of Philosophy* 22, no. 1 (1992): 105–132; and Velleman, "Love as Moral Emotion." *Ethics* 109, no. 2 (1999): 338–374.

seeing the target of attention as *worthy* of attention. Moreover, respect is partially constituted by certain behavioral dispositions. Generally speaking, if we respect something we will be disposed to preserve it or cherish it, and we will, at minimum, take ourselves to have reasons not to destroy it.[49]

Stephen Darwall argues that philosophers often conflate two kinds of respect. What he calls *recognition respect* consists in "a disposition to weigh appropriately in one's deliberations some feature of the thing in question and to act accordingly."[50] This kind of respect can take a wide variety of objects, such as persons, the environment, a court of law, and the like. A person may be an object of recognition respect qua person, but also qua father, professor, child, and so on.[51] In addition, a person may be a target of what Darwall calls *moral recognition respect*: if some feature x is an appropriate object of moral recognition respect, failing to give x adequate consideration would be to do something morally wrong.[52]

Darwall also points out that there is another attitude we call "respect," which is distinct from recognition respect but which also plays an important role in morality. *Appraisal respect* takes persons as its object and involves a positive evaluation of the person as a person or as someone who occupies a particular role or engages in a specific activity. What grounds this kind of respect are features that merit positive evaluation.[53] Unlike recognition respect, appraisal respect comes in degrees.

If one fails to recognize Darwall's distinction between these two kinds of respect and if one thinks that all persons deserve

---

49. See Joseph Raz, *Value, Respect, and Attachment* (Cambridge: Cambridge University Press, 2001), 162.
50. Darwall, "Two Kinds of Respect," 38.
51. Ibid., 38.
52. Ibid., 40.
53. Ibid., 38.

respect, then apt contempt looks impossible. However, once we acknowledge the distinction between recognition respect and appraisal respect, it is clear that appealing to the respect we owe all persons cannot provide us with an overriding reason to forgo all contempt.[54] If all persons qua persons are owed respect, it is clearly recognition respect that they are owed and not appraisal respect.[55] But contempt is not incompatible with recognition respect; there is no reason to suppose that the contemnor will, for example, always fail to acknowledge the moral or legal rights of those they condemn. Thus an ethic of contempt is not incompatible with an ethical system that demands we respect all persons as persons.

Kant, Contempt, and the Social Virtues

To better understand how contempt can be morally valuable even if we assume that all persons are owed respect, it will be helpful to consider, in more detail, Kant's own views on contempt. In the *Groundwork*, Kant famously expresses skepticism regarding the possibility of emotions as moral motives.[56] Moreover, some of Kant's writings have led commentators to conclude that he thinks contempt is an especially objectionable emotion. But there are other passages that suggest that Kant may not be the critic of contempt that many assume. (I will not attempt to provide a definitive scholarly exegesis of Kant's position on respect and contempt here. Instead, I will show that those who appeal to Kant in defending the claim that contempt is always a nasty or inapt emotion have not taken into account all that he says about contempt,

---

54. For more on this point see Mason, "Contempt as a Moral Attitude," 265.
55. Darwall, "Two Kinds of Respect," 38.
56. Immanuel Kant, *Groundwork of the Metaphysics of Morals*, trans. and ed. Mary Gregor, with an introduction by Christine Korsgaard (Cambridge: Cambridge University Press, 1998), sec. I.

respect and the conditions under which we should refrain from *showing* respect to another.)

Kant insists that we owe all persons respect, and he sometimes suggests that this respect precludes responding to persons with contempt:

> The *respect* that I have for others or that another can require from me (*observantia aliis praestanda*) is therefore recognition of a *dignity* (*dignitas*) in other human beings, that is, of a worth that has no price, no equivalent for which the object evaluated (*aestimii*) could be exchanged—Judging something to be worthless is contempt.[57]

He stresses that this respect is incompatible with having contempt for another: "To be *contemptuous* of others (*contemnere*), that is, to deny them the respect owed to human beings in general, is in every case contrary to duty; for they are human beings."[58] As he makes clear, failing to fulfill duties of respect does not simply evince a *lack of virtue* but is, instead, vicious; when we fail to perform our duties of respect we wrong others and violate their rights.[59] He seems to be insisting that our duty to respect persons renders contempt always inapt.

But if we look beyond these frequently quoted passages, a more nuanced position emerges. For example, Kant writes: "At times one cannot, it is true, help inwardly *looking down* on some in comparison with others (*despicatui habere*); but the outward manifestation of this is, nevertheless, an offense."[60] Kant here wants to distinguish between "being contemptuous" (which he

---

57. Kant, *Metaphysics of Morals*, 6:462.
58. Ibid., 6:463.
59. Ibid., 6:464.
60. Ibid., 6:463.

thinks is incompatible with respect) and "looking down on some in comparison to others." But as I've characterized it, the heart of contempt involves precisely this downward-looking comparative evaluation. In this passage, Kant suggests that this attitude is "natural" and is not, by itself, open to moral assessment. Moreover, he describes some vices (e.g., haughtiness) as "contemptible."[61] But if we can't help but to contemn some forms of badbeing and if certain faults *merit* contempt, in what sense is Kant a critic of contempt?

Kant expresses concern about the outward manifestations of contempt. Specifically, he focuses on punishments that express contempt such as drawing and quartering and cutting off a person's nose.[62] These punishments, even if meted out only to those who deserve them, "make a spectator blush with shame at belonging to the species that can be treated that way."[63] For Kant, these kinds of punishments contravene our duties of respect because they express complete and utter disregard for persons. To punish a person by drawing and quartering is to treat the individual as a mere object or as someone who utterly and completely lacks moral worth rather than as a person with dignity. But to express concerns about punishments such as drawing and quartering need not amount to a flat rejection of an ethic of contempt. Even defenders of an ethic of contempt would have reason to object to the punishments he describes.

There are other features of Kant's moral system that should lead us to question the standard anti-contempt reading of his work. While he thinks that every person ought to be respected,

---

61. Kant, *Lectures on Ethics*, trans. Louis Infield (Indianapolis: Hackett Publishing Company, 1981), 238. It is interesting to note that much of what Kant says here fits nicely with my own account of the vices of superiority.
62. Kant, *Metaphysics of Morals*, 6:463. This passage is also discussed in Mason, n. 8.
63. Ibid.

he also insists that how we demonstrate this respect should vary. Different forms of respect are to be shown to others in accordance with differences of "age, sex, birth, strength, or weakness, or even rank and dignity."[64] Thus how we ought to show respect toward the virtuous may be very different from how we ought to show respect toward the vicious. Kant doesn't elaborate on these differences but we can speculate about what he might have had in mind. For one thing, the vicious may deserve punishment, and he famously argues that punishing the guilty is one way for the state to demonstrate respect for criminals.[65]

Just as humane punishment is compatible with recognition respect for the person punished, looking down upon and withdrawing from those who evince vices of superiority is compatible with having recognition respect for them. We can gain a better understanding of this point by considering what Kant writes about the social virtues. He characterizes the social virtues (agreeableness, tolerance, mutual love, and respect) as necessary not to promote what is best for the world "but only to cultivate what leads indirectly to this end."[66] These social virtues are not to be valued for their own sakes, nor are they simply instrumentally valuable as a means to the end of virtue:

> [The social virtues] are, indeed, only *externals* or by-products (*parerga*), which give a beautiful illusion resembling virtue that is also not deceptive since everyone knows how it must to be taken. *Affability, sociability, courtesy, hospitality,* and *gentleness* (in disagreeing without quarreling) are, indeed, only

---

64. Ibid., 6:468.
65. For a helpful recent overview of Kant's views on punishment, see Nelson Potter, "Kant on Punishment," in *The Blackwell Guide to Kant's Ethics,* ed. Thomas E. Hill (Chichester, UK: Wiley Blackwell, 2009).
66. Kant, *Metaphysics of Morals*, 6:473.

tokens; yet they promote the feeling for virtue itself by striving to bring this illusion as near as possible to the truth.[67]

Kant's insight here is important. These virtues are ways of *appearing virtuous* and are valuable as *tokens* or *illusions* of true virtue. By showing esteem, deference, and other signs of appraisal respect, even when this respect is not warranted, we pay tribute to the person as someone who is capable of someday meriting esteem and deference.

Given this presumption in favor of good manners and the appearance of respect, it is interesting to consider what Kant says about how we should comport ourselves around the vicious. While we cannot entirely avoid them, and while we ought to recognize that our judgments concerning persons' virtues and vices are always based on incomplete evidence, he insists that one must not keep company with those whose vices are "scandals":

> But if the vice is a scandal, that is, a publicly given example of contempt for the strict laws of duty, which therefore brings dishonor with it, then even though the law of the land does not punish it, one must break off the association that existed or avoid it as much as possible, since continued association with such a person deprives virtue of its honor and puts it up for sale to anyone who is rich enough to bribe parasites with the pleasures of luxury.[68]

How is it that associating with the wicked could deprive virtue of its honor? Kant suggests that *showing respect* for a non-vicious person by associating with him and manifesting the social virtues in one's relations with him is valuable not in itself or because it will

67. Ibid.
68. Ibid., 6:474.

bring about some valuable state of affairs but as a *token of virtue*. These tokens of virtue are important, he thinks, because human beings will aspire to be worthy of them. He assumes that most persons are neither perfectly virtuous nor completely vicious, and when we interact with decent persons, these tokens of virtue have what we might call "aspirational value." That is, they inspire most people to be worthy of them and thus indirectly cultivate virtue. But when we offer these tokens of respect to the vicious, they take on a very different meaning. To manifest the social virtues in our dealings with those who give every indication of vice is to make a mockery of these tokens' expressive and aspirational value.

To better appreciate his insight, consider the signs of respect that some think we ought to show toward the flag: according to the US flag code, one should never carry the flag horizontally, allow it to touch the ground, or fly it without illumination at night. The flag code codifies tokens of respect that have symbolic value. What would we think of someone who showed this kind of deference toward the flag of the National Socialist German Workers Party? Showing these signs of respect toward the Nazi flag does not seem to be intrinsically disvaluable, nor will it necessarily lead to negative consequences, but it is clear that expressing respect toward the Nazi flag is morally objectionable. Such behavior is objectionable because what the flag stands for is so obviously unworthy of these signs of respect. Similarly, *showing* respect (i.e., manifesting the social virtues) toward someone who is clearly vicious may not be bad in itself and may not lead to any negative consequences, but it is morally objectionable due to the social meaning of these tokens of respect. Moreover, when directed toward those who cannot or will not change their ways, the aspirational value of these tokens of respect will not be realized; under these conditions, tokens of respect are incapable of inspiring targets to change their ways.

Kant does not elaborate on his claim that one should break off one's association with those whose vices are scandals. He clearly thinks that we should not keep their company or treat them in ways that would express the social virtues of affability, decorum, courtesy, and so forth. And we should behave in these ways *because* we see these persons as *low* for spectacularly violating strict laws of duty. But withdrawing from another and refusing to give him the signs of respect that we would give others because we see him as low in virtue of some fault is, according to the account defended in chapter 1, to harbor contempt for the person. Thus insofar as Kant suggests that we should withhold signs of respect from the vicious he leaves ample room in his moral system for apt contempt.

My arguments here do not address Kant's more general worries about emotions as moral motives. But they do call into question the standard interpretation of Kant as a staunch critic of contempt. Once we look beyond the passages most often cited in the secondary literature, we should conclude that Kant is not the unyielding defender of an anti-contempt ethic that he is usually taken to be. If he is right, an ethic of respect and an ethic of contempt are, in fact, compatible.

4.4.3 Contempt and Comparisons

Some Kantians object to the interpersonal comparisons that structure contempt. As we have seen, contempt is reflexive and involves the subject making a direct comparison between herself and the object of her contempt; contempt presents its target as comparatively low. Some have argued that comparisons of this kind are always morally suspect, and insofar as contempt involves these comparative evaluations we ought to dismiss contempt as an inapt attitude *tout court*. Allen Wood is representative of this position. Wood argues that Kant's Formula of Humanity renders *any* interpersonal comparative evaluations confused at best and vicious at worst. The Categorical Imperative, on Wood's reading, "implies that all the normal (comparative and competitive) measures of people's self-worth—wealth, power, honor, prestige, charm, charisma, even happy relationships with others—are expressions of an utterly false sense of values."[69] This is because of the fundamental moral equality of persons: all persons have the same dignity or worth as any other; comparative or competitive measures of persons' worth are always inapt.[70]

Wood points out that Kant's doctrine is sometimes interpreted as allowing that we owe minimal respect to everyone, but beyond that minimal level, respect must be earned by good conduct or through some other non-moral excellence. But he rejects this reading of Kant and insists that the worth of our rational nature is absolute and cannot be diminished or increased.[71] For Wood, to claim that even some respect must be earned is to confuse our true worth (our dignity) with a "comparative-competitive conception of self-worth."[72]

According to Wood's Kant, it is *"contrary to ethical duty"*[73] to look down on some in comparison to others. Since both the virtuous and the vicious have absolute worth as rational agents, a person's worth never varies in comparison to others; moral comparisons are, for Kant, always contrary to duty. Wood cites the following passage from *The Metaphysics of Morals* in support of his claim:

> Humility in *comparing oneself with other human beings*... is no duty; rather, trying to equal or surpass others in this respect,

---

69. Wood, *Kant's Ethical Thought*, 133.
70. Ibid.,132.
71. Ibid., 135.
72. Ibid.
73. Ibid. Emphasis in original.

believing that in this way one will acquire an even greater inner worth, is *ambition (ambitio)*, which is directly contrary to one's duty to others, while belittling one's own moral worth merely as a means to acquiring the favor of another, whoever it may be (hypocrisy and flattery) is false (lying) humility, which is contrary to one's duty to oneself since it degrades one's personality.[74]

While Wood takes this passage to show that it is contrary to duty to look down on some in comparison to others, the text does not support this interpretation. Kant does not here claim that it is *contrary to duty* to make these kinds of comparisons; instead, he states that we do not have a *duty* to compare ourselves to others. As we have seen, Kant thinks that we often can't help but make interpersonal comparisons. If we can't help but to make these kinds of comparisons, then looking down on some in comparison to others can't, in fact, be contrary to duty.

But putting the problems with Wood's reading of this passage to one side, Kant is clearly troubled by interpersonal comparisons. In his *Lectures on Ethics* he writes: "There are two methods by which men arrive at an opinion of their worth: by comparing themselves with the Idea of perfection and by comparing themselves with others. The first of these methods is sound; the second is not, and it frequently leads to a result diametrically opposed to the first."[75] If we compare ourselves to the idea of perfection, we will always come up short and strive to better ourselves. If, on the other hand, we compare ourselves to other persons, we may come to a false sense of our own virtue by comparing ourselves only to those we antecedently know are moral

---

74. Ibid. Originally from Kant, *Metaphysics of Morals*, 6:435–436.
75. Kant, *Lectures on Ethics*, 215.

cretins.[76] Moreover, since it is easier to deprecate others than improve ourselves, when we compare ourselves to our moral equals or superiors we tend to downgrade other persons' good qualities rather than attempting to better ourselves.[77]

Kant is right to stress that interpersonal comparisons can go wrong and that we can deceive ourselves by comparing ourselves to those we antecedently judge to be our inferiors or by disparaging the good qualities of our superiors.[78] Nevertheless, he fails to appreciate that interpersonal comparisons are necessary for moral knowledge. To see this, let's begin by considering the value of *intra*personal moral comparisons and then move to the value of *inter*personal comparisons.

As many have noted, much of our knowledge of the world comes to us through a process of comparing one thing to another. David Hume, for example, asserts that human beings "always judge more of objects by comparison than from their intrinsic worth and value."[79] And he emphasizes the general connection between comparisons and knowledge: "all kinds of reasoning consist in nothing but a comparison, and a discovery of those relations, either constant or inconstant, which two or more objects bear to each other."[80]

Do we ever have reasons to compare *persons* to one another? Those who insist that it is always wrong or disvaluable to compare

---

76. "The Idea of perfection is a proper standard, and if we measure our worth by it, we find that we fall short of it and feel that we must exert ourselves to come nearer to it; but if we compare ourselves with others, much depends upon who those others are and how they are constituted, and we can easily believe ourselves to be of great worth if those with whom we set up comparison are rogues." Ibid., 215.
77. Ibid., 216.
78. Some contemporary social psychologists echo Kant's claim. See, for example, Benoit Monin, "Holier than Me? Threatening Social Comparison in the Moral Domain," *International Review of Social Psychology* 20, no. 1 (2007): 53–68.
79. David Hume, *A Treatise of Human Nature*, 238.
80. Ibid., 50.

ourselves to others often fail to distinguish between the different *kinds* of comparisons we may make. To make what we might call "intrapersonal diachronic moral comparisons" involves comparing one's current moral status to one's past moral status and who one wants to be in the future. It is difficult to imagine why anyone would want to reject these sorts of comparisons as disvaluable. If we never engaged in intrapersonal diachronic comparisons, then we would surely be morally worse for it. A person could not hope to improve herself (e.g., become kinder or less selfish) if she never compared the person she is now to the person she once was or the person she strives to be. Nor would genuine moral change be possible; for some change in behavior or character to count as a genuine moral progress, one would have to have backward-looking comparative attitudes directed toward the person one once was.[81] The genuinely reformed rogue should, for example, look back on his earlier self with feelings of regret and possibly shame and self-contempt; if one were never prone to these sorts of backward-looking comparisons, then one's improvement could be called into question. In short, the very possibility of moral improvement and moral change depends upon our engaging in intrapersonal comparisons.

But if we accept that *intra*personal comparisons can be a valuable source of moral knowledge, then there is no reason to reject *inter*personal comparisons as always morally objectionable. To acknowledge the value of intrapersonal moral comparisons while insisting that interpersonal moral comparisons are always disvaluable is to fall into a form of solipsism that ought to be rejected. For in comparing ourselves to others we can learn things about our

---

81. Linda Zagzebski argues against the possibility of instantaneous moral transformations using a similar line of reasoning. See chap. 2 of *Virtues of the Mind: an Inquiry into the Nature of Virtue and Ethical Foundations of Knowledge* (New York: Cambridge University Press, 1996).

moral status that we could not learn simply by making diachronic intrapersonal comparisons. We may make mistakes about which standards we ought to endorse or what we can legitimately expect from others. By engaging in interpersonal moral comparisons we may potentially correct these mistakes. Even Kant acknowledges the importance and unavoidability of interpersonal moral comparisons in the *Metaphysics of Morals*: "It is indeed natural that, by the laws of imagination (namely, the law of contrast), we feel our own well-being and even our good conduct more strongly when the misfortune of others or their downfall in scandal is put next to our own condition, as a foil to show it in so much the brighter light."[82] And he goes on to affirm the importance of judging others and giving the judgments of others uptake in the *Lectures on Ethics*: "Men are meant to form opinions regarding their fellows and to judge them. Nature has made us judges of our neighbours so that things which are false but are outside the scope of the established legal authority should be arraigned before the court of social opinion... The man who turns a deaf ear to other people's opinion of him is base and reprehensible."[83]

None of this is to deny the dangers of interpersonal comparisons. We can compare ourselves to the wrong people or come to mistaken conclusions about where we stand vis-à-vis others. Moreover, these comparisons, if expressed, have the potential to shame those we compare ourselves to. For all these reasons we should be cautious in making interpersonal comparisons and even more circumspect in expressing any comparisons we do make. But we shouldn't rid ourselves of these comparisons altogether. By

---

82. Kant, *Metaphysics of Morals*, 6:460.
83. Kant, *Lectures on Ethics*, 230–231. Kant goes on to write that since we are ignorant of others' dispositions, we cannot tell whether or not they are "punishable before God," but this does not preclude making judgments of others: "We cannot judge the inner core of morality: no man can do that; but we are competent to judge its outer manifestations." 230.

making interpersonal comparisons we can gain moral knowledge that cannot be gained by relying on intrapersonal comparisons alone.

4.4.4 Withdrawal and Moral Address

Many are suspicious of contempt's characteristic withdrawal. Withdrawal, it seems, cannot be a form of what some have called *moral address*.[84] Like recognized forms of moral address, contempt makes a *demand* on its target, but unlike other forms of moral address, contempt communicates this demand through *withdrawal*.[85] As one commentator sees it, contempt's characteristic withdrawal has much in common with disgust's aversion: "[t]he sort of recoil that contempt involves is no more a form of address than the recoil of disgust is some sort of appeal to putrid food."[86] Given this description, we might wonder whether the withdrawal that partially constitutes contempt undermines its moral value.

Simple withdrawal often evinces a lack of moral maturity or worse. In his published diaries, we learn that President Ronald Reagan was not above using "the silent treatment" as a way of sanctioning friends and family members. In response to his son, Ron, hanging up on him during a heated telephone call, the seventy-two-year-old Reagan writes: "I'm not talking to [Ron] until he apologizes for hanging up on me."[87] On the face of it, we have reason to object to this kind of withdrawal. For a father to

---

[84] I take the term "moral address" from Gary Watson. See Watson, "Responsibility and the Limits of Evil: Variations on a Strawsonian Theme," in *Responsibility, Character and the Emotions: New Essays in Moral Psychology*, ed. Ferdinand Schoeman (Cambridge: Cambridge University Press, 1987). The idea of moral address also plays an important role in Darwall, *Second-Person Standpoint*.

[85] Darwall, *Second-Person Standpoint*, 67, n. 4.

[86] David Sussman, "Shame and Punishment in Kant's Doctrine of Right," 315.

[87] *The Reagan Diaries*, ed. Douglas Brinkley (New York: HarperCollins, 2007), 149. This passage is cited in Nicholas Lemann's review of the published diaries

use the silent treatment on his son in order to sanction a minor slight may seem petty and manipulative.

Moreover, recent research suggests that the long-term effects of withdrawal can be devastating. Ostracism, social exclusion, and rejection all threaten our basic need to belong. When this fundamental need is not met, people very often show signs of serious illness and distress.[88] Although all hostile interactions threaten belonging, withdrawal threatens it more clearly and more strongly than other negative social encounters. An angry rebuke, for example, may be threatening, but it involves some level of interaction, albeit negative, between the angry person and the target of his anger.

In addition, direct confrontation offers a level of specificity that is absent in many cases of withdrawal. A target of an angry rebuke typically comes away with some understanding of the perceived wrong. Even if one thinks that the accuser is mistaken, one at least has some sense of what one was *thought* to have done wrong. But withdrawal often occurs without any explanation of the reason for withdrawal or even an acknowledgment that the other is withdrawing. The ambiguity of silence contributes to the devastating effects of exclusion and withdrawal.[89]

Although withdrawal is objectionable for these reasons, our social practices and interpersonal relationships reveal a widespread reliance on withdrawal as a form of communication. On the political stage, states often ostracize other states. In the 1980s, for example, a number of nations imposed trade sanctions

---

"O Lucky Man: The Diaries of Ronald Reagan," *New Yorker* May 28, 2007. http://www.newyorker.com/arts/critics/books/2007/05/28/070528crbo_books_lemann

88. See Roy Baumeister and Mark Leary, "The Need to Belong: Desire for Interpersonal Attachments as a Fundamental Human Motivation," *Psychological Bulletin* 117, no. 3 (1995): 497–529.

89. Kipling D. Williams, Joseph P. Forgas, William von Hippel, Lisa Zadro, "The Social Outcast: An Overview," in *The Social Outcast: Ostracism, Social Exclusion, Rejection, and Bullying*, ed. Kipling D. Williams, Joseph P. Forgas, and William von Hippel (New York: Taylor & Francis Group, 2005), 323.

on South Africa in order to help bring about an end to apartheid. Interpersonal ostracism of various kinds is widely inflicted as a penalty, and it is very commonly used as a form of social control. Parents of young children are encouraged to use "time-outs" since they are considered more humane than corporal punishment. And despite the negative consequences associated with the silent treatment, it is widely used within personal relationships.

Can we ever *address* a person through withdrawal? The answer to this question seems to be a rather straightforward yes. Anyone who would deny that withdrawal could serve as a form of address would need to sharply distinguish between verbal communication and non-verbal communication. But it is difficult to see the reasons for drawing this distinction. We can communicate in a wide variety of ways, and there is no good reason to deny that withdrawal can be communicative. The controversial issue is whether withdrawal can ever be a form of *moral* address. Those who claim that some emotions are modes of moral address often begin by pointing out that a liability to certain emotions presupposes a kind of relationship between the subject and the target. For example, resentment is not merely expressive of an isolated, inner state of the resenter; instead, it both expresses a claim (or makes a demand) and, at the very same time, *calls for a response* from its target. Gary Watson argues that constraints on moral address come from the normative felicity conditions of making a demand. As Watson points out, demanding something requires that the utterance is understood as a demand. So, to the extent that I resent you, I am making a demand on you, and my resentment presupposes that you understand this demand.[90] When my

---

90. The claim is not that the resenter must *believe* the object of her resentment understands the demand inherent in the resentment. Rather, the claim is that resentment, as a form of moral address, presupposes that the object of resentment understands the demand. For more on this point, see Darwall, *Second-Person Standpoint*, 75.

resentment is completely successful, my target understands that I am addressing a claim and gives the claim uptake. That is, she takes the content of the claim seriously and treats it as a *claim* whether or not she agrees with its content.

To return to our question, in some cases withdrawal is not a form of moral address. If I see a convicted child molester in my neighborhood and I actively avoid him and refuse all communication with him, I may be addressing him, but I may also be viewing him merely as a disgusting contaminant that I need to avoid for my child's safety.[91] Disgust is, I think, an attitude that should not be characterized as a form of moral address. In responding with disgust, I am certainly *judging* the pedophile, but I'm not *issuing a demand* or *making a claim*. Moreover, my judgment of him does not call for a response. In fact, to see someone as disgusting is to preclude the very possibility of a coherent response. Disgust presents its object as a contaminant and therefore as incapable of a response that could be given uptake.[92] Any response that the target of disgust could offer would be unwelcome because contagions should be kept at arm's length. We don't want slime talking back to us (this is the stuff of horror movies!), nor do we want those we deem disgusting responding to our evaluation of their disgustingness. Moreover, if the message implicit in disgust is that its object is a contaminant that must be avoided, it is difficult to see how

---

91. There is a scene in the film *Little Children* (dir. Todd Field, 2006) that offers a good example of this kind of withdrawal: A known pedophile comes to swim in the local public pool on a hot summer day. When concerned parents spot him, they call their children out of the pool until only the child molester remains in the water. While the parent's actions certainly have an expressive component, I'm inclined to say that they did not *address* the man through their actions. Instead, they simply viewed him as a contaminant to be given a wide berth.

92. See Miller, *Anatomy of Disgust;* and Martha C. Nussbaum, *Hiding From Humanity: Disgust, Shame and the Law* (Princeton: Princeton University Press, 2004). The psychologist Paul Rozin has done extensive work on the eliciting conditions of disgust. See Paul Rozin and April Fallon, "A Perspective on Disgust," *Psychological Review* 94, no.1 (1987): 23–41.

this message could be given uptake because it is not clear what would count as taking this claim seriously.

Unlike disgust, apt contempt can be a form of moral address. Contempt involves making a claim and this claim may be addressed to the target through contempt's characteristic withdrawal. Contempt does not present its target as a contaminant but as a person of comparatively low status. Unlike disgust, it is possible to give contempt uptake. If a target of contempt believes that the contempt directed at him is apt, then he will respond with shame and an attempt to ameliorate his character. And this character change may give the contemnor a reason to rationally overcome her contempt through a process of forgiveness.[93]

If contempt is to serve as a form of moral address, then the target must be capable of giving contempt uptake. This in turn presupposes that he has certain basic capacities: the target must be able to understand what it means to fail to meet a standard and must be able to change his ways if he comes to accept the claim implicit in contempt. If a person is unable to understand what it means to fail to meet a standard or is utterly unable to take steps to address his fault, then one could not morally address him through one's contempt.

There are several aspects of its characteristic withdrawal that make contempt a particularly risky form of moral address. Even when it *is* intended as address, withdrawal can easily be interpreted as a form of *manipulation* or *coercion*. To manipulate or coerce another is to fail to respect her autonomy. At minimum, respecting a person's autonomy involves seeing and treating the person as capable of deliberation and responding to reasons and thus able to take responsibility for herself and

---

93. I return to the issue of forgiveness in chap. 6.

her life. Coercion is incompatible with this basic form of respect because when one person coerces another—by demanding, for example, "Your money or your life!"—the coercer uses the threat of force to get his victim to do what he wants rather than allow the person to deliberate and rationally assess her reasons for action. In paradigmatic cases, the coerced person comes to see a normally disagreeable option as her only real alternative. While I wouldn't normally take the mugger's *demand* for my money as a reason to hand over my wallet, when he puts a gun to my head, I do.

Likewise, when one person manipulates another he unfairly (and usually surreptitiously) influences the victim's options. In extreme cases, manipulation is indistinguishable from coercion. If, for example, a mother threatens to kill herself if her daughter gets married, this is very similar to paradigmatic forms of coercion involving gun-to-the-head demands. The only difference is that in standard cases of coercion the threat is made to the person being coerced, whereas in this example the manipulator threatens to harm herself if her daughter refuses to cede to her demand. Of course, this manipulation will only come off if the daughter sees the mother's suicide as something that would seriously set back her own interests. Thus, in this case at least, the line between coercion and manipulation is quite thin.

Is it unfairly manipulative or coercive to address another with contempt? One is, after all, presenting the target with a difficult choice: reform or be seen as someone low and to be avoided. Given our fundamental desire for esteem and deference, the possibility of withdrawal may function like the threat of a gun to the head. But unlike paradigmatic examples of coercion and manipulation, when one responds to another with apt contempt, one is not attempting to *use* the painfulness of the emotion as a mere tool to get the target to do what one wants. This sort of contempt would fail to satisfy the aptness conditions set out in the first section of this chapter because one wouldn't be responding with contempt for defensible reasons. The contemned is presented with a tough choice, but when contempt is apt, he has brought this hard choice on himself and there is nothing manipulative or coercive about contempt's withdrawal.

It is true that contempt's withdrawal may be misinterpreted. Silence and withdrawal are multiply ambiguous in ways that other forms of address are not. The ambiguity of withdrawal makes it easy for manipulative or coercive withdrawers to deny that they are withdrawing at all. And the deniability that withdrawal affords is part of what makes it so devastating to targets. But while the ambiguity of withdrawal can be disorientating, this disorientation can also be constructive. As targets think about what elicited the withdrawal, they may, like Darcy, come to recognize contemptible aspects of their characters that they had long overlooked. Moreover, there need not be anything subterranean about contempt. While the withdrawal characteristic of contempt is often ambiguous, this doesn't mean that the contemnor is intentionally trying to keep the target in the dark. Given that silence has the potential to be misinterpreted, the person who contemns excellently will make it clear to the target why she holds him in contempt. This explicitness, while socially awkward, offers an additional defense against the charge of manipulation or coercion.

4.5 DO WE HAVE AN OBLIGATION TO CONTEMN?

Contempt, as explained in section 4.3, has both instrumental and non-instrumental value. Moreover, the objections that are commonly raised against contempt do not give us reason to accept an anti-contempt ethic. Should we conclude that we *ought to* contemn the contemptible? Consider the following argument:[94]

1. We must feel some affective attitude in response to the badbeing and wrongdoing we face.
2. We ought to respond with the attitude that best answers the badbeing or wrongdoing we face.
3. Apt contempt does the best job of answering certain forms of badbeing (especially the vices of superiority).
4. Therefore, we ought to respond to certain forms of badbeing with apt contempt (especially the vices of superiority).

According to the first premise, we must feel something in response to the badbeing and wrongdoing we face; avoiding emotions altogether is not a viable option for creatures like us. Of course, there are a wide variety of affective attitudes we could harbor including some that are muted or barely discernable, and there is certainly no reason to suppose that these attitudes must be "negative emotions." My point is merely that we must feel *something* in response to the wrongdoing and badbeing we encounter. The question isn't "should we experience affective attitudes in response to wrongdoing and badbeing?" but rather "which affective attitudes should we feel?"

According to the second premise, we ought to adopt the attitude that *best* answers the wrongdoing or badbeing we confront. I have agued that both wrongdoing and badbeing damage our personal and moral relationships, and it is incumbent upon us to answer this relational damage in order to mitigate or, more optimistically, repair it. Since various forms of badbeing and

---

94. I am grateful to Achille Varzi and Akeel Bilgrami for their suggestions concerning how to frame this argument and for a helpful discussion of these issues.

wrongdoing damage our relationships in different ways, we ought to respond with the attitude or attitudes that best answers the wrongdoing or badbeing that we encounter.

The third premise states that apt contempt does the best job of answering the vices of superiority.[95] An attitude *answers* a fault or action when it is apt and mitigates the damage wrought. I have argued that contempt does a better job than neighboring affective attitudes of answering the superbia at the heart of the vices of superiority. Of course, a full defense of this claim would require comparing contempt to *every other* possible response to superbia, and this is not a task I can take on here. I have, however, argued that contempt does a better job than resentment, disgust, hatred, and disappointment in answering the vices of superiority, and since these are the clearest alternatives to contempt, I think we have good reason to believe that contempt does the best job of answering these vices. Unless critics give us a reason to think that some other attitude does a better job of answering the superbia at the heart of the vices of superiority, we have sufficient reason to accept the third premise.

Given all this, it looks like we ought to respond to certain faults—especially the vices of superiority—with contempt. However, some will argue that we have independent reason to reject the conclusion of this argument due to a problem it inherits from the second premise. This premise presupposes that affective oughts are coherent; that is, it presumes that it makes sense to say things like "Tracy *ought* to feel contempt for her father" or "Seth *ought* not feel contempt for Tracy." However, some philosophers

---

95. It is worth stressing that apt contempt must be *fitting* (this is contempt's first aptness condition), and as I argued in chap. 2, whether a particular token of contempt fits its target depends upon the relationship between the subject and the target. So contempt may be an apt response for you to have toward someone, but it may not be an apt response for me to take up toward the same person.

deny the possibility of affective oughts; we cannot, according to these critics, coherently claim that some person ought to experience some emotion.

The coherence of affective oughts turns on whether oughts require direct voluntary control. We arguably have direct control over at least some of our actions, and many think that action oughts are coherent for this reason. However, we lack this kind of control over our emotions. If ordered to close the kitchen door or offered payment to take out the garbage we can, under normal conditions, simply go to the kitchen and close the door or take out the garbage. Things are different when it comes to our emotions: if you order me to feel sad or offer to pay me to feel jealous, I cannot just feel sad or jealous no matter how much I want to obey the order or receive the payment. I lack the kind of control over my emotions that I have over at least some of my actions.

We may accept this point without denying that we do exercise *some* agency over our emotions. We can, over time, revise our emotions and encourage ourselves to experience some and discourage ourselves from experiencing others.[96] Cognitive therapy is premised on the possibility of persons exercising this sort of indirect control over their affective lives; those undergoing this kind of therapy are prompted to consider and revise their irrational beliefs and thought processes, and in this way indirectly revise their emotions. The therapy would not have the success it has in treating depression and anxiety disorders if persons were unable to exercise this kind of agency over their emotions. We may also exercise our emotional agency by controlling our environment; we may, for example, avoid situations that are especially likely to

---

96. Nancy Sherman expresses some skepticism regarding this claim in "Taking Responsibility for our Emotions," *Social Philosophy and Policy* 16, no. 2 (1999): 294–323.

leave us feeling angry or nervous. And we may also manage our emotions through medication, meditation, pretense, and so on. In short, we do exercise agency over our affective lives, but the kind of control we have over our emotions is indirect, and our agency in this realm is most effectively exercised over relatively long periods of time.

Many philosophers think that if one ought to φ, then one must have the power to φ or "ought implies can." What is within our power is, of course, a topic of much debate. Some may argue that the "can" in the "ought implies can" (OIC) principle presupposes the subject's immediate and direct control; in other words, we cannot be said to have the power to φ unless we have immediate and direct control over our φ-ing. If oughts require this sort of immediate control, then affective oughts will be impossible. For the type of indirect agency we have over our emotions is not sufficient to satisfy this condition. Others may argue that the OIC principle does not presuppose immediate voluntary control; as long as we have indirect control over our emotions and have the power to revise them over time, affective oughts are not undermined by the OIC principle. Yet others may question whether we should accept the OIC principle in the first place.

A complete resolution of these issues would take us far away from the central concerns of this book, and so I will not attempt to tackle these issues here. Since there is debate about whether affective oughts run afoul of the OIC principle, I remain neutral on the possibility of affective oughts. We do, however, have reason to accept a somewhat weaker claim: we ought to strive to cultivate contempt and other hard feelings so that we are ready respond aptly to wrongdoing or badbeing. Striving to cultivate emotions is under our direct voluntary control in a way that experiencing an emotion is not.

In light of these considerations, we may revise our argument as follows:

1. We must feel some affective attitude in response to the badbeing and wrongdoing we encounter.
2. We ought to strive to cultivate the attitude that best answers the badbeing or wrongdoing we face.
3. Apt contempt does the best job of answering certain forms of badbeing (especially the vices of superiority).
4. Therefore, we ought to strive to cultivate apt contempt in order to answer certain forms of badbeing (especially the vices of superiority).

We ought to strive to cultivate apt contempt—as well as other hard feelings—so that we are in a position to answer the badbeing that we encounter.

We do not have a reason to contemn all those that evince superbia. Contempt's fittingness conditions are relationship dependent, and the aptness of a particular token of contempt depends upon the relationship between the subject and target. Moreover, we do not necessarily have reason to contemn in every case where contempt would be apt. Just as we don't have reason to value all that is valuable, we don't have reason to disvalue all that is disvaluable. However, we do have reason to answer bad being or wrongdoing when it seriously damages our relationships with other persons or threatens to undermine persons' integrity or self-esteem. There is no recipe or algorithm for determining when relational damage counts as serious, but there are some general guidelines for distinguishing between cases of superbia that significantly damage our relationships and those that do not. If A's superbia or other contempt-meriting fault threatens to undermine B's integrity or self-esteem (or the integrity or self-esteem of some other person or persons), then B has *pro tanto* reason to respond to A with contempt. For this condition to be satisfied, there must be some connection between A and B: A may be a good friend of B, B's father, or fellow citizen; A may even be an institution with which B frequently interacts. But if A is a person on the other side of the world in a culture that is far removed from B's culture, then, barring some special story, there is little reason to suppose that A's superbia will threaten B's integrity or self-esteem; under these conditions, B would not have *pro tanto* reason to respond with contempt.

* * *

Many have dismissed contempt as always disvaluable because of the bad consequences that often follows its expression. As I noted in the Introduction, married partners who respond to one another with contempt during their arguments are more likely to separate than those who express anger or frustration. This result seems to support the widely held view that contempt is a nasty or immoral emotion that undermines, rather than strengthens, our relationships with other persons.

In some cases, contempt's negative consequences may be part of its distinct value. Perhaps it was a good thing that contemptuous couples were more likely to separate than their resentful counterparts. Perhaps the focused attention and engagement characteristic of resentment kept some troubled couples together when separation would have provided a better resolution to their marital problems. There is a lot we don't know about the couples in these psychological studies. Most significantly, we don't know whether the contempt they expressed was apt. Without this information, this research cannot shed much light on the question of contempt's value. Contempt's corrosive power is undeniable. Nonetheless, what is deniable, and what should, in fact, be denied, is the claim that all corrosive emotions are necessarily morally objectionable. When apt, even destructive emotions like contempt have moral value, and we should attempt to cultivate them.

In arguing that contempt has an important role to play in our moral lives, I do not mean to dismiss or ignore the damage done by inapt contempt. Contempt certainly has a dark side, and in chapter 5 I will explore the moral dangers of inapt contempt as it is evinced in racism and the power of counter-contempt as a response.

Chapter 5

Contempt, Racism, and Civility's Limits

Some may worry that my moderate defense of contempt has ignored two important social facts: first, contempt is especially likely to be directed toward members of stigmatized groups. Second, members of stigmatized groups suffer the most from being held in contempt. In fact, some have argued that contempt structures a wide variety of oppressive institutions and practices, and is at the heart of racism, sexism, and heterosexism.[1] If members of stigmatized groups are especially likely to be on the receiving end of contempt and are vulnerable to greater suffering from being held in contempt, then some will conclude that this gives us decisive reason to accept an anti-contempt ethic (despite the arguments I've offered in favor of an ethic of contempt).

I think those who would argue against an ethic of contempt on these grounds are making a mistake. The contempt that underlies racism and other forms of oppression is clearly inapt according to the conditions outlined in chapter 4 and is utterly without positive value. But just because we have reason to reject some forms of contempt as disvaluable, it doesn't follow that contempt never makes a positive contribution to our moral lives. Moreover, the best response to inapt, race-based contempt is to marshal a robust *counter-contempt* for those who harbor this objectionable attitude. While members of stigmatized groups may more frequently find

---

1. See, for example, David Haekwon Kim, "Contempt and Ordinary Inequality."

themselves targets of inapt contempt and may find this experience particularly painful, it actually provides an additional reason to favor an ethic of contempt over an anti-contempt ethic: an anti-contempt ethic will not provide the resources necessary for *answering* the inapt contempt directed toward members of stigmatized groups.

My aims in this chapter are twofold: first, focusing on anti-black racism in the United States, I offer an account of contempt's role in racism and argue that the best way of answering racist contempt is by responding with apt contempt. Second, I consider whether this counter-contempt, and apt contempt more generally, should ever be publicly expressed. Some suggest that our interactions with one another (even when we confront the disrespectful and vicious) should always be conducted *civilly*. What people usually mean by this is that we should not express contempt or other hostile emotions in our communications. Showing respect by conforming to norms of civility may help create a stable public life by smoothing over discord and sustaining debate and conversation, but what are civility's limits? Using the case of responding to racist contempt with counter-contempt as an illustrative example, I sketch an account of the limits of civility. While civility is valuable, many of its defenders overemphasize the role it should play in our collective lives. Racist contempt, and inapt contempt more generally, calls for an aptly contemptuous—that is, uncivil—response.

5.1 CONTEMPT AND ANTI-BLACK RACISM: THE CASE OF THE OBAMA BUCKS CARTOON

From slavery to Jim Crow to various forms of bias, the relationships between American blacks and whites have long been structured by feelings of contempt. Instead of reviewing the history of anti-black contempt here, I propose that we begin thinking about race-based contempt by considering a contemporary example: In October 2008, at the height of the US presidential race, the leader of a Republican group in California sent out a newsletter containing a cartoon that depicted then-candidate Barack Obama on a food stamp with the words "Obama Bucks" emblazoned on the bottom. In the cartoon, Obama is presented with a donkey's body and is surrounded by watermelon, ribs, and a bucket of Kentucky Fried Chicken. Tim Kastelein, a Democrat from Minnesota, originally created the cartoon in an attempt at satirizing Obama's critics. Unaware of the satirical intent behind the cartoon, Diane Fedele, president of California's Chaffey Community Republican Women, Federated, sent the cartoon to members of the group along with the following message: "Obama talks about all those presidents that got their names on bills. If elected what bill would he be on???? Food stamps, what else?" After Fedele came under scrutiny by the press, she reported that she circulated the image without any racist intent and claimed that the cartoon was just a playful riff on Obama saying he didn't look like the past presidents on American currency.[2]

Through its hackneyed invocation of old stereotypes, the cartoon clearly expresses race-based contempt for Obama. By depicting him on a "$10 food stamp" and surrounding him with images of products stereotypically associated with African Americans, Obama is negatively compared to past presidents. The cartoon presents blacks as greedy recipients of governmental aid, and Obama is ridiculed as someone who does not deserve to be taken seriously as a presidential candidate.

2. "I never connected," she told a local newspaper. "It was just food to me. It didn't mean anything else." Michelle DeArmond "Inland GOP Mailing Depicts Obama's Face on Food Stamp," *Press Enterprise* (San Bernardino, CA), October 16, 2008.

The kind of racism expressed by the Obama Bucks cartoon is certainly not the only or even the most common form of racism; many cases of anti-black racism are far subtler than Fedele's ham-fisted attempt at humor. Nor is the cartoon the most reprehensible recent example of anti-black racism. Unfortunately, we still encounter brutally violent displays of racism, such as the 1998 murder of James Byrd Jr. who was dragged to his death by three white supremacists in Jasper, Texas. Nor is racism is restricted to individuals; corporations and other institutions may also express racism through their policies and actions. Nevertheless, I submit that the case of Fedele and the Obama Bucks cartoon is illustrative of a common form of anti-black racism that has endured in the United States since the time of slavery. By distributing the cartoon with a snide note, Fedele expressed a morally objectionable attitude toward Obama qua black man and toward black persons more generally.[3]

How should we characterize what is objectionable about Fedele's attitude? In an influential series of papers, Jorge Garcia develops the view that racism is constituted by intrinsically disvaluable attitudes—primarily hatred and contempt. In order to understand what is objectionable about Fedele's attitude, let's begin by considering Garcia's account of racism as a vice.

5.2 RACE-BASED CONTEMPT AS A VICE

Garcia defends what he calls a volitional conception of racism. He develops his account over several papers, but I focus on just one aspect of Garcia's views: his understanding of the attitudes that constitute racism and his account of what makes these attitudes

---

3. I will use the terms "race-based contempt" and "racist contempt" synonymously to refer to the kind of contempt expressed through the Obama Bucks cartoon.

vicious. Garcia argues that racism is best understood as a kind of *race-based disaffection*:

> My own view is that racism, in its root, consists in racial disregard or even ill-will. Hate, ill-will, is, at least, the core of the phenomenon. A morally lesser, but still grave, related form of racism consists in racially based or racially informed disregard—that is, an indifference to another's welfare on account of the racial group to which that person is assigned.[4]

There are, Garcia argues, two main forms of racism associated with two distinct attitudes: one kind of racism is characterized by hatred and ill will, while the other type is characterized by disregard and contempt.[5] These unfitting and disvaluable attitudes play a role in several distinct vices: the first kind of racist evinces the vice of "malevolence," and insofar as hard feelings motivate one to deny people of color their rights or the respect that they are owed, this kind of racist is also unjust.[6] The second kind of racist manifests the vice of moral disregard or "indifference." This kind of racist may also be unjust insofar as one fails to acknowledge and respect the rights of the persons one contemns.[7]

According to Garcia, a morally decent person would never hate or contemn anyone, for any reason. This is made clear in his discussion of the difference between race-based preferential treatment and racial disregard: "Of course we may not deny people even gratuitous favors out of hatred or contempt, whether or not race-based,

---

4. J. L. A. Garcia, "Philosophical Analysis and the Moral Concept of Racism," *Philosophy and Social Criticism* 25, no. 1 (1999): 13.

5. Garcia sometimes suggests that the latter form of racism is actually a mode of the former. See "The Heart of Racism," 9.

6. Garcia, "Current Conceptions of Racism: A Critical Examination of Some Recent Social Philosophy," *Journal of Social Philosophy* 28, (1997): 29.

7. Ibid.

but that does not entail that we may not licitly choose to bestow favors instead on those to whom we feel warmly."[8] In this passage and others, Garcia suggests that harboring contempt or hatred for someone is always intrinsically disvaluable. The "of course" which prefaces his remark is telling, for Garcia seems to take it as obvious that contempt is intrinsically disvaluable and that harboring and expressing contempt is always morally objectionable.

Garcia would likely interpret the Obama Bucks cartoon as expressive of the second form of racism he identifies: the racism of contempt. While Fedele may have aimed to make blacks suffer through her actions, it is more likely that she simply didn't care enough about their interests to consider whether they would find the cartoon offensive. If Fedele regularly evinced this lack of good will toward blacks, she could, according to Garcia's account, be characterized as manifesting injustice. One way race-based contempt may be unjust is when it involves withholding from a person "the respect she is owed and the deference and trust that properly express that respect."[9] Garcia says very little about what respect requires, and in a footnote states that he will make no attempt to offer an account of when insufficient respect constitutes injustice.[10] The difficulty with this move is that he takes for granted what he is purporting to establish: namely, that contempt is unjust insofar as it precludes the respect that we owe everyone as a matter of justice.[11]

---

8. Garcia, "The Heart of Racism," 14.
9. Ibid., 10.
10. "I will not try to identify minimal levels of good will such that having less is against the virtue of benevolence, nor minimal levels of respect such that less offends against justice. I doubt these levels can be identified in abstraction, and it will be difficult or impossible for us to determine them even in minutely described particular situations. Throughout, I generally restrict my talk of disrespect and other forms of disregard to cases where the levels are morally vicious, offending against the moral virtues of benevolence and justice, respectively." Ibid., n. 19.
11. While Garcia rejects Kant's moral theory, his brief remarks suggest that he is covertly appealing to a Kantian (or at least Kantian-sounding) notion of respect for persons. He writes, for example, that this sort of racism is incompatible with respect

As I argued in chapter 4, we have reasons to doubt that an ethic of respect is incompatible with an ethic of contempt in the way that Garcia suggests. We cannot fully explain the moral badness of contempt simply by appealing to our duties to respect because the demands of respect do not rule out harboring some feelings of contempt. Moreover, by dismissing all forms of contempt as morally objectionable, Garcia's volitional account of racism leaves no conceptual space for apt contempt. This is a problem because marshalling apt contempt is the best way of answering the moral trouble created by race-based contempt.

Those who harbor race-based contempt evince superbia: they see themselves as having a comparative high status in virtue of their race, they desire that this status be recognized, and they often attempt to exact esteem and deference from others by dishonoring members of the despised race. Being a target of this kind of contempt can have significant consequences. As W. E. B. Du Bois noted more than one hundred years ago, targets of anti-black racism often come to see themselves through the lens of white contempt. Under such circumstances, blacks are unable to attain true self-consciousness. What Du Bois referred to as the "double consciousness" of the American Negro is structured by contempt. It marks a "world which yields him no true self-consciousness, but only lets him see himself through the revelation of the other world. It is a peculiar sensation, this double-consciousness, this sense of always looking at one's self through the eyes of others, of measuring one's soul by the tape of a world that looks on in amused contempt and pity."[12] As Du Bois makes clear, race-based

---

since "caring little about those she assigns to a certain racial group, [this racist] will distain them and their rights as beneath notice, therein breaching that respect for others and their dignity which the virtue of justice demands." "Current Conceptions of Racism," 29.

12. W. E. B. Du Bois, *The Souls of Black Folk* (Mineola, NY: Dover Publications Inc., 1994), 2.

contempt, even a comparatively "gentle" contempt—which is close to pity—has the potential to seriously undermine its target's self-esteem.

Race-based contempt is sustained through a host of negative stereotypes, and contemporary psychologists have studied the damage caused by these stereotypes. To take one illustrative example from a well-known line of research, Claude Steele has shown that negative stereotypes can impair persons' performance on various tasks. "Stereotype threat" is a kind of anxiety experienced by those who find themselves in circumstances that could potentially confirm a negative stereotype about their social identity. While members of any group are vulnerable to stereotype threat, it is an especially acute problem for those, like blacks, whose social identities are contoured by numerous negative stereotypes. Consider, for example, the stereotype that blacks are less intelligent than whites. Steele has found that when blacks encounter a situation in which they may be seen through the lens of this stereotype, that is, a situation in which their intelligence is called into question or explicitly assessed, they tend to experience an increased level of anxiety. In this state of heightened anxiety, their performance is negatively affected. For example, blacks perform worse on standardized tests if they are told it is a measure of intellectual ability than if they are led to believe that the test was designed to measure the psychological processes of verbal problem solving.[13]

As the theoretical and empirical research makes clear, targets of race-based contempt must cultivate defenses against being a target of this attitude or risk a loss of self-esteem and poor performance. One way of attempting to shore up one's self-esteem would

---

13. Claude M. Steele and Joshua Aronson, "Stereotype Threat and the Intellectual Test Performance of African Americans," *Journal of Personality and Social Psychology* 69, no. 5 (1995): 797–811.

be to distance oneself from the negative stereotypes directed toward one's race. If one's group is stereotyped as unintelligent, for example, one could strive for academic excellence and do one's best to outperform others. However, this is not likely to be a particularly effective way of avoiding the consequences of stereotypes. Race-based contempt is focused not just on the supposedly undesirable *actions* of members of racial groups but on the *persons* themselves. If you are seen as low in virtue of your race, attempting to win esteem by outperforming others is unlikely to be successful; under these conditions, your successes are not likely to redound to your favor. Instead, you will likely be interpreted as the beneficiary of good luck or some other external factor. Also, given that contempt takes whole persons as its object, it is unlikely that any specific achievement—even if acknowledged—will be seen as giving a reason for revising contempt.

A second way of attempting to avoid the loss of self esteem and poor performance associated with being a member of a stigmatized group is to respond with anger.[14] Angrily challenging the stereotypes that define one's social identity may give targets a sense of control and draw attention to the unfairness of being interpreted in this way. But while anger has a role to play in responding to race-based injustices, it cannot fully answer the superbia at the heart of race-based contempt. In addition, when reasons for anger are ever-present, as they are under circumstances of racial injustice, we might worry about the demands anger places on the attention of the oppressed. In societies marred by a great deal of racism, responding with anger would impose serious psychological costs on those who are already victims of oppression. Anger's patterns of focus and engagement would lead subjects to

---

14. See Macalester Bell, "Anger, Oppression, and Virtue," in *Feminist Ethics and Social and Political Philosophy: Theorizing the Non-Ideal*, ed. Lisa Tessman (New York: Springer, 2009), 165–183.

use many of their affective resources responding to the targets of their anger. For these reasons, anger is not always the best way of responding to race-based contempt.

The best defense against the threat of diminished self-esteem that comes from being a target of race-based contempt is to marshal a defiant counter-contempt for racists—if targets of racist contempt can disengage and dismiss the racists as low, then their self-esteem is less likely to be compromised by the racists' contempt.[15] One's self-esteem cannot be threatened by others' contempt if one sees the contemnors as low and unworthy of appraisal respect. Mustering apt contempt for racists can protect members of stigmatized groups from the pain and loss of self-esteem associated with being a target of race-based contempt.

Today, many philosophers would express reservations about the suggestion that blacks, qua targets of race-based contempt, have reason to answer racist contempt with their own apt counter-contempt. For Garcia, to respond to racists with contempt is to make what is, at bottom, the *very same* moral error that racists make: the mistake of responding to another person with an intrinsically disvaluable emotion. But philosophers concerned about the effects of anti-black racism have not always taken such a dim view of counter-contempt. In his famous speech, "What to the Slave is the Forth of July?" Frederick Douglass makes it clear that contempt can be an apt response to racist defenders of slavery. Douglass delivered his speech at a time when there was active debate about which methods abolitionists should use to end slavery. According to the moral suasion approach favored by William

---

15. Velleman argues that a good way for members of stigmatized groups to protect themselves against feelings of shame is to marshal contempt for those doing the stigmatizing: "A better defense against racist remarks is to muster a lively contempt for the speaker and hearers, since regarding others as beyond one's social pale is a way of excluding them from the notional audience required for the emotion of shame." See "The Genesis of Shame," 46.

Lloyd Garrison, abolitionists should dispassionately set out their arguments against slavery and keep any hard feelings they might harbor about the practice and the practitioners to themselves.[16] Douglass is not convinced:

> At a time like this, scorching irony, not convincing argument, is needed. Oh! Had I the ability, and could I reach the nation's ear, I would, to-day, pour out a fiery stream of biting ridicule, blasting reproach, withering sarcasm, and stern rebuke. For it is not light that is needed, but fire; it is not the gentle shower, but thunder. We need the storm, the whirlwind, and the earthquake. The feeling of the nation must be quickened; the conscience of the nation must be roused; the propriety of the nation must be startled; the hypocrisy of the nation must be exposed; and its crimes against God and man must be proclaimed and denounced.[17]

Douglass recognized that there is a limit to the work that "convincing argument" can do in confronting the racist contempt of those who defended the practice of slavery. While civil debate and discussion has its place in bringing about social change, by 1852 Douglass was convinced that the time for civil argument about the morality of slavery had long past. Instead of dispassionately offering arguments in defense of their position, abolitionists should be encouraged to respond to defenders of slavery with biting contempt. This contempt, Douglass suggests, is a fitting, reasonable, and morally appropriate response to racist defenders of slavery.

---

16. For an analysis of Douglass's speech and its historical context, see James A. Colaiaco, *Frederick Douglass and the Fourth of July* (New York: Palgrave Macmillan, 2006).

17. Frederick Douglass, "What to the Slave is the Forth of July?" Rochester, New York, July 5, 1852.

Garcia's account of racism cannot adequately explain what is morally objectionable about Fedele's actions and the attitude they express. While Garcia is right to stress that racism is closely connected to contempt and other hostile attitudes, the problem with racist contempt is not that contempt is intrinsically disvaluable. Moreover, Garcia's account of the badness of racism does not leave conceptual space for the positive contribution that contempt can make in answering race-based contempt.

Garcia is not the only philosopher to posit a tight connection between racism and contempt. John Arthur has offered an account of racism as race-based contempt, yet unlike Garcia, he does not assume that contempt is always a nasty or intrinsically disvaluable attitude.

5.3 RACE-BASED CONTEMPT AS UNFITTING

According to Arthur, racism is best characterized as harboring contempt toward persons in virtue of their race.[18] Someone harbors contempt "in virtue of" a person's race when the target's race plays a role in the explanation of the subject's contempt, whether or not the subject is aware that race plays this explanatory role.[19] Thus if Obama's blackness partially explains the contempt Fedele expressed through her dissemination of the Obama Bucks cartoon, then her attitude can be appropriately classified as racist even though she denies the charge of racism. Harboring contempt for someone in virtue of her race is distinct from harboring contempt for someone who happens to be a member of a particular

---

18. John Arthur, *Race Equality, and the Burdens of History* (New York: Cambridge University Press, 2007).
19. Ibid., 14–15.

race.[20] A subject may harbor non-racist contempt for a target that happens to be black as long as the target's race plays no explanatory role in the subject's contempt.

What makes harboring contempt for someone in virtue of his or her race criticizable is that this attitude is *unfitting*:

> Instead of thinking of racism as some form of *moral* defect for which the person should always be held responsible, we should instead see racism as an epistemological defect. Even if it has no consequences, racial contempt in the form of racial hostility or indifference is defective because it is unjustified. And because of that fact, because of its inappropriateness, we have reason to condemn it even if it is otherwise harmless and the person who has it is blameless.[21]

Arthur's argument here is rather compressed, but the conclusion he draws is clear: racism is an epistemic fault rather than a moral failing. We have reason to criticize race-based contempt because it fails to fit its target.

To support his characterization of racism, Arthur encourages us to think about a case of a "reluctant racist"—a person whose upbringing led him to harbor race-based contempt that he now regrets. If this person tries to overcome his attitude but fails, then he is not blameworthy:

> Although he is still a racist, it seems clear that it would be wrong to blame such a person. He is like a person who is born with an inclination to be violent, or a kleptomaniac who feels a strong desire to steal worthless junk.... A reluctant racist,

---

20. Ibid., 41.
21. Ibid., 17–18.

if anything, might be admired for his ability to deal with problems ordinary people are lucky enough never to face. The core of racism and its normative force is therefore epistemic. Merely having the attitude is by itself not an indication of any defect other than the fact that the attitude is unjustified.[22]

Ordinary racists are usually responsible for their race-based contempt due to decisions that they have made in the past (e.g., decisions to socialize with prejudiced people or to cultivate friendships only with people of the same race).[23] The reluctant racist that Arthur imagines is different: this person, through the accident of being born to racist parents, has ended up harboring race-based contempt that he does not endorse. This attitude did not come about through his choices, and given that he now stands against it, Arthur insists that he shouldn't be blamed for it. The possibility of the reluctant racist is supposed to show that racism is an epistemic, rather than a moral, fault. Again, the reluctant racist is still racist insofar as he harbors race-based contempt, but given his history, he should not be blamed for his racism.

Unlike Garcia, Arthur is not committed to the view that contempt is always morally objectionable, and his account is compatible with my claim that the best way of answering race-based contempt is by directing apt counter-contempt toward the racist. But while Arthur's account of racism is, for these reasons, preferable to Garcia's account, it has problems of its own. Specifically, Arthur has not adequately defended his claim that race-based contempt is solely an epistemic fault. For Arthur, since the reluctant racist could not control his history, did not make choices that led to his racist attitudes, and now stands against his race-based contempt, he should not be held responsible for these attitudes.

22. Ibid., 19.
23. Ibid., 19.

It is not entirely clear whether he thinks it is the reluctant racist's lack of control over his past or the fact that he now stands against his former attitudes that renders him blameless for his racism. Some have questioned whether direct voluntary control is a necessary condition for moral responsibility (see Introduction). We often resent the person with a quick temper even if we believe that he doesn't have direct control over his anger at the moment of his outburst, and we may have good reason to think this resentment is justified.[24] Consideration of cases like this may give us reason to abandon the control condition. Even if we reject the control condition, we may still concede that the reluctant racist is *less* blameworthy than the ordinary racist. In struggling to stand against his attitudes, the reluctant racist is at least *trying* to overcome his race-based contempt, and this attempt should mitigate his blameworthiness to some extent.

But Arthur goes on to argue that the example of the reluctant racist gives us reason to conclude that racism is an epistemic, rather than a moral, fault. And this is a claim that we must reject. Someone could have an incontrovertibly moral fault (e.g., stinginess or meanness, instilled in her since childhood, unconnected to any of her autonomous choices that she struggles against), and we might think that in this case, as in the case of the reluctant racist, the person is not fully blameworthy for her fault. But this doesn't render stinginess an epistemic rather than a moral fault. Just because one's history may sometimes excuse and mitigate one's blameworthiness, it doesn't follow that one's fault is epistemic rather than moral. One cannot conclude that some fault is not a moral fault simply because one may be excused or exempted from blame for evincing the fault.

---

24. For defenses of this position, see Robert M. Adams, "Involuntary Sins" and Angela Smith, "Responsibility for Attitudes: Passivity and Activity in Mental Life."

Furthermore, Arthur gives us an account of the badness of racism that we should reject. For Arthur, harboring race-based contempt is structurally analogous to evincing other forms of unfitting contempt, for example, harboring contempt for someone in virtue of his arrogance when the target is actually just shy due to a childhood trauma. I think we should resist this characterization of the badness of racism. In ordinary (non-pathological) cases of unfitting emotions, when an epistemic error is pointed out, the subject makes some effort to overcome his emotion.[25] If, for example, you learn that your colleague's reticence to speak is due to her shyness and not her arrogance, you will strive to overcome any hard feelings you originally felt. Race-based contempt, on the other hand, is especially recalcitrant, and it is in this respect fundamentally different from many other cases of unfitting attitudes. Pointing out that the target does not merit contempt simply in virtue of his race is unlikely to lead the contemnor to revise his attitude. The recalcitrance of race-based contempt suggests that unlike ordinary cases of unfitting emotions, racist contempt is, in some way, self-serving. The person who manifests race-based contempt is one who *holds on* to his unfitting attitude long after being given evidence that supports a very different response.

Moreover, race-based contempt is structured by a host of stereotypes and false beliefs with a long social history. It is, in this respect, utterly different from ordinary cases of unfitting emotions. If you contemn someone for her arrogance but it turns out that the target is really just shy, your unfitting contempt could conceivably be the result of an accidental misinterpretation of the

---

25. As I noted in chap. 4, we don't have immediate and direct control over our emotions, so when we discover that our emotions are unfitting, this may not immediately extinguish them. Nevertheless, over time, we will slowly overcome emotions that we believe are unfitting (unless we suffer from a mood disorder or some other pathological condition).

target. But it is surely not an *accident* that Obama is the target of race-based contempt nor is it an accident that this contempt is expressed through the invocation of familiar stereotypes. Given its recalcitrance and dependence on stereotypes, Arthur is wrong to characterize the badness of race-based contempt solely in terms of its lack of fittingness. Race-based contempt is *inapt* and not simply unfitting.

5.4 RACE-BASED CONTEMPT AS INAPT

Race-based contempt presents persons as comparatively low in virtue of their presumed race. The problem with race-based contempt is not, as Garcia would insist, that contempt is a nasty or immoral emotion, nor is the problem merely one of unfittingness as Arthur maintains. Instead, race-based contempt is objectionable because it fails to meet the aptness conditions outlined in chapter 4. If racism can be characterized as a vice, it is surely a vice of superiority. To see a person as comparatively low simply because of his or her perceived race is to manifest unfounded ill will and superbia. This attitude is fundamentally at odds with the respect and affective openness characteristic of unimpaired moral relations.

On a minimally acceptable morality, our moral relationships are characterized by respect and affective openness. We acknowledge that everyone is owed a basic form of moral consideration, and we will only act in ways that are, in principle, justifiable to others (see chap. 4).[26] To be affectively open does not mean that we love and appreciate the good qualities of all persons. Instead, the affectively open person will not respond to others with hostility or ill will unless she has been given good reason to do so; she

---

26. See, for example, T. M. Scanlon, *What we Owe to Each Other* (Cambridge, MA: Belknap Press of Harvard University Press, 1998).

will be *open* to appreciating the good qualities of persons unless she has reason to abandon her openness.

Race-based contempt for blacks is structured by a number of negative stereotypes that interfere with this affective openness.[27] The Obama Bucks cartoon, for example, trades on stereotypes of blacks as gluttonous, poor, greedy, welfare recipients, and so on, and these stereotypes obviously mis-present their targets. To the extent that one sees persons through the lenses of these stereotypes, then one is not open to appreciating their good qualities. The person prone to race-based contempt closes herself off to persons of the despised race and is unable to enjoy affectively open relationships with them.

Affective openness cannot be reduced to the more familiar notions of recognition or appraisal respect. It does not involve recognizing persons' moral or political rights, nor can it be equated with esteem or deference. To be affectively open is to recognize the other's normative powers (i.e., her powers to give reasons, including reasons for or against adopting certain attitudes). To harbor race-based contempt for a person is to deny her the power to shape one's attitudes toward her; the negative stereotypes that structure race-based contempt do not allow those in their grip to see the stereotyped person as fully in possession of normative powers.

One important feature of race-based contempt is that it targets individuals qua group members. As a result, a token of racist contempt directed at an individual has the potential to dishonor not just that person but members of the group more generally. African Americans are a heterogeneous group and obviously differ in terms of culture, politics, values, and so on. Nevertheless,

---

27. For a discussion of the moral problems posed by stereotypes, see Lawrence Blum, "Stereotypes and Stereotyping: A Moral Analysis," *Philosophical Papers* 33, no. 3 (2004): 251–289.

African Americans do share a common history and a common experience of race-based contempt, which is, in turn, structured by a common set of derogatory stereotypes. Individuals can be dishonored by racist contempt in much the same way as individuals may be dishonored by arrogance or hypocrisy. But there is also a sense in which *all* African Americans are dishonored by race-based contempt, even when the contempt is directed toward an individual.

Consider, once again, the Obama Bucks cartoon: through Fedele's circulation of the cartoon, Obama was denied the esteem and deference that he merited as an individual and in this way was dishonored. But in addition, *all* African Americans were dishonored by the contempt expressed through the cartoon: if a person is inaptly contemned on the same basis that you (or a relative) have been contemned in the past or may reasonably anticipate being contemned in the future—in this case, on the basis of being black—then you are also dishonored by this contempt. That is, you are, as a member of the despised race, not given the esteem and deference that you merit. If you come to learn about this token of racist contempt, and you identify with being black, this race-based contempt has the potential to undermine your self-esteem as an African American. Of course, the Obama Bucks cartoon is a special case insofar as it involves the expression of contempt for a public figure who occupied an important symbolic position as the first black American presidential nominee, but while Obama's status as a public figure made the expression of contempt particularly striking and garnered the attention of the press, it isn't what makes the cartoon injurious to African Americans as a group. Instead, what makes this cartoon injurious to blacks qua blacks is the fact that Obama was contemned on the *basis* of being black; other blacks have experienced contempt on this basis in the past or can reasonably be expected to experience this kind of contempt in the future, and this is why race-based contempt dishonors all blacks.

In short, targets of race-based contempt are seen as low in virtue of a trait that should have no bearing on their status. This sort of attitude has the potential to undermine targets' self-esteem; those who are contemned in this way may come to see themselves as having a lower status than others solely in virtue of their race.

The best way of responding to racist contempt is with apt counter-contempt. This attitude can help protect the self-esteem of members of targeted races and will answer the superbia inherent in this attitude. The person who harbors race-based contempt sees himself as having a high status in virtue of his race, desires that this status be recognized, and often attempts to exact esteem and deference from others on this basis. Responding to the racist with apt contempt corrects his status claim and helps to restore the equilibrium between the esteem and deference he takes himself to deserve and the esteem and deference he actually merits.

When race-based contempt is publicly expressed, as in the case of the Obama Bucks cartoon, public expression of apt counter-contempt may be called for. The damage wrought by a public expression of race-based contempt—especially if it is directed toward a high-profile person with whom many in the stigmatized race may identify—can be fully answered only by a public expression of counter-contempt. Many will baulk at this suggestion. Contemptuous criticism is an *uncivil* response, and even those who acknowledge that racists merit contempt may insist that we have overriding reasons to refrain from expressing uncivil criticism. Civility requires that we *show* everyone that we think they are worthy of esteem, including those we believe don't actually merit it. But should we always be civil in our interactions with others? What are the limits to civility?

5.5 CONTEMPT AND CIVILITY

In his speech, "What to the Slave is the Fourth of July?" Frederick Douglass responds to slavery's defenders with dismissive scorn and sarcasm. Some of his fellow abolitionists objected to the tack Douglass took in his address: respectful engagement and dispassionate presentation of arguments against slavery, rather than dismissive contempt for slavery's defenders, was thought to be the only way to realize the ends of the abolitionist movement. Many contemporary ethicists would likely express similar reservations about Douglass's tone. Today, civility is often touted as a kind of master-value that should regulate all public discussion of difficult social issues. When a moral issue is debated in a public forum, invariably someone will stress the importance of having a civil discussion and remind the group that persons can disagree without being disagreeable.[28]

The civil person is one who shows respect for others through her actions. In particular, civility involves showing the esteem and deference characteristic of appraisal respect; good manners and civility are supposed to show that one thinks one's interlocutor merits esteem and deference even when one disagrees the person's views. Since civility is communicative, and what we are able to communicate depends upon the background norms and conventions of our society, the civil person will follow the conventions

---

28. One popular philosophy blog has a "Be Nice" comment policy, and remarks that are deemed uncivil are not published: "Our main rule: BE NICE. Engage arguments, but do not insult people you're arguing with. When engaging with arguments, do so respectfully. Don't attribute nasty motivations to people unless they really make it clear that they have those motivations. Try to be as charitable as possible. Abusive comments may be deleted, including but not limited to sexist and racist comments. Repeatedly abusive posters may be blocked. Why do we have this policy? Because we think it's the best way to facilitate productive dialogue. We might be wrong. But it's our blog and our policy." http://feministphilosophers.wordpress.com/our-policies.

of her society for showing respect.[29] Thus what civility requires in one society may be very different from what civility requires in another. Civility is important for lubricating social relations generally, but it is particularly important in helping us navigate disagreement, especially moral disagreement, about contested and controversial issues. Civility helps facilitate smooth social relations by reminding targets that they are regarded as worthy of respect.[30] The displays of respect characteristic of civility help keep debate and discourse on difficult issues from breaking down.[31]

While we have good reasons to be civil to one another, not everything deserves a civil response; some opinions and behaviors are simply beyond the pale. How do we determine civility's limits? One might think that individuals should decide which sorts of views or opinions do not deserve a civil response based on how objectionable they are. Douglass believed that chattel slavery was such a great and obvious evil that its defenders were

---

29. See, for example, Cheshire Calhoun, "The Virtue of Civility," *Philosophy & Public Affairs* 29, no. 3 (2000): 251–275. Calhoun writes: "The function of civility, I will suggest, is to *communicate* basic moral attitudes of respect, tolerance, and considerateness. We can successfully communicate these basic moral attitudes to others only by following socially conventional rules for the expression of respect, tolerance, and considerateness," 255. Similarly, Sarah Buss argues that good manners involve the expression of respect. See "Appearing Respectful: On the Moral Significance of Manners," *Ethics* 109, no 4 (1999): 795–826.

30. Here's how Calhoun describes the moral value of civility: "First, civility signals others' willingness to have us as co-participants in practices ranging from political dialogues, to campus communities, to funerals, to sharing public highways. Second, for those who are not already coerced into sharing social practices with us, civility may be a precondition of their willingness to enter and continue in cooperative ventures with us. Third, civility supports self-esteem by offering token reminders that we are regarded as worth respecting, tolerating, and considering. Finally, civility, particularly toward members of socially disesteemed groups, protects individuals against the emotional exhaustion of having to cope with others' displays of hatred, aversion, and disapproval," 266. Of course, norms of civility obviously can't *prevent* race-based or other forms of inapt contempt, but when such contempt is expressed, it can be labeled uncivil. I don't see this as offering much in the way of protection for the socially disesteemed, but Calhoun disagrees.

31. Ibid.

not owed a civil response. So too, it seems as though the moral badness of, say, child pornography puts its defenders outside the bounds of civility and renders them vulnerable to uncivil criticism from others. Who is and isn't owed a civil response would seem to depend on how objectionable the attitude, action, or practice being defended is; the more objectionable the view, the less plausible it is to insist on civility.

While civility has an important role to play in regulating our social interactions, when persons publicly express superbia in such a way as to undermine others' self-esteem, then they are not owed a civil response. To respond civilly to such persons is to risk condoning the superbia they express, thereby further damaging moral relations. A civil response to an expression of race-based contempt affirms the contemnor's claim of status superiority and the target's status inferiority, and responding in this way is morally objectionable.

Against this, some have objected that we misunderstand the nature and value of civility if we claim that the limits of civility ought to be determined by a consideration of the moral badness of the attitude expressed or practice defended. Cheshire Calhoun, for example, argues that the limits of civility must not be left up to the discretion of individuals: "In the midst of disagreement over what is morally intolerable (and thus does not deserve a civil response), it is a display of *intolerance* to insist on using one's own judgment to decide what deserves a civil response."[32] Nor can we rely on ethicists to distinguish between what merits a civil response and what does not; in making their arguments about the bounds of civility, ethicists will appeal to premises and make assumptions that not everyone will accept. Since not everyone will accept these starting points, one expresses intolerance for the views of others in using this method to determine civility's limits.[33]

32. Ibid., 270. Emphasis in original.
33. Ibid.

According to Calhoun, we should determine the bounds of civility by appealing to *social consensus*: we need not respond civilly to a person who expresses an abhorrent attitude if there is "social closure on its intolerability" (i.e., a general consensus that the attitude expressed or practice defended is beyond the moral pale): "At that point, civility would not further the work of enabling the non-like-minded to continue political dialogue or social interaction."[34] For example, I do not need to worry about showing signs of deference or respect to the child pornographer since we have, arguably, reached consensus in this society that creating and viewing child pornography is abhorrent. If, however, there is disagreement in one's moral community about the intolerability of some attitude, action, or practice, then we owe its defenders a civil response. Even if I think that eating factory-farmed meat is obviously wrong and have convincing arguments that I believe demonstrate its wrongness, I should remain civil in my criticisms of the practice since there is currently disagreement in this society about the moral propriety of the practice. Since the moral propriety of slavery was still actively debated in the United States when Douglass delivered his Fourth of July speech in 1852, Calhoun would insist that he owed defenders of slavery a civil response and may be criticized for his tone. Today we have achieved social closure on the intolerability of slavery and no longer need to respond to its defenders in a civil manner, but there is still disagreement concerning the tolerability of the kind of race-based contempt expressed in the Obama Bucks cartoon. While many people see the attitude expressed in the cartoon as clearly intolerable, others see it as an innocuous form of politically incorrect humor. That Fedele felt comfortable openly distributing the cartoon to members of her political group belies the fact that there is still debate concerning whether this

---

34. Ibid., 271.

kind of light hearted expression of race-based contempt is beyond the moral pale. Thus, while we may have reason to criticize Fedele, our criticisms ought to be expressed in a civil manner, which precludes any expression of contempt.

When a person lives in a world where social closure on the intolerability of some intolerable practice has not yet been achieved, she must choose between being civil and acting with integrity.[35] A person with integrity will stand up for what she values and denounce what she disvalues even if this means acting in an uncivil manner. But the fact that civility sometimes comes at the cost of persons' integrity does not, according to Calhoun, undermine civility's value. This is because the practice of morality is deeply social: not only do we want to arrive at correct moral judgments, but we also strive for convergence and mutual agreement. We want to achieve what we might call a "progressive moral consensus." That is, we want to get things right and also get others to agree with us about what is right and wrong, vicious and virtuous. According to Calhoun, though, achieving this kind of consensus "requires regulating moral dialogue so that conversations do not break down."[36] Since incivility is likely to lead to conversational breakdown, and since our only hope for achieving a progressive moral consensus is through open conversation, civility helps us, collectively, achieve our aims, even when it comes at the cost of the integrity of some. According to this line of argument, we should forgo publicly expressing contempt, even when it is apt, in order to help us achieve a progressive moral consensus and achieve morality's ends.

What should we think of this argument? Calhoun is right to stress that morality is a social practice that aims at mutual agreement. When, for example, I judge that factory farming is morally

---

35. Ibid., 274.
36. Ibid., 273.

indefensible, I clearly desire that others come to accept this position so that we can work together to end it. And it is certainly plausible to suppose that norms of civility help smooth over discord and keep conversations from breaking down. However, Calhoun seems to assume that we can achieve progressive moral consensus *only* through conversation and dialogue, and this assumption should be rejected. There is reason to think that *disrupting* dialogue may also, in the long term, help bring about a progressive moral consensus, and contempt's characteristic withdrawal has a role to play in creating disruption and discord that can ultimately lead to this kind of moral consensus.

Why do some philosophers assume that achieving a progressive moral consensus always requires dialogue and debate? The claim can be understood either descriptively or normatively. According to the descriptive interpretation, the only path to eventual convergence and agreement is through respectful dialogue and conversation; we simply cannot achieve moral consensus in any other way. But it is far from obvious that respectful conversation is, in fact, the only way to achieve this consensus. Consider a historical example: there is now broad agreement that chattel slavery is abominable, but 150 years ago there was difference of opinion and a great deal of debate concerning the morality of slavery. Did the progressive moral consensus we have achieved regarding this issue come about through a process of respectful conversation and civil argumentation? While we would need the assistance of historians and sociologists to provide a complete answer to this question, even a cursory look back at our history reveals that scorn, angry protest, bloodshed, and war played a much larger role than respectful conversation in bringing about our current consensus concerning the indefensibility of slavery. While some abolitionists urged a path of civil argument and respectful debate, others expressed plenty of uncivil scorn and anger for slavery and its defenders. Douglass makes it clear that he thinks achieving a progressive moral consensus in this domain in 1852 requires sarcasm and vitriol rather than civil debate and discussion, and his Fourth of July speech aimed to disrupt the dialogue concerning the moral propriety of slavery rather than help smooth over discord and encourage dispassionate exchange of reasons. Other cases of uncivil responses to slavery's defenders can be found throughout the abolitionist literature. Consider just a couple of examples:

> See your Declaration Americans!!! Do you understand your own language? Hear your language, proclaimed to the world, July 4th 1776—⇒ "We hold these truths to be self evident— that ALL MEN ARE CREATED EQUAL!! that they are endowed by their creator with certain unalienable rights; that among these are life, liberty, and the pursuit of happiness!!" Compare your own language above, extracted from your Declaration of Independence, with your cruelties and murders inflicted by your cruel and unmerciful fathers and yourselves on our fathers and on us—men who have never given your fathers or you the least provocation!!!!!![37]

> But while I trust that I have some experimental and saving knowledge of religion, it would be a great pleasure to me to have some one better qualified than myself to lead my mind in prayer and meditation, now that my time is so near a close. You may wonder, are there no ministers of the gospel here? I answer, No. There are no ministers of *Christ* here. These ministers who profess to be Christian, and hold slaves or advocate

---

37. David Walker, *Appeal to the Coloured Citizens*, reprinted in *American Protest Literature*, ed. Zoe Trodd (Cambridge MA: Belknap Press of Harvard University Press, 2006), 84.

slavery, I cannot abide them. My knees will not bend in prayer with them while their hands are stained with the blood of souls.[38]

While these examples from the history of the abolitionist movement don't establish that the consensus we've achieved regarding the morality of chattel slavery was born through uncivil speech, they do call into question the assumption that this consensus could have come about only through respectful moral dialogue.

Kwame Anthony Appiah has recently argued that moral revolutions, such as the change in opinion regarding chattel slavery, happen not because of a process of civil dialogue and debate but through changes in honor codes.[39] Practices and activities that were once socially acceptable become *dishonorable*. Uncivil, contemptuous speech has a central role to play in shaping what activities and practices people see as honorable and dishonorable. Getting people to regard some practice as dishonorable is not simply a matter of getting the majority to see the persuasiveness of arguments for or against it. As Appiah points out, in many cases the arguments for or against the practice are widely known. Instead, a progressive moral consensus is achieved when people come to see those who participate in the practice as contemptible. If Appiah's analysis of moral revolutions is accurate, then we have additional reasons to reject the descriptive interpretation of Calhoun's argument.

But perhaps Calhoun's insistence that reaching a progressive moral consensus requires moral dialogue and conversation is best interpreted not as making an unsupported descriptive claim about how this kind of consensus does, in fact, come about but rather as a normative claim about the process we should use in attempting to bring about moral consensus. Maybe the respect we owe to all

38. John Brown, "Prison Letters," reprinted in *American Protest Literature*, 103.
39. See Appiah, *The Honor Code*.

persons qua persons requires a civil exchange of reasons; it is only through civil conversation that we can achieve the end of mutual agreement in a respectful manner. If, for example, I attempt to get you to appreciate the evil of factory farming by coercing or manipulating you into seeing it as abominable, we may well achieve a kind of consensus, but I have brought this about in a way that fails to respect you as a person. Dialogue, it may be argued, is the only way to achieve progressive moral consensus while at the same time giving all persons the recognition respect that they are due.

Indeed, respectful exchange of reasons is one way of bringing about mutual agreement while respecting persons, but it is not the *only* respectful way of achieving this end. It would be disrespectful to manipulate or coerce you into accepting what I see as the right position on some moral issue, but it is not disrespectful to help you appreciate the reasons you have to accept the position. And this is precisely what apt contempt does: it helps put the target in a position to appreciate the reasons he has to change his ways. Being on the receiving end of contempt is often disorientating and highly disruptive, but disruption, in itself, is not always disrespectful. For through a process of withdrawal and disruption a person can come to appreciate the reasons she has to change her ways. To put someone in a position to appreciate her reasons for accepting some view or changing her ways is not to *cause* or manipulate her to change. We routinely use a variety of means to get people to appreciate their reasons. In fact, those who champion civility often defend it in precisely this way: good manners and a civil tone are thought to ease people into a position where they are able to engage in dialogue and dispassionately determine which side has the strongest reasons. In other words, civility is a way of putting persons into a position where they can come to appreciate the reasons they have to be for or against something. While civility may sometimes be the best way to get people to appreciate their reasons, it is not the only respectful means of putting people into this position. Expressing apt contempt toward those who evince the vices of superiority is also a way of putting targets in a position to appreciate their reasons.

While many contemporary ethicists extol civility and see it as a kind of master value that should regulate the way we express our opinions concerning all contentious moral issues, we do not owe everyone a civil response. Civility may, in some circumstances, help usher in a progressive moral consensus, but it can come at a high price: responding in a civil manner to those who express race-based contempt is to condone this abhorrent attitude and it puts the self-esteem of members of the race in jeopardy. Civility is not the only way to achieve a progressive moral consensus; this consensus can also be respectfully brought about through contempt's characteristic disruption.

* * *

In some cases, contempt deserves its reputation as a morally ugly emotion. Race-based contempt can fundamentally damage our moral relationships and undermine targets' self-esteem. But to defend an ethic of contempt is not to defend the view that race is a justifiable basis for hierarchical evaluations of persons. We can distinguish between apt and inapt contempt; only the former has a positive role to play in our moral lives.

Apt counter-contempt answers racist contempt and helps to mitigate some of its damage. When an expression of racist contempt threatens to undermine the self-esteem of members of the moral community, it calls for an uncivil response. Incivility is not always something to be lamented; in fact, responding in an uncivil manner to those who express racist contempt is often the best way of answering this objectionable attitude.

Chapter 6

Contempt, Forgiveness, and Reconciliation

As I have argued, contempt has a positive role to play in our moral lives, and we have reasons to prefer an ethic of contempt to an anti-contempt ethic. Nevertheless, under some conditions we may have good reasons to overcome apt contempt through a process of forgiveness. While philosophers have become increasingly interested in forgiveness, there is little in current discussions of the topic that sheds light on what is involved in overcoming contempt through forgiveness and what sorts of considerations provide good reasons to forgive. This lack of attention stems from a fundamental problem with the standard philosophical conception of forgiveness. After offering a diagnosis of this problem, I present an account of what is involved in overcoming contempt through forgiveness and what sorts of considerations provide reasons for this kind of forgiveness.

While this chapter is primarily focused on interpersonal forgiveness, my account has implications for a related set of issues in our social lives. Like individuals, institutions may express superbia, and contempt is often the best way of answering this attitude. We may sometimes, however, have reasons to overcome our apt contempt for institutions through a process analogous to forgiveness. I consider how reparations and memorials may address—and fail to address—apt contempt for institutions.[1]

---

1. This chapter incorporates material from my paper, "Forgiving Someone for Who They Are (and Not Just What They've Done)," *Philosophy and Phenomenological Research* 77, no. 3 (2008): 625–658.

6.1 A PROBLEM WITH THE STANDARD ACCOUNT OF FORGIVENESS

Bishop Joseph Butler defined forgiveness as the overcoming of excesses of resentment.[2] Influenced by Butler, many philosophers have understood forgiveness exclusively as the overcoming of resentment on moral grounds, and this Butlerian conception has become the basis of the standard philosophical account of forgiveness.[3] Although this description of forgiveness is intuitively plausible, some have argued that the standard account is overly narrow. Norvin Richards articulates this objection as follows:

> [A]bandoning resentment does not constitute forgiving, because a person can stop resenting and still have a hostile attitude of another kind...neither must it be resentment that one is forswearing: it should also count as forgiveness to abandon contempt for someone or disappointment in him. Taken together, these suggest that to forgive someone

---

2. Joseph Butler, "Upon the Forgiveness of Injuries," in *The Whole Works of Joseph Butler* (London: Thomas Tegg, 1826), 78–89; in "Joseph Butler on Forgiveness: A Presupposed Theory of Emotion," *Journal of the History of Ideas* 62, no. 2 (2001): 233–244, Paul Newberry argues that Butler did not actually define forgiveness as the *overcoming* of resentment but as the checking of revenge. Similar correctives of the standard interpretation of Butler's views have been given by Andrea Westlund, "Anger, Faith, and Forgiveness," *Monist* 92, no. 4 (2009): 507–536; and Ernesto V. Garcia, "Bishop Butler on Forgiveness and Resentment," *Philosophers' Imprint* 11, no. 10 (2011), http://quod.lib.umich.edu/cgi/p/pod/dod-idx/bishop-butler-on-forgivenes s-and-resentment.pdf?c=phimp;idno=3521354.0011.010 . Even if Butler thought that forgiveness involves the moderation of resentment and not its complete elimination, he did not seem to recognize that forgiveness might involve the moderation of *other* emotions beyond resentment. This is the point I wish to stress.

3. See, for example, Jeffrie Murphy, *Forgiveness and Mercy*; Pamela Hieronymi, "Articulating an Uncompromising Forgiveness"; R. J. O'Shaughnessy, "Forgiveness," *Philosophy* 42 (1967): 336–352; H. J. N. Horsburgh, "Forgiveness," *Canadian Journal of Philosophy* 4, no. 2 (1974): 269–282; and Elizabeth Beardsley, "Understanding and Forgiveness," in *The Philosophy of Brand Blanshard*, ed. P. A. Schilpp (La Salle, IL: Open Court, 1980), 247–258.

for having wronged one is to abandon all negative feelings toward this person, of whatever kind, insofar as such feelings are based on the episode in question.[4]

On Richards's account, to forgive is not simply to overcome one's resentment for the offender. Instead, genuine forgiveness involves the forgiver overcoming *all* hostile or "negative" emotions directed toward the target. Although he offers an important challenge to the standard account of forgiveness, Richards retains two central elements of the received view: (1) the belief that forgiveness is a possible response to wrongdoing but not to badbeing, and (2) the insistence that the emotions overcome through forgiveness must be based on a specific act or particular episode. In later sections of this chapter, I challenge both assumptions.[5]

Other philosophers have begun to acknowledge that the standard account of forgiveness is overly narrow. Jeffrie Murphy recounts Butler's definition of forgiveness as the overcoming of resentment on moral grounds before going on to offer the following caveat:

> I have now been persuaded by Norvin Richards and others, however, that it is a mistake to define forgiveness so narrowly. It is more illuminating—more loyal to the actual texture of our moral lives—to think of forgiveness as overcoming a variety of negative feelings that one might have toward a

---

4. Norvin Richards, "Forgiveness," 79.
5. In "Forgivingness," *American Philosophical Quarterly* 32, no.4 (1995): 289–306, Robert C. Roberts has a discussion of the range of emotions one may overcome through forgiveness. But in the end, Roberts argues that the emotion overcome through forgiveness is anger. More recently, Howard Wettstein has noted that our affective responses toward wrongdoing are multiple and philosophers should not focus exclusively on resentment. See "Forgiveness and Moral Reckoning," *Philosophia* 38, no. 3 (2010): 446.

wrongdoer—resentment, yes, but also such feelings as anger, hatred, loathing, contempt, indifference, disappointment, or even sadness. There is no reason to think that even this list is complete.[6]

Despite the lip service paid to this expanded definition of forgiveness, philosophers (including Murphy and Richards) have not fully defended the claim that we can extend the notion of forgiveness in this way, nor do they acknowledge the ramifications of broadening the standard account. In particular, they have not acknowledged that expanding our characterization of forgiveness in this way ought to change *what reasons count as morally good reasons to forgive*.

Moral theorists have not recognized the need to revise the standard account of our reasons to forgive because they are reticent to accept as "moral emotions" the wide variety of hard feelings that one might have toward wrongdoing or badbeing. While Murphy lists hatred, loathing, and contempt as possible responses to immorality, philosophers have traditionally regarded these as *inapt* emotions, which have no proper role in the psychological life of the morally mature. Given this understanding of the negative emotions, moral agents should either: (1) strive to extirpate these emotions as much as possible, regardless of whether they have morally good reasons to overcome them, or (2) simply ignore these emotions. As I have argued, I think this prejudice against hard feelings is unwarranted. Once we recognize the important role these emotions may play in our moral lives, we will be in a better position to understand when they should be overcome through a process of forgiveness.

In what follows, I conceptualize forgiveness as the overcoming of resentment and contempt, and I refer to this

---

6. Jeffrie Murphy, *Getting Even* (Oxford: Oxford University Press, 2003), 59.

characterization of forgiveness as "the expanded account." According to the expanded account, for *x* to forgive *y*, *x* must overcome her resentment and/or contempt for *y* on moral grounds. Of course there may well be *other* attitudes that can and should be overcome through a process of forgiveness (e.g., indifference, disappointment, sadness, and distrust), and so my expanded account will remain overly narrow. However, by conceptualizing forgiveness in this way I hope to establish that if we accept the expanded account, then we must revise the standard account of morally good reasons to forgive. I use the unfortunately awkward term "forgiveness-R" to denote forgiveness as the overcoming of resentment and the equally awkward "forgiveness-C" to denote forgiveness as the overcoming of contempt.

Part of my task in this chapter is to make the case that forgiveness-C is a genuine form of forgiveness. In discussions, I have experienced some resistance to this idea and will discuss specific worries concerning the coherence of forgiveness-C later in the chapter, but it may be worth pausing here to consider this objection in its most general form. Why think that overcoming a negative emotion other than resentment ought to count as forgiveness? Moreover, what explains the philosophical presumption that forgiveness must be directed toward specific *actions* and not toward an offender's character as such?[7]

Richards and Murphy offer one strategy for responding to those who are skeptical of my claim that forgiveness-C is a genuine form of forgiveness: imagine someone who was insulted and responded with contempt but did not resent any of the offender's

---

7. Charles Griswold notes that we forgive the person and not the action, yet he, like many others, assumes that we always forgive persons for their actions: "We forgive the agent, not the deed (even though we forgive the agent for doing the deed)." See "Debating Forgiveness: A Reply to My Critics," *Philosophia* 38, no. 3 (2010): 463. He also makes a similar claim in *Forgiveness: A Philosophical Exploration*.

actions. Suppose this person eventually overcame her apt contempt for what looked like morally good reasons.[8] Would we really want to deny that this person had forgiven her offender? Conversely, suppose that someone claimed to have forgiven someone but still harbored contempt for the person. Wouldn't we be skeptical of the claim that the person had forgiven? Reflecting on these types of cases may be enough to convince some that forgiveness-C is a genuine mode of forgiveness, but even more can be said in defense of this claim.

Recall Murphy's list of possible attitudes that can be overcome through forgiveness: resentment, anger, hatred, loathing, contempt, indifference, disappointment, and sadness. Is there something special about resentment such that overcoming it and it alone deserves to be called forgiveness? I think not. Consider what these attitudes have in common. In addition to being described as "negative emotions,"[9] these are all attitudes that *separate* persons from one another. The reason why overcoming resentment is a paradigmatic case of forgiveness is that resentment functions as a barrier between persons. If I resent you, I will resist spending time in your company, I will not give you the benefit of the doubt or sympathize with your plight. I will think of you as the person who wronged me, and I may bring up your wrongdoing repeatedly. In short, my attention to what you have done will drive a wedge between us. Resentment is an attitude that is commonly overcome through forgiveness because resentment separates persons from one another, thereby making forgiveness possible. But the other emotions on Murphy's list also constitute barriers between persons. Insofar as these other

---

8. I will take up the issue of what sorts of reasons ought to count as morally good reasons to forgive-C in sec. 6.4.

9. See the introduction for a discussion of the use of the term "negative emotion."

attitudes serve to separate us from one another, they ought to be included in the class of attitudes that one can overcome through a process of forgiveness.

To see this, it might be helpful to consider an example that everyone would agree should *not* count as a case of forgiveness. Suppose that Sam, for some unknown reason, routinely experiences happiness whenever he is wronged. He realizes that this is an aberrant response, and he attempts to overcome this feeling through what he describes as a process of "forgiveness." While we might think Sam is right to try and overcome his feeling of happiness at being wronged, we would deny that Sam's activity is properly characterized as a process of forgiveness. Why? Happiness is not the sort of attitude that can be overcome through forgiveness because happiness is not an attitude that constitutes a barrier between the victim and the offender. Being happy does not focus one's attention on the flaws of the offender nor does it motivate aggressive confrontation or cool withdrawal. Forgiveness, on the other hand, involves removing attitudinal barriers between persons.

What then accounts for the tendency of philosophers to insist that forgiveness must be directed toward a person's *actions* and not the person herself? I suspect that the answer to this question has to do with the theological roots of some of our intuitions about forgiveness. Augustine's views concerning the attitudes we ought to take toward wrongdoers are particularly relevant:

> For this reason, the man who lives by God's standards, and not by man's, must needs be a lover of the good, and it follows that he must hate what is evil. Further, since no one is evil by nature, but anyone who is evil is evil because of a perversion of nature, the man who lives by God's standards has a duty of

"perfect hatred" towards those who are evil; that is to say, he should not hate the person because of the fault, nor should he love the fault because of the person. He should hate the fault, but love the man. And when the fault has been cured there will remain only what he ought to love, nothing that he should hate.[10]

Augustine argues that we should love what is good and hate what is evil. But since God created persons, they cannot be evil in themselves. Rather, any evil associated with persons must be the result of the person's freely chosen actions. Augustine contends that we ought to hate the fault but love the person. Thus, according to his prescriptions, any negative emotion that we harbor toward wrongdoers is properly directed toward that person's *actions*. And, as the quotation suggests, when we forgive someone, our forgiveness must be for the individual's actions rather than for who he or she is as such.

However, philosophical discussions of interpersonal forgiveness should not be constrained by its theological roots. In fact, when we look at our actual forgiveness practices and how we talk about forgiveness, the tendency for philosophers to treat forgiveness as an activity directed at actions and not persons seems even more misplaced. We typically say, for example, "I forgive you" or ask "please forgive me" rather than "I forgive your stepping on my toe last week" or "please forgive my borrowing your favorite shirt without asking on Thursday."[11]

---

10. Augustine, *City of God*, trans. Henry Bettenson (London: Penguin Books, 2003), 556.
11. I owe this observation about our forgiveness practices to an anonymous reviewer.

6.2 THE FUNDAMENTAL FEATURES OF FORGIVENESS

In the previous section I argued that Butler's account of forgiveness is unsatisfactory insofar as he characterizes forgiveness exclusively as the overcoming or moderation of resentment. Despite this flaw in his account, he is right to describe forgiveness in terms of the forgiver overcoming or moderating her negative emotions toward the wrongdoer. Articulating precisely what it is to "overcome" an emotion through forgiveness is difficult, but it need not mean completely eliminating the emotion. On my view, to overcome an emotion is to no longer be led or dominated by it.[12] But genuine forgiveness requires more than simply overcoming one's negative emotions in this sense. As several philosophers have noted, for one person to genuinely forgive another, the would-be forgiver must overcome her negative emotions for the right sorts of reasons while simultaneously maintaining her commitment to morality, self-respect, and respect for the offender.[13] In this section, I will argue that two conditions must be met if an instance of overcoming apt contempt is to count as forgiveness-C.

First, to count as forgiveness, one must *actively* overcome one's negative emotions. For example, if someone overcomes her resentment or contempt due to a head injury or pharmacological intervention, this would not count as forgiveness. In fact, it is not clear that we should describe such an agent as having *overcome* her feelings at all since to overcome one's feelings involves at least some activity on

---

12. Murphy seems to have a similar view of what it is to overcome a negative emotion through a process of forgiveness. See Murphy and Hampton, *Forgiveness and Mercy*, chaps. 1 and 3. See also Andrea Westlund, "Anger, Faith, and Forgiveness."
13. See Hieronymi, "Articulating an Uncompromising Forgiveness"; and Murphy and Hampton, *Forgiveness and Mercy*.

the part of the person doing the overcoming. Genuine forgiveness must be what I term *agential*. Forgiveness is agential when an agent intentionally overcomes her hard feelings for good reasons.[14]

Additionally, many philosophers claim that for a process to count as forgiveness, the forgiver must maintain certain views about the wrong done and the wrongdoer. Specifically, it is often thought that the forgiver must maintain her view that the act in question was a moral wrong that the wrongdoer can legitimately be held responsible for, and that she, as a member of the moral community, should not have been wronged.[15] A person who forgives yet who also wishes to retain her commitment to morality must maintain these views; her forgiveness must be what I term *non-complicit*. Such a person does not tacitly condone the wrong and therefore is not complicit in it.

Since apt contempt is a response to *badbeing* rather than *wrongdoing*, the conditions that must be met for forgiveness-R to be non-complicit are not identical to the conditions required for non-complicit forgiveness-C. An instance of non-complicit forgiveness-C would require that the forgiver maintain the following three commitments:

1. Because of a morally flawed character, the target of contempt has failed to live up to an important standard.
2. The target of contempt is a member of the moral community who can be held responsible for her character.

---

14. Hieronymi describes forgiving for good reasons as an "articulate account" of forgiveness in "Articulating an Uncompromising Forgiveness," 530. However, I think "agential" better captures the idea that genuine forgiveness must result from some activity on the part of the forgiver.

15. These conditions are very close to Hieronymi's conditions that must be met if an instance of forgiveness is to be what Hieronymi terms "uncompromising," in "Articulating an Uncompromising Forgiveness," 530–531. I argue that these conditions must be revised if we accept the expanded account of forgiveness.

3. The subject can legitimately expect or demand that the target live up to the standard in question.

To forgive-C is to overcome one's apt contempt for good reasons. To give up any of the above commitments is to deny the aptness of the contempt. But if one's contempt is not apt, then overcoming this contempt cannot count as forgiveness. To see this, let's consider each condition in turn: (1) to give up the commitment that the object of contempt failed to live up to an important standard because of her flawed character is analogous to completely excusing a wrongdoer or judging that no wrong was done. You may have come to relinquish the first commitment because you have come to see that you were mistaken in believing the target's character was flawed, or you may come to see that the failure to meet the relevant standard was completely excusable. In such cases, one's contempt would be inapt and should be overcome. If, however, you overcome your contempt by relinquishing the first commitment, you cannot be said to have genuinely forgiven-C that person. (2) Suppose you claim to have forgiven-C someone, but you give up the second commitment, meaning that you no longer see the contemned as a member of the moral community who can be held responsible for her character. Perhaps you have given up this commitment because you discover that (unbeknownst to you) the individual in question grew up in an extremely abusive home. If the abuse was serious, you may decide that the former object of your contempt was not completely responsible for the trait you find contemptible. But if you overcome your feelings of contempt by relinquishing this second commitment, you have excused the target of your contempt, not forgiven her. (3) Suppose you claim to have forgiven someone, but you relinquish the third commitment above, that is, you no longer think that you were in a position to legitimately hold the target of your contempt to the standard in question. Perhaps you mistakenly thought that the standard partially constituted your relationship with the offender, but you realized later that it did not. But to overcome your contempt by relinquishing this third commitment is not to forgive-C. If you relinquish this commitment, your contempt is no longer apt, but you have not forgiven the target.

What sorts of reasons are good reasons to forgive on the expanded account of forgiveness?

6.3 THE STANDARD ACCOUNT OF OUR REASONS TO FORGIVE

Reasons to forgive are considerations that call for or justify forgiveness. Forgiveness is possible only in cases where the hard feelings that are overcome were originally apt. Given this, we always have prima facie reason *not* to overcome our apt hard feelings through forgiveness.[16] Thus in saying that someone has a reason to forgive, I do not mean to suggest that they therefore have an *overriding* reason to forgive; the person may also have good reasons to continue harboring negative emotions toward the offender. For example, if the offense was particularly heinous, there may not be any moral considerations strong enough to trump considerations in favor of the person maintaining her hard feelings. So in judging someone to have good reasons to forgive, we are not thereby claiming that the person in question has an obligation to forgive.[17] In order to determine when forgiveness

---

16. An analogous point also seems to hold with regard to our beliefs: if we are justified in believing that *p*, then we have *prima facie* reason to continue to believe that *p*. These reasons can, of course, be overridden by other reasons.

17. It is important to avoid thinking about forgiveness as obligatory in order to retain the idea that forgiveness is always a "free gift." I will say more about this in what follows.

is praiseworthy (or even justified) and when it is not, we need an account of the morally good reasons to forgive.[18]

Oscar Wilde is reported to have said "Always forgive your enemies; nothing annoys them so much." But forgiving a person simply in order to irritate him is not something that seems to merit high moral praise. In fact, some might argue that such a stance is so far removed from central cases of forgiveness that we should deny that Wilde's type of forgiveness is really forgiveness at all. I mention Wilde's quip to motivate my claim that the moral evaluation of a particular token of forgiveness requires an assessment of the *reasons* the forgiver forgives.

The reasons most often cited in the popular press as reasons to forgive are what we might term *prudential reasons*. For example, the forgiver might decide to forgive so that she is able to move on with her life without the burden of harboring unpleasant emotions such as contempt or resentment.[19] To forgive someone for

---

18. Not only can reparative activities *give* victims reasons to forgive, they can also *provide* these reasons. To provide a reason involves enacting the reason in such a way as one can reasonably expect that it will be given uptake qua reason. To give a reason involves simply pointing to the reason or giving evidence for the existence of a reason. For more on this distinction, see Macalester Bell, "Forgiveness, Inspiration, and the Powers of Reparation." In this chapter, though, I focus on how reparative activities can *give* reasons to forgive.

19. The popular television therapist Dr. Phil advocates this type of reason to forgive in his *Life Law #9: There is Power in Forgiveness*. Dr. Phil writes: "Hate, anger and resentment are destructive, eating away at the heart and soul of the person who carries them. They are absolutely incompatible with your own peace, joy and relaxation. Ugly emotions change who you are and contaminate every relationship you have. They can also take a physical toll on your body, including sleep disturbance, headaches, back spasms, and even heart attacks. Forgiveness sets you free from the bonds of hatred, anger and resentment.... Forgiveness is not about another person who has transgressed against you; it is about you. Forgiveness is about doing whatever it takes to preserve the power to create your own emotional state. It is a gift to yourself and it frees you. You don't have to have the other person's cooperation, and they do not have to be sorry or admit the error of their ways. Do it for yourself." "Dr. Phil's Ten Live Laws" http://drphil.com/articles/article/44/. Given the ubiquity of prudential reasons to forgive in the popular discourse on the subject, it would be disingenuous to claim that those who overcome an emotion for these sorts of reasons do not *really* forgive.

a prudential reason will not necessarily be morally objectionable. However those who forgive for these reasons do not, generally speaking, merit moral praise. Forgiving for prudential reasons seems too self-regarding to merit the high praise we usually accord forgiveness. This is not to deny that there may be cases of forgiveness that do merit high moral praise and for which we have both self-regarding and other-regarding reasons to forgive. But if one forgives *merely* for prudential reasons, one's forgiveness is (at least) morally suspect.

Let's turn now to the two most commonly cited, non-prudential, reasons to forgive-R and consider whether they can serve as reasons to forgive-C.

6.3.1 Repentance

The sincere repentance of the offender has traditionally been thought of as a paradigmatic reason to forgive. According to Murphy's influential characterization, repentance involves the wrongdoer repudiating his past behavior: "In having a sincere change of heart, he is withdrawing his endorsement from his own immoral past behavior; he is saying, 'I no longer stand behind the wrongdoing, and I want to be separated from it. I stand with you in condemning it.'"[20]

Repentance is the clearest way in which a wrongdoer can separate himself from his past wrongdoing. For Murphy, morally good reasons to forgive must not compromise the agent's self-respect, respect for others, or respect for the moral order.[21] Murphy claims that wrongdoers send degrading messages to

---

We can, with the folk, refer to this as forgiveness. However, it is not the kind of morally exemplary forgiveness that is the focus of this chapter.
20. Murphy, *Forgiveness and Mercy*, 26.
21. Ibid., 24.

their immediate victims and to society at large through their actions.[22] To forgive someone who continued to endorse the message sent by his wrongdoing would manifest a serious lack of self-respect on the part of the forgiver. But sincere repentance serves to cleanly separate the repented wrongdoer from the message sent by his wrongdoing. Given this separation between the *immoral act* and the *repented agent*, the victim may forgive the wrongdoer without thereby condoning the message sent by the wrongdoing. In short, Murphy suggests that repentance severs the connection between the wrongdoer and the message sent by his wrongdoing, and thereby allows the victim to forgive the wrongdoer without condoning the message sent by his actions.

In considering whether repentance so construed can give a reason to forgive-C, some interpretive work is required. Murphy's characterization of repentance as a reason to forgive depends upon a prior assumption: that through their *actions*, wrongdoers send degrading messages to the world at large. But apt contempt is focused on persons, not actions. If repentance, as Murphy understands it, is to serve as a reason to forgive-C, then it must be the case that the *character* of the contemned is capable of sending degrading messages. The suggestion that one's character is capable of "sending messages" may strike us as rather forced—how could one's character be capable of sending any messages at all? The oddness of this suggestion may, in fact, be sufficient reason to reject Murphy's analysis of repentance as a reason to forgive-C. If one's character cannot send messages, then repentance, as Murphy characterizes it, cannot serve as a reason to forgive-C.

Even if we could make sense of the idea that our characters are capable of sending degrading messages, an offender who expressed remorse for just his *actions* (and not for his character)

---

22. Ibid., 25.

would give his victim no reason to overcome her contempt for him. To see this, let's return to the example of Tracy's contempt for her father in *The Philadelphia Story* (see chap. 4). Suppose Seth comes to realize that it was inappropriate to publicly berate Tracy for her selfishness and blame her for the breakup of his marriage. Let's imagine that Seth comes to feel remorse for his actions and expresses his sincere repentance to Tracy. While Seth is genuinely sorry for his *actions*, i.e., unfairly criticizing Tracy, he has not paused to consider whether his actions reveal anything about his character. If Seth were to express remorse just for what he had done (and not for who he is as a person), then his repentance would not give Tracy reason to overcome her contempt through forgiveness.[23]

6.3.2 Excuses and Good Intentions

Butler points out that it is very rare for one person to injure another out of pure malice; we are more likely to harm each other out or carelessness or ignorance, and these mitigating circumstances or excuses ought to count as reasons to forgive.[24] On his account, the fact that someone inadvertently hurt you gives you good reason to overcome your resentment for that person though a process of forgiveness.[25]

---

23. An anonymous reviewer suggested that genuine repentance does not involve simply rejecting one's past act but also involves rejecting the self that made such an act possible. However, I think we should distinguish between deep and shallow repentance. I return to this issue in sec. 6.4.

24. Butler, "Upon the Forgiveness of Injuries."

25. Many will object that excuses can never count as reasons to forgive since excuses necessarily exculpate the "wrongdoer" from moral responsibility. If the apparent wrongdoer were not actually responsible for the act in question, then it would seem that there is nothing for the supposed victim to forgive since no wrong was done in the first place. On this view, excuses completely block the attribution of wrongdoing and because of this, cannot function as reasons to forgive. Murphy writes as if all excuses worked in precisely this way. In *Forgiveness and Mercy* he explains what he

Butler argues for this claim as follows: legitimate excuses such as mistakenness, inadvertence, and carelessness are good reasons to forgive because everyone is prone to these liabilities.[26] Since we are all vulnerable to these forms of human frailty, we have two ways of regarding others and ourselves. We can stand firm and be intolerant of both our own minor mistakes and the mistakes of others. This intolerance of human limitations would lead one to be an impatient and hostile person. Alternatively, we can be easy on ourselves for minor mistakes, and only hard on others. In this case, we would be guilty of making an exception of ourselves without any good reason. Thus a person who is unwilling to forgive ordinary failings exhibits one of two equally bad character flaws: intolerance of human frailty, or hypocrisy.

It is sometimes suggested that the fact that the wrongdoer "meant well" should also count as a reason to forgive. While Murphy insists that excuses cannot function as reasons to forgive, he does allow that in some cases, the fact that the agent meant well can give a reason to forgive:

> It is hard to view the friend who locks my liquor cabinet because he knows I drink too much as on exactly the same

---

takes to be the difference between excusing and forgiving as follows: "[W]e may forgive only what it is initially proper to resent; and, if a person has done nothing wrong or was not responsible for what he did, there is *nothing to resent* (though perhaps much to be sad about). Resentment—and thus forgiveness—is directed toward *responsible wrongdoing*; and therefore, if forgiveness and resentment are to have an arena, it must be where such wrongdoing remains intact—i.e., neither excused nor justified" (20). While some excuses operate in the way Murphy suggests, many do not. If I say something hurtful to a friend and later try and excuse my behavior by truthfully saying, "I'm sorry, I didn't know that comment would be so hurtful to you," it is not at all clear that this excuse completely severs me from culpability for what I said. At most, this excuse *mitigates* the wrongfulness of my action by showing that I acted a bit less badly than I may have appeared to. If some excuses mitigate rather than absolve, then it looks as if there is nothing incoherent about the claim that some excuses can give reasons to forgive.

26. Butler, "On the Forgiveness of Injuries."

moral level as the person who embezzles my funds for his own benefit—even though both are violating my rights. Thus the case for forgiving the former (at least the first time) strikes me as having some merit.[27]

Thus the fact that the offending agent acted out of paternalistic motives can, in at least some cases, give the victim reason to forgive.

While we might object to the idea that excuses and good motives can count as morally good reasons to overcome one's resentment, I would like to bracket these issues and consider whether a legitimate excuse or the offender's good motives could ever count as a reason to overcome one's *contempt* through forgiveness. For forgiveness-C to be non-complicit, the forgiver must maintain the three commitments outlined on page 236–7. Given that non-complicit forgiveness-C requires that the forgiver maintain these three commitments, the offender's good motives cannot count as a reason to overcome one's contempt through forgiveness. If the offender's motives really are good, then the forgiver cannot reasonably maintain all three commitments. Specifically, it is difficult to see how one could maintain the commitment that someone has a character flaw and is responsible for this character flaw, and yet at the same time see her motives as good. Although there is nothing incoherent about the possibility of someone with a morally flawed character occasionally acting from good motives, there is no reason to think that the good motives of such a person ought to serve as a reason to forgive-C. Since apt contempt is a response to the target's flawed character, her particular motives for action (understood as distinct from her

---

27. Hampton and Murphy, *Forgiveness and Mercy*, 26.

character) cannot be relevant when determining if there is reason to forgive-C her.

Can an excuse give a good reason to forgive-C? While all of us occasionally harm others though mistake or inadvertence, this is irrelevant to whether or not we have reason to overcome our apt contempt for another. Suppose Seth responded to Tracy's apt contempt by citing all of the times she inadvertently hurt him. Even if Seth's allegations were true, this would not give Tracy reason to overcome her contempt for her arrogant and hypocritical father. In short, we have no reason to suppose that excuses give us good reasons to overcome our apt contempt through a process of forgiveness.

6.4 REASONS TO OVERCOME CONTEMPT THROUGH FORGIVENESS

The best reasons to forgive-C will involve the offender taking responsibility for and acknowledging his faults and taking steps to transform the objectionable features of his character. By taking responsibility for his faults and attempting to transform them, the offender shows that he cares about the standards he has failed to meet. The three commitments that must be maintained for non-complicit forgiveness-C will constrain what reasons will count as good reasons to overcome one's contempt through forgiveness.

In what follows, I consider what I take to be the two main reasons to forgive-C.

6.4.1 Character Transformation

The first reason to forgive-C is that the target has taken steps to transform the contemptible aspects of his character. Actual or attempted character change is a good reason to forgive-C because character transformation offers clear evidence that the contemned has come to accept responsibility for his character flaws and revile these deficits in character. If the target is able to improve these deficits, then the contemnor can overcome her contempt without condoning the faults that initially gave rise to contempt. Further, to forgive for this reason indicates that the forgiver is responsive to the fact that the object of her contempt is a member of the moral community and capable of change.

Some might object that if a person truly transforms her character, then it is simply no longer appropriate to feel contempt for her. Just as some excuses totally exculpate the wrongdoer, a person who completely transforms her character would seem to no longer merit contempt. This description of the case suggests that forgiving someone who transforms herself is no longer elective but obligatory. Insofar as we think that forgiveness ought to be a "free gift," then it looks as if forgiving someone because he has transformed his character cannot count as a case of genuine forgiveness. Let's call this the *free-gift objection*.

It is important to note that this transformation of character cannot be so radical that we feel pressure to judge that the transformed individual is literally a *new person*. If this were the case, then non-complicit forgiveness may not be possible because the would-be forgiver might lack the grounds for holding the "new" person responsible for his "old" character. Nonetheless, I suspect that the requisite transformation of character could be rather dramatic before we would need to worry about the personal identity of the transformed target. Even if we put such cases to one side, there is still the possibility of what we might term "total moral transformation." Is it coherent to forgive someone because he has undergone a total moral transformation or has shown signs that he is on the road to such a transformation?

It is worth noting that the free-gift objection does not pose a problem just for cases of forgiveness-C; this objection can be pressed against any account of forgiveness that emphasizes the importance of *forgiving for reasons*. Consider, for example, what Cheshire Calhoun says about repentance as a reason to forgive-R:

> Those who find repentance important do so because sincere repentance makes forgiveness both risk free and rational. In undergoing a repentant change of heart, the wrongdoer makes herself someone who will not injure us this way again. In breaking the connection between her wrongdoing and her true self, the reformed person ceases to be an appropriate object of resentment. Only by refusing to accept either the sincerity or sufficiency of repentance can resentment retain a legitimate foothold. The point is this: *to the extent that repentance is allowed to count in favor of forgiving, to that extent the wrongdoer ceases to be viewed under a damning description, and forgiving ceases to be elective.*[28]

Calhoun's point is that insofar as the sincere repentance of the wrongdoer counts as a good reason to forgive, forgiving a person who sincerely repents will be obligatory rather than elective. For if sincere repentance separates the wrongdoer from the wrong done in such a way that continued resentment would be *inapt*, then it looks as if the victim *ought* to overcome her resentment through a process of forgiveness. Forgiving the repentant agent is no longer a free gift but a moral obligation.

Calhoun is making a specific point about forgiveness-R, not forgiveness-C, but her general point is applicable to cases of

---

28. Cheshire Calhoun, "Changing One's Heart," *Ethics* 103, no. 1 (1992): 81, emphasis added.

overcoming one's contempt for someone who has undergone a process of character transformation: if someone has undergone a total moral transformation, then it seems inapt to continue to harbor feelings of contempt toward her. If contempt would no longer be appropriate, then it may seem that we have an obligation to overcome our contempt for her. But overcoming our contempt for someone because it is no longer appropriate does not look like a case of genuine forgiveness; forgiveness in this case is no longer elective.

This objection relies upon a controversial account of the nature of character judgments. Specifically, it depends on the undefended assumption that one's character is constituted solely by one's current dispositions. If character judgments were nothing more than evaluations of a person's current dispositions, then when those dispositions change (as in the case of the person who has undergone a total moral transformation), continued contempt would cease to fit the target. But we should reject the assumption that our character judgments ought to track only persons' current dispositions. While a person's present dispositions are partially constitutive of her character, they are meaningful only when illuminated by her history and knowledge of her past dispositions and previous actions.[29] If we insist that an individual's character is partially constituted by her previous actions, dispositions, and commitments, then a total moral transformation will not completely remove the grounds for continued contempt, but it will give a good reason to forgive-C the person. Moreover, this would explain why forgiveness-C involves

---

29. Something like this idea seems to be behind Aristotle's discussion of the difficulty of character change. See *Nicomachean Ethics*, 3.5. Some might worry that my appeal to "previous actions" in this sentence suggests that what contempt is really tracking is bad actions and not bad character. I think this is incorrect. In most cases, we come to have knowledge of someone's character *through* her actions. But it doesn't follow from this that the object of our contempt is a person's actions.

forgiving a person for who she *is*, not simply for who she *was*. For who a person now *is* cannot be completely separated from who that person once *was*.

6.4.2 Shame

I have suggested that the best way for offenders to show respect for the standards they have failed to meet is for them to take responsibility for their faults and attempt to change them. If this is correct, then the genuine moral shame of the offender is another important reason to forgive-C. The offender's shame can give a powerful reason to overcome one's contempt because, through feeling shame, the offender simultaneously takes responsibility for his character, acknowledges his character flaws, and shows some desire to improve himself.

Unlike what we might term "simple repentance," which involves the subject taking responsibility only for what he has *done*, shame involves the subject taking responsibility for the person he *is*. We may come to feel shame for a wide variety of personal attributes and associations, such as our appearance, lineage, or accent. However, we may also come to feel shame in response to our moral failings or blemished character; this is what John Rawls terms "moral" shame. We are liable to what Rawls calls "natural shame" when we fail to achieve excellence in personal characteristics we cannot control, such as our appearance or intelligence, whereas we feel moral shame when we fail to achieve a particular moral excellence, such as self-command.[30]

---

30. John Rawls, *A Theory of Justice*, rev. ed. (Cambridge, MA: Belknap Press, 1999), 444–446. For another helpful discussion of moral shame and the distinction between moral shame and guilt, see Jeffrie Murphy, "Shame Creeps Through Guilt and Feels like Retribution," *Law and Philosophy* 18 (1999): 327–344.

We may have reason to reject Rawls' characterization of shame.³¹ Nonetheless, we should retain his central idea that moral shame tracks failings of character rather than wrong action. While different persons will experience shame in different ways, shame is typically experienced as a deeply painful emotion. The psychological pain of this mode of self-reflection creates a desire for some kind of relief. Shame can lead the subject to seek relief from these painful feelings by motivating her to improve her character.³² While guilt is typically associated with a desire to make amends, shame is typically associated with a desire to change who one is. Of course I do not mean to suggest that *all* instances of shame have this feature, but insofar as an offender's shame does include a desire to change the parts of his character that are connected to his contemptible vices, this should count as a reason to forgive-C him.³³

An offender's desire to change his character ought to count as a reason to forgive-C because this shift in attitude is partially constitutive of many types of character transformation. Consider, for example, a miser: stinginess or miserliness is a character flaw because the miser takes a particular attitude toward herself and the world. The stingy person refuses to see that others' needs and

---

31. Rawls's characterization of moral shame is too narrow. We can and do feel moral shame for failing to achieve excellences of character but also for failing to meet even minimal moral standards. We may be liable to feelings of moral shame when we fail to be the very best persons we can be, but we also may feel moral shame in response to being a complete moral failure. Further, as John Deigh has pointed out, we may be liable to feelings of moral shame because of *who we are* understood independently of what standards we may or may not have lived up to. See John Deigh, *The Sources of Moral Agency* (New York: Cambridge University Press, 1996).

32. Many philosophers have suggested that shame motivates us to reform or rebuild our damaged characters. See Allan Gibbard, *Wise Choices, Apt Feelings*, 293; and Bernard Williams, *Shame and Necessity*, 94. Herbert Morris writes, "[T]he steps that are appropriate to relieve shame are becoming a person that is not shameful," in "Persons and Punishment," *Monist* 52, no. 4, (1968): 489.

33. I qualify this claim further in what follows.

desires ought occasionally to override her own self-interested desire to hoard. The miser fails to notice the harm occasioned by her stinginess, and in part, this is what makes the miser's character abhorrent. But suppose the stingy person comes to see that the needs and desires of others should occasionally trump her own desires to hoard. This recognition and shift in attitude is transformative even if her outward behavior does not undergo an immediate change. If the miser recognizes her stinginess and has a genuine desire to change, she has ceased to have the attitude characteristic of a complete miser, and this is moral progress. Thus, insofar as moral shame includes a desire to transform one's character flaws, the moral shame of the offender may give a reason to forgive-C.

While the moral shame of the offender can give a reason to forgive-C, a further qualification is in order. If a person is regularly ashamed of her failings but continues to live her life in exactly the same way as she has in the past, then we have reason *not* to treat her shame as a reason to forgive-C. But if a formerly shameless person comes to feel moral shame concerning her faults, this should count as a reason to forgive-C. In short, whether or not the shame of the offender should count as a reason to forgive-C will partly depend upon the past history of the offender.

Taking the moral shame of the offender as a reason to forgive is not incompatible with maintaining the three commitments necessary for an uncompromising forgiveness-C. Moreover, it is possible that the offender's moral shame could serve as independent confirmation of the forgiver's judgment that the offender has failed to live up to an important standard due to a character flaw for which he could appropriately be held responsible. Hence, there seems to be no reason why the moral shame of the offender should not count as a reason to forgive-C. More importantly, if

I am right to insist that the desire for moral growth or character transformation is closely associated with feelings of shame, and if the moral growth of the offender gives us good reasons to forgive, then it looks as if the genuine shame of the offender ought to give us a good reason to forgive-C.

Some might wonder whether the kind of character transformation I've discussed in this section is really much different from repentance (properly understood). Specifically, someone might insist that repentance has force as a reason to forgive-R only if it involves a commitment to repudiating and transforming the negative character trait from which the wrongful action sprang. If this were correct, then there would not be a salient difference between the sincere repentance of the offender and the kind of character transformation I have been discussing.

Murphy describes the repentant person as undergoing a change of heart that involves standing against his own immoral past behavior. I submit that someone could undergo what Murphy describes as a change of heart concerning her past *behavior* without coming to see (let alone take responsibility for or attempt to change) the underlying character flaws that her behavior revealed. If this is correct, then this form of repentance could not serve as a reason to forgive-C.

To see this, consider the following two cases:

> *The Case of Jane's Inconsiderate Behavior*: Jane borrows Colleen's favorite dress. While wearing it at a dinner party, Jane accidentally knocks over her wine glass thereby leaving a red stain down the front of the dress. She returns the dress wrinkled and soiled. Colleen sees the stain and resents that Jane would return her dress in such a condition. Colleen confronts her, Jane realizes her behavior was wrong, and expresses her remorse. Colleen takes herself to have reason to forgive Jane.

The Case of Jane's Inconsiderateness: This case is identical to the one described above, except that in this case, Jane is routinely self-involved and careless with other people's belongings. Colleen responds with anger about her dress but what she most strongly feels is contempt for Jane. "What kind of person," she thinks, "could regularly show so much arrogance and so little concern for others? Who does Jane think she is?!" Colleen confronts Jane, and Jane repents and says that she is very sorry about the red wine stain. Jane's repentance suggests that she has come to see that her actions in this case were wrong, but Jane does not seem to recognize what her actions reveal about her as a person. Moreover, Jane does not take responsibility for her faults or make any effort to change her ways. Colleen does not take herself to have a reason to forgive Jane.

These examples suggest that we can distinguish between simple and deep repentance. Simple repentance involves feeling sorry about one's actions while deep repentance involves feeling sorry for who one is as a person and how one's character may have manifested itself in one's actions. In each case described above, Jane repents. In the first example, her simple repentance is accepted as a reason to forgive, but in the second case it is not. What I wish to deny is the suggestion that only deep repentance can give a reason to forgive-R. In some cases, wrong behavior is just wrong behavior and does not implicate any of the offender's character traits (as in the Case of Jane's Inconsiderate Behavior). In these sorts of cases, simple repentance may well give a reason to forgive the wrongdoer. But, as I've been arguing throughout this book, sometimes what we care about is not a person's action in isolation but what the action expresses about who the offender is as a person. In the first case, Colleen does not think Jane's inconsiderate behavior expresses anything about Jane's character; Colleen is simply angry that Jane returned her dress in such sorry shape. But in the second case, there is something else at stake: Jane's (resentment-worthy) behavior seems to express a contemptible sort of arrogance.

6.5 DO WE GENUINELY FORGIVE IN OVERCOMING CONTEMPT?

Some people have suggested that forgiveness-C is not really a form of forgiveness because it is difficult to see how one could *ask* for forgiveness-C; having a bad character trait, it is claimed, is not the kind of failure for which one could coherently *ask* forgiveness.[34] Behind this objection lurks the assumption that asking for (and granting) forgiveness is an essential aspect of interpersonal forgiveness. Moreover, if the proper responsiveness to being an object of contempt involves the contemned ameliorating his or her character or at least professing a genuine desire to change, then asking for forgiveness-C seems to be beside the point. If asking for forgiveness-C is somehow incoherent or pointless, and if it is true that asking for forgiveness is central to our forgiveness practices, then we may have some reason to conclude that forgiveness-C is not really a type of forgiveness.

Other critics have expressed concerns about what we forgive someone *for* when we overcome our contempt. When we forgive someone for what they have done, it is perfectly clear what we are forgiving them for. If you break a promise to me and I later come to forgive you, it is clear that I have come to forgive you for the act of breaking your promise. What then do we forgive someone for

---

34. In her helpful comments on an earlier version of this chapter, Andrea Westlund raised this worry and the following worry about my proposal.

in cases of forgiveness-C? As I have argued in previous sections, I think that when we overcome our contempt for someone through a process of forgiveness, we are forgiving the person for his or her character flaws. But the suggestion that we may forgive someone for his or her character flaws may strike us as presumptuous or arrogant. How can we claim to forgive someone for her character traits? If the idea of forgiving someone for her character traits is morally abhorrent, then we may decide that forgiveness-C is not really a form of forgiveness after all. Again, I think this worry is an important one and will return to it momentarily.

When it comes to forgiveness-R we have a pretty good idea whose "business" it is to forgive and whose business it isn't. Most philosophers think that a person has standing to forgive-R if he or she is victim of wrongdoing. A third party to the wrongdoing may well feel indignation toward the wrongdoer but not resentment, and would not, therefore, have standing to forgive-R. Yet it seems like many people would have standing to forgive-C since many could be in the position to aptly harbor contempt for the target. This puts forgiveness-C on rather different footing than forgiveness-R; forgiveness-R seems to be the kind of moral project for which there are strict and clear-standing requirements. If the standing requirements of forgiveness-C are not similarly restricted, this may give us reason to conclude that forgiveness-C is not actually a type of forgiveness after all.

In light of these worries about forgiveness-C, it may seem that overcoming one's contempt should be understood not as a mode of forgiveness, but as a *precondition* for entering into the type of relationship in which forgiveness can be properly sought and granted. Contempt involves withdrawal or disengagement from the target of contempt, and this form of disengagement may be understood as a kind of withdrawal from the very sort of engagement that repentance and forgiveness requires. If this is correct, then overcoming our contempt for an offender should not be understood as a form of forgiveness but as a precondition for the type of interpersonal relationship that is itself a precondition for forgiveness.[35]

It is worth pointing out that even if we characterize forgiveness-C as a precondition for forgiveness, we would still need some way to distinguish between cases where a person has good reasons to overcome her contempt and cases where she does not. At the very least, I have shown that the standard account of the good reasons to forgive cannot help us determine what sorts of reasons would be good reasons to overcome contempt. My arguments here could be read as contributing to the debate by offering an analysis of one, rarely discussed, precondition for forgiveness.

But I *do* want to insist that overcoming one's contempt should sometimes be characterized as part of a process of forgiveness rather than as a precondition for forgiveness. Forgiveness has an especially esteemed place in the catalog of possible responses to immorality, and in some cases, overcoming apt contempt deserves the honorific of "forgiveness." Moreover, while contempt is structurally distinct from resentment and while the reasons to forgive-R are distinct from the reasons to forgive-C, this does not give us reason to conclude that forgiveness-C is not a type of forgiveness. Our responses to immorality are more nuanced and complex than current philosophical discussions of forgiveness would suggest. Those who maintain that forgiveness must be defined solely in terms of the overcoming of resentment rather than contempt ought to defend this claim. In the absence of such a defense, I can think of no reason to accept the thesis that forgiveness must be characterized solely in terms of overcoming resentment.

---

35. Westlund suggested just this possibility in her comments.

Moreover, I find nothing incoherent about the possibility of an offender asking for forgiveness-C. While asking for forgiveness-C will certainly not replace the hard work of character transformation, the victim may not immediately recognize that the offender has transformed himself. In these circumstances, asking for forgiveness is not beside the point. Instead, it is a way of announcing that one has changed or is the process of changing one's character. In asking for forgiveness-C, the offender might say something like, "I know I've been a jerk in the past. But I've changed my ways, and I ask you to forgive me." In making a plea of this kind, the offender acknowledges his inferior status; he recognizes that doesn't deserve esteem or positive appraisal, and through his prostration he affirms the victim's relative superiority in relation to the relevant standards.

Some critics have argued that forgiveness is a highly interpersonal activity that depends upon a special sort of relationship between victim and offender, and that feeling contempt for another makes this sort of relationship impossible. But it is important to remember that when we forgive, we seek to overcome a negative emotion that was initially apt. When our contempt for another is apt, it *presupposes* some kind of relationship between the contemnor and the contemned, rather than precluding such a relationship. Contempt involves holding a person to a standard, and when our contempt is morally appropriate we must be justified in holding the person to the standard in question. Since apt contempt is an interpersonal emotion, the activity of overcoming contempt through forgiveness will also be interpersonal.

In fact, it seems to me that forgiveness-C is a more deeply interpersonal activity than forgiveness-R. Accepting an expanded account of forgiveness may require us to rethink what it means to *overcome* an emotion through forgiveness. While we can overcome our resentment for another without any movement toward reconciliation, overcoming contempt will require us, at least in many cases, to "re-engage" the offender. This is because of the fundamental differences between resentment and contempt. As we have seen, contempt is characterized by withdrawal or disengagement. Hence, part of overcoming one's contempt will involve one overcoming this disengagement and re-engaging (or fully engaging for the first time) the former object of contempt.[36] What it means to *overcome* a hard feeling through forgiveness will turn on the structure of the emotion to be overcome.

Finally, let's turn to the question of the standing requirements for forgiveness-C. When does a person have standing to forgive-C? To answer this question, I think we will need to consider particular cases and ask ourselves who could legitimately demand that the target meet the standard at issue. Anyone who could legitimately demand that the target meet the standard has standing to forgive-C, and those who could not legitimately make this demand would not have standing to forgive-C. If the relationship between the contemnor and contemned was seriously damaged by the offender's faults, and if overcoming contempt restores or repairs this relationship, then the process of overcoming contempt merits the honorific "forgiveness." The suggestion that numerous people may have standing to forgive-C will strike many as counterintuitive. But once we appreciate that many relationships are damaged by wrongdoing and badbeing, we should acknowledge that the strict standing conditions that some insist upon ought to be loosened; many people may indeed have the standing to forgive.[37]

---

36. I do not mean to suggest that every case of forgiveness-C will require us to fully reconcile with the offender. There may well be cases of genuine forgiveness-C where full reconciliation is either impossible or unreasonable.

37. For a detailed discussion of standing and forgiveness, see Glen Pettigrove, "The Standing to Forgive," *Monist* 92, no. 4 (2009): 583–603.

6.6 CONTEMPT, SYMBOLIC REPARATIONS, AND SOCIAL RECONCILIATION

My account of what is involved in overcoming contempt through forgiveness may shed some light on a related set of issues in our social lives. Like individuals, institutions such as universities, businesses, and governmental organizations may be targets of apt contempt insofar as they express superbia through their policies and actions.[38] Institutions may express superbia in a number of different ways. Perhaps most clearly, superbia may be expressed through blatantly racist policies and practices such as the forced relocation and internment of Japanese Americans during World War II or the use of slave labor. Responding to institutions with contempt may be the best way of answering the objectionable attitudes that they express through their policies.[39]

Often, people must rely on the very institutions they hold in contempt, and it is difficult to withdraw from an institution that one is dependent upon. Thus people often end up engaging, interacting, and relying on institutions at the same time that they seek to distance themselves from them. While not all forms of engagement are in tension with contempt's characteristic withdrawal, relying on and making oneself vulnerable to the target of one's contempt while seeking to withdraw from it is an unstable

---

38. For a discussion of the messages sent by institutions, see Thomas Hill, "The Message of Affirmative Action," *Social Philosophy and Policy* 8, no. 2 (1991): 108–129.

39. Some may wonder if contempt for institutions is properly characterized as contempt on my account since I have argued that contempt is a person-focused emotion. While I will not take a stand on whether we should regard institutions as persons, it is clear that they are person-like. In particular, institutions are capable of expressing a wide variety of attitudes, including superbia. Given this, institutions may be fitting, reasonable, and apt targets of contempt. Admittedly, contempt for institutions will lack some of the features of paradigmatic cases of contempt. Specifically, institution-directed contempt may lack the reflexivity that contempt has when it is directed toward persons. For more on derivative forms of contempt, see chap. 1.

response, which can lead to feelings of cynicism that may be corrosive to our collective lives. This is especially true when large groups of people come to harbor contempt for important social institutions.

Like individuals, institutions may respond well or poorly to the contempt directed toward them. When they make appropriate reparative gestures, institutions give persons reasons to overcome their contempt. While we may not wish to describe this process as one of "forgiveness," forgiveness-C provides a model for thinking about what sorts of projects could give good reasons to overcome contempt for institutions. In recent years, philosophers and political theorists have explored the moral dimensions of a number of reparative activities that may play a role in confronting past wrongdoing (e.g., reparations, truth commissions, memorials, public apologies, commemorations, official condemnations, etc.). I will focus on the possibilities and limitations of reparations and memorials in addressing apt contempt for institutions.

Earlier, I argued that if an offender seeks forgiveness-C, he ought to show the right sort of responsiveness to the contempt directed at him. Signs of character transformation, or at least a strong desire to change, may give persons good reasons to overcome their contempt. So too, institutions must show signs of transformation or at least the desire to change in order to give persons reasons to overcome their apt contempt. But how can institutions express this sort of responsiveness? Perhaps offering cash payments may provide a way for institutions to express their deep repentance. Commenting on the reparations paid to Japanese American survivors of internment camps, Jeremy Waldron writes:

> The point of these payments was not to make up for the loss of home, business, opportunity, and standing in the community,

which these people suffered at the hands of their fellow citizens, nor was it to make up for the discomfort and degradation of their internment. If that were the aim, much more would be necessary. The point was to mark—with something that counts in the United States—a clear public recognition that this injustice did happen, that it was the American people and their government that inflicted it, and that these people were among its victims. The payments give an earnest of good faith and sincerity to that acknowledgement. Like the gift I buy for someone I have stood up, the payment is a method of putting oneself out, or going out of one's way, to apologize.[40]

And so cash payments may offer a way for institutions to signal their good faith and sincere desire to repair their relations with the persons they serve. Following Waldron, we can distinguish between compensatory and symbolic reparations. Compensatory reparations attempt to provide victims with sufficient funds to compensate them for their losses, whereas symbolic reparations offer public acknowledgment of past wrongdoing and express a desire to move forward in a just manner. As Waldron argues, there are reasons to object to compensatory reparations, but can symbolic reparations appropriately address institution-focused contempt?[41]

Whether reparative activity is able to appropriately address apt contempt depends upon the attitude expressed by the

---

40. Jeremy Waldron, "Superseding Historic Injustice," *Ethics* 103, no. 1 (1992): 6–7.

41. Many of Waldron's objections to compensatory reparations focus on the metaphysical and practical difficulties associated with attempting to return people to the state that they would have been in if not for the injustice. We obviously can't know how people would have behaved in the possible world where the injustice did not take place, and making *predictions* about how persons would have acted lacks moral authority. These worries do not pose problems for symbolic reparations.

activity. What attitudes do cash payments express? While institutions may intend to convey that they have taken responsibility for their superbia, changed their practices, and are willing to work to repair relations with those who hold it in contempt, it is unlikely that cash payments will actually send those messages. Most often, we offer cash payments for services rendered. Put more cynically, we usually offer cash payments to buy people off. If cash payments normally express these sorts of attitudes, it is unlikely that symbolic reparations will be able to express the kind of message that would give people reasons to overcome their apt contempt. Perhaps it is possible for cash payments to signal the giver's transformation and commitment to do better, but the conventional meanings of cash payments make this difficult.

More to the point, cash payments do not address the specific damages wrought by institutions that express superbia through their policies and actions. Cash payments can be made without members of the institution reflecting on the history or character of the institution or making any attempt to change its culture or take responsibility for its past. For these two reasons, cash payments must be supplemented by other reparative gestures in order to give persons reasons to overcome their contempt. On their own, cash payments will likely send insulting or degrading messages, and they will not give persons reasons to overcome their contempt.

Memorials offer another way of addressing institution-focused contempt. In recent years, discussions of memorials, such as the Vietnam Veterans Memorial, have figured prominently in philosophical treatments of political and social reconciliation.[42] In order to explore how memorials may address—and fail to

---

42. See, for example, Charles Griswold, *Forgiveness: A Philosophical Exploration*, chap. 5.

address—apt contempt, I'd like to focus on a trio of small projects that the University of North Carolina has recently undertaken in an attempt to confront its past and address the hard feelings that some harbor for the university.

The University of North Carolina at Chapel Hill has a long and complicated history of racial injustice. Slave labor was used in the construction of university buildings, many administrators owned slaves, and there is evidence that the university paid local slave owners to use their slaves as "college servants."[43] For many years, the role that slave labor played in the construction and administration of the university was not officially acknowledged. The lack of attention paid to the university's history of relying upon slave labor was thrown into relief by the way the university memorialized *other* aspects of its history. For example, the most prominent statue on campus, now called *Silent Sam*, is a memorial to fallen Confederate soldiers, and some of the buildings on campus are named in honor of high-ranking members of the Ku Klux Klan.[44] Given its racist history, and the way in which the university has memorialized and celebrated this history, some have come to hold the university in contempt.

In an attempt to address its racist past, the university has recently undertaken several memorial projects: a plaque has been added to the campus cemetery, *The Unsung Founder's Memorial* was erected on McCorkle Place lawn, and two interactive museums were created and posted on the university's website.

The first memorial is a plaque erected in the "black section" of the Old Chapel Hill Cemetery, located on what is now the eastern

---

43. UNC University Library, *Slavery and the Making of the University: The College Servants*, http://www.lib.unc.edu/mss/exhibits/slavery/servants.html.

44. William Saunders graduated from the university in 1854. He had a successful law career and served as the Secretary of the State and was appointed to a university trusteeship. After the war, he became one of the first state leaders of the Ku Klux Klan. Saunders Hall is named after him.

edge of the university's campus. The cemetery has been in use since 1798, and many students, faculty, and administrators are buried there. Since there were no separate black cemeteries in Chapel Hill at the time of its creation, the cemetery is segregated, and two of its six sections are reserved for blacks: a brick wall separates the black and white sections. Some of the graves in the black section are marked by weathered stones, and there is no way of knowing who is buried beneath them. Most likely, these are the graves of slaves owned by people associated with the university. Many of the graves in this section of the cemetery have been vandalized, and headstones have been broken. The newly mounted plaque in the black section of the cemetery reads: "African Americans are buried here in the western section of the community cemetery. Some individuals were enslaved and others were free persons. Many worked for the university. These workers contributed to the growth of the university during its first century and helped Carolina become a leading public university."[45]

The second memorial project is a collection of online, interactive museums that chronicle the university's history.[46] In the Slavery and the Making of the University exhibition, university archivists catalog the role that slaves played in the creation and administration of the university. Through the use of text and photographs, the exhibit vividly documents the racism that characterized much of the university's past. Another online exhibition, The Carolina Story: A Virtual Museum of University History, lists some of the demeaning treatment inflicted upon blacks during the period of segregation that followed the American Civil War.

---

45. For more on the history of the cemetery, see University of North Carolina at Chapel Hill, *Silent Sentinels of Stone: Old Chapel Hill Cemetery*, http://www.ibiblio.org/cemetery/index.html.

46. Some might object to calling these museums memorials since they aim to do far more than memorialize the past. Nevertheless, there are features of these museums that are clearly memorializing.

In a section titled, "African Americans and Segregation," a photograph of a man, Ben Boothe, is presented along with the following description:

> North Carolina's African Americans faced tremendous financial difficulties in the late nineteenth century. Sometimes they submitted to demeaning treatment for a few pennies. Ben Boothe, an African American resident of Chapel Hill, allowed students to hit him on the head with a fist or a board for five cents. He would never flinch. For another five cents, he crowed like a rooster. Faculty suspected that college servant Tom Kirby secretly sold whiskey to students.[47]

The photograph and accompanying text paints a powerful portrait of university life in the postwar period. Nonetheless, the last sentence of this description is rather strange given the apparent aims of the exhibition.

The third, and most prominent, memorial project is *The Unsung Founder's Memorial*, created by Do-Ho Suh, which now sits on the McCorkle Place lawn in front of the alumni building. Suh is a South Korean artist who is especially well known for his site-specific sculptures and works involving small figures. The memorial consists of a black granite tabletop surrounded by five stone seats, supported by a number of miniature stone figures. These figures represent the people of color who helped to build and administer the university. Encircling the tabletop is the following inscription: "The Class of 2002 honors the University's unsung founders, the people of color bond and free, who helped build the Carolina that we cherish today."

---

47. UNC University Library, *The Carolina Story: A Virtual Museum of University History: African Americans and Segregation*, http://museum.unc.edu/exhibits/segregation/ben-boothe-died-1891.

One way of interpreting these three memorials is to see them as part of the university's ongoing attempt to be responsive to those who have come to hold it in contempt because of its history of racism. The university had, through its policies and programs, expressed race-based contempt for the slaves who helped create the university and for blacks more generally. Through these projects, though, the university has attempted to acknowledge its racist past and move toward a better future. Do these memorials successfully address persons' institution-focused contempt and give persons reasons to overcome their apt contempt?

The memorials vary in their reason-giving power. Arguably the least successful memorial of the three is actually the most prominent and celebrated one: *The Unsung Founder's Memorial*. The placement of this memorial on the campus' central quad is appropriate, but it is dwarfed in size and scale by the statue *Silent Sam*, located a few steps away. The former hugs the ground, while the later sits high above the quad on a pedestal. The *Unsung Founder's Memorial* is a working memorial designed to function as a table. There are relatively few benches on Chapel Hill's campus, and public seating on the quad is a welcome addition. However, the utilitarian nature of the memorial undermines its ability to appropriately address persons' apt contempt; there is something troubling about seeing people eating, literally, on the backs of the small stone figures at the base of the table. This is supposed to be a memorial that recognizes the many nameless and forgotten slaves who long served the university without public recognition. By representing these slaves as anonymous, indistinct, small supports for a large stone table used for picnics, the memorial ends up reinforcing the very contempt the university showed toward blacks in the past. As some observers have noted, should one sit at the table as the memorial invites, one cannot actually see the figures at the base of the table; these figures are located at one's feet, and one is likely to inadvertently kick dirt and dust into their faces.[48] Given that showing the soles of one's shoes and kicking dirt into a person's face are widely recognized gestures of contempt, the memorial ends up tacitly reinforcing, rather than addressing, the university's history of race-based contempt. Moreover, as others have observed, the memorial does not explicitly mention that many of those who worked to create and run the university were slaves.[49] Instead, it is dedicated to the workers "bond and free." Given the Southern practice of ambiguously referring to enslaved people as "servants," the memorial would have been more effective if it had been less coy about the persons it is supposed to be acknowledging. Finally, the memorial was the class of 2002's senior gift to the university. As with all senior gifts, members of the graduating class chose the memorial through a voting procedure: the memorial received 44.9 percent of the seniors' votes, while a scholarship for underprivileged students garnered 28 percent of the votes, and a marquee for a campus building received 27.1 percent of the votes.[50] Although university officials did provide matching funds and space on campus for the memorial, its design and creation were not the direct result of administrative action. Because of this, the memorial cannot address the contempt that some may harbor for the university; it is unclear whether the memorial expresses the views of the administration, and it was chosen by a meager percentage of graduating seniors. In short, *The Unsung Founder's Memorial* does not give persons reasons to overcome their apt

---

48. See, for example, the comments of Yonni Chapman in "UNC-Chapel Hill Examines Race and History," Cynthia Greenlee-Donnell, *Independent Weekly* (Chapel Hill, NC), October 18, 2006, http://www.indyweek.com/indyweek/unc-chapel-hill-examines-race-and-history.

49. See, for example, the remarks of student Janell Jack, in ibid.

50. Jamie Dougher, "Senior Class Gives Nod to Unsung Founders," *Daily Tarheel*, October 12, 2001, http://www.dailytarheel.com/index.php/article/2001/10/senior_class_gives_nod_to_unsung_founders.

contempt for the university. If anything, the utilitarian nature of the memorial, its scale, its inscription, and the way the public is encouraged to interact with it reinforces the contempt that the university historically showed to the free and enslaved blacks that helped build the university.

Let's look now at the other two memorial projects recently undertaken by the university. The online exhibitions have the potential to tell the neglected story of the role of enslaved and free blacks in the history of the university. By choosing to feature Boothe's story and prominently displaying his photograph, The Carolina Story presents an unflinching look back at the humiliating treatment that some black members of the university community endured. The combination of the photograph and text makes the degrading treatment vivid, and by making this tale part of its official history, the university is clearly taking responsibility for its past.

Nevertheless, these exhibitions do not, in their current form, adequately address the apt contempt that some may harbor for the university. There seems to be a strange carelessness in the way in which some of the sensitive material is presented. The story of Boothe is offered in the same breath as an allegation that one of the "university servants," likely a slave, was alleged to have sold alcohol to the students. This juxtaposition expresses a lack of concern about the appalling way Boothe was treated by members of the university community, and not enough attention is given to the reasons why he might have felt the need to demean himself in this way.

In addition, structural features of these online exhibitions undermine their ability to address institution-focused contempt. First, the materials related to the university's history of slavery are spread over at least two different websites with no easily navigable links between them. Second, the creators of these museums note that they will change and evolve over time. Thus there is no guarantee that the page devoted to the story of Boothe will continue to be part of the museum a month or a year from now. Finally, one must be especially interested in the topic to find and visit the online exhibits. Unlike *The Unsung Founder's Memorial*, which has a prominent location on the main campus quad, one must search for the online museums. There is no direct link to the exhibits from the university's homepage, and it is likely that only those who are looking for them will come across the exhibits after navigating through multiple webpages.

The final memorial is the plaque erected in the Old Chapel Hill Cemetery. While this is the simplest and least ambitious memorial, it is arguably the most successful in addressing persons' contempt. Many of the graves in the black section of the cemetery are unmarked, and others have been vandalized over the years leaving them bereft of headstones. Given the elaborate markers and monuments in the white section of the cemetery, the black section seems comparatively sad and neglected. By clearly describing the history of the cemetery and reminding people of the important role slaves played in the creation of the university, the plaque directly addresses the university's contemptible past. Unlike *The Unsung Founder's Memorial*, this simple plaque makes it explicit that slave labor was used in the building and running of the university. Unlike The Carolina Story exhibit, this memorial is visible to all passersby and is intended as a permanent addition to the campus. Admittedly, this memorial is very small, and it does not go far enough in expressing shame or deep repentance for the university's past, but it is a gesture that goes some way toward addressing persons' apt institution-focused contempt.

The University of North Carolina at Chapel Hill has, in recent years, made several attempts to take responsibility for its racist past and move forward toward a better future. I have argued that some of these reparative gestures have more successfully addressed those who hold it in contempt than others. As I write, some protesters are calling on the university to move the statue *Silent Sam* from the main quad to the cemetery. Others would like to see a plaque added to the statue noting what the Confederate soldiers were seeking to defend.[51] It is obvious that the university's efforts at addressing its past have not been wholly successful, but it is clearly making an effort to right historic wrongs.

* * *

If we accept an expanded account of forgiveness, then we will need to re-evaluate some truisms concerning forgiveness. We must also accept that there will be different reasons to forgive depending upon the particular hard feelings to be overcome. If we are to forgive only when we have morally good reasons to do so, then we should examine the strength of our reasons to forgive and perhaps change our forgiveness practices. For example, as victims of wrongdoing or badbeing we should be careful to articulate to ourselves and to others precisely what attitudes and emotions we experience. Subjects and targets of hard feelings ought to have a clear understanding of precisely what emotions or attitudes are to be overcome in order to know what sorts of considerations will count as morally good reasons to forgive.

Wrongdoing and badbeing create moral trouble that persists across time, but persons can change the ways in which the present is affected by the past. Contempt is an apt response to superbia,

---

51. Lana Douglas, "UNC's Confederate Statue Draws New Protest," *News & Observer*, September 2, 2011, http://www.newsobserver.com/2011/09/02/1454360/sam-is-silent-his-detractors-arent.html.

but targets may give us reasons to overcome our contempt through their shame and character transformation. Institutions that previously merited contempt may also change over time. Through various reparative activities, these institutions may address those who hold them in contempt and work to give persons reasons to leave their contempt behind.

Conclusion
"Contempt Is Not a Thing to be Despised"

None but the contemptible are apprehensive of contempt.
La Rochefoucauld

Contempt is not a thing to be despised.
Burke

Contempt may go terribly wrong; people may contemn for the wrong reasons and evince faults structured by inapt contempt. But even though contempt can be experienced in vicious and disvaluable ways, this does not give us reason to adopt an anti-contempt ethic. Despite its dangers, contempt has a unique power: it can *answer* the threats posed by superbia. Through its characteristic withdrawal and downward-looking comparative evaluations, contempt answers what is objectionable about superbia in such a way as to mitigate its damage.

There are other ways of dealing with those who evince vices of superiority: we may try to convince ourselves that we are not dishonored by their attitudes or that this dishonor doesn't matter. In responding in these ways we are not answering the threats posed by superbia but are instead attempting to ignore them. But closing our eyes to superbia and its dangers is not to confront these threats and is not the best way of responding to them. It is better to face these dangers head on, and this requires the cultivation of contempt. It would be nice if no one ever evinced the vices of superiority, and in such a world contempt would not play the defensive role I've described. But we shouldn't respond to real and pressing threats in this world by pretending that they don't exist, and this is why we should prefer an ethic of contempt to an anti-contempt ethic.

Contempt can be a fitting, reasonable, prudent, and morally appropriate response to those who harbor superbia. It answers badbeing and is the best defense against the dangers posed by faults like arrogance, hypocrisy, and racism. When contempt satisfies the aptness conditions outlined in chapter 4, it is an attitude that we should strive to cultivate.

The arguments offered in this book provide reasons to reject disvalue monism.[1] Those who defend an ethic of resentment and reject an ethic of contempt presume that there is only one basic kind of disvalue, that of the resentment-worthy. Defenders of this view seem to have two options when it comes to responding to superbia: they may argue that all persons who genuinely evince vices of superiority have *also* performed some resentment-worthy acts and thereby merit resentment on this basis, or they may insist that those who evince superbia but have not wronged anyone do not merit any hard feelings at all. The former strategy is mistaken insofar as it misconstrues the moral badness of the vices of superiority. Those who evince these vices impair their relationships whether or not they perform any resentment-worthy actions. Not only would we misconstrue Tartuffe's faults if we regarded him as simply resentment-worthy for his wrongdoing, but responding to him with just resentment would not answer his faults. For much of what is objectionable

---

1. For an argument defending the claim that there are different kinds of moral value based on a classification of evaluative adjectives, see Richard B. Brandt, "Moral Valuation," *Ethics* 56, no. 2 (1946): 106–121.

about Tartuffe cannot be reduced to instances of culpable wrongdoing. Does he violate Dorine's moral rights by insisting that she use his handkerchief to protect her modesty? Probably not. But in hypocritically making a spectacle of his apparent piety he still evinces a fault that impairs his relationship with her and threatens her integrity and self-esteem, all of which calls for some response. If Tartuffe expressed simple repentance for his actions without reflecting upon what they revealed about who he is as a person, this would not give Dorine or anyone else reason to forgive him. Adopting an ethic of resentment while rejecting an ethic of contempt leaves persons unable to aptly respond to badbeing. As I have argued, the second strategy fails to take seriously the threats posed by those who evince these vices. Given superbia's potential to damage our personal and moral relations, we clearly have reason to stand against it. The resentment-worthy is one important mode of disvalue but the contemptible is another.

Those who defend an ethic of resentment usually take what we might term a *top-down* approach to moral psychology: they begin with a specific account of the nature of morality and from there argue that resentment and its close cousins have a privileged role to play in our moral lives.[2] I have taken a different tack, which may be described as a *bottom-up* approach: rather than beginning with a substantive account of the nature of morality and arguing from this robust starting point to claims about the privileged status of a small set of emotions, a bottom-up approach begins with a detailed investigation of the hard feelings themselves and considers what role these emotions might play in a minimally acceptable morality. By carefully considering the ways

2. Those who I think take a top-down approach include Stephen Darwall, *Second-Person Standpoint;* Allan Gibbard, *Wise Choices, Apt Feelings;* and R. Jay Wallace, *Responsibility and the Moral Sentiments.*

in which various hard feelings differ from one another, we come to a clearer sense of what these emotions *do*. Hard feelings are, I've argued, responses to distinct types of threats. Contempt is, for example, a response to the threats posed by superbia, disgust is a response to threats posed by contaminants, resentment is a response to the threats posed by wrongdoing, and so on. With a clear understanding of how various hard feelings present their targets and what threats they seek to answer, we may step back and consider whether these perceived threats really are dangerous and how a particular hard feelings may answer its associated threat.

Taking a bottom-up approach helps us understand the moral dimensions of a host of emotions, which are generally ignored within contemporary moral psychology and, at the same time, allows us to come to a deeper appreciation of the moral trouble created by badbeing and wrongdoing. Rather than privileging one class of emotions as the "moral emotions" according to one's preferred normative system, a bottom-up approach leads us to a richer understanding of the wide variety of affective responses that may play a positive role in our moral lives. Thus my bottom-up defense of contempt is one piece in a larger reclamation project. By carefully considering the nature of under-explored emotions such as contempt, shame, and disgust, we have the opportunity to rethink the role that emotions should play in an adequate moral psychology, which takes seriously the wide variety of threats that we face as moral agents. Rather than characterizing hard feelings as helpmates to independently justified moral theories, a bottom-up approach takes seriously the defensive work that hard feelings do.

Despite the many charges leveled against it, contempt has an important role to play in our contemporary moral lives. While undeniably corrosive and sometimes dangerous, contempt answers a range of real and serious threats; when it is apt, contempt is not, as Burke notes, "a thing to be despised,"[3] but is, instead, the best way of responding to the superbia at the heart of the vices of superiority.

---

3. Burke, "Letters on a Regicide Peace," in *The Writings and Speeches of Edmund Burke,* Beaconsfield Edition, vol. 5 (Boston: Little Brown and Company, 1901), 436.

BIBLIOGRAPHY

Unless noted, all websites cited in this bibliography were accessed and checked for accuracy on August 1, 2012.

Abramson, Kate. "A Sentimentalist's Defense of Contempt, Shame, and Disdain." In *The Oxford Handbook of Philosophy of Emotion*, edited by Peter Goldie, 189–213. Oxford, New York: Oxford University Press, 2009.

Adams, Robert Merrihew. "Involuntary Sins." *Philosophical Review* 94, no. 1 (1985): 3–31.

———. *A Theory of Virtue: Excellence in Being for the Good*. Oxford: Oxford University Press, 2006.

Alston, William. "Emotion and Feeling." *Encyclopedia of Philosophy*, vol. 2. Edited by Paul Edwards. New York: Macmillan, 1967.

Appiah, Kwame Anthony. *The Honor Code: How Moral Revolutions Happen*. New York: W. W. Norton, 2010.

Aristotle. *Rhetoric*. In *The Rhetoric and the Poetics of Aristotle*. Translated by Rhys Roberts and Ingram Bywater. New York: McGraw-Hill Companies, 1984.

———. *Politics*. Translated by C. D. C. Reeve. Indianapolis: Hackett Publishing Company, 1998.

———. *Nicomachean Ethics*. Translated by Terence Irwin. Indianapolis: Hackett Publishing Company, 1999.

Arthur, John. *Race Equality, and the Burdens of History*. New York: Cambridge University Press, 2007.

Augustine. *City of God*. Translated by Henry Bettenson. London: Penguin Books, 2003.

Austen, Jane. *Pride and Prejudice*. New York: Simon & Schuster, 2004.

Baumeister, Roy, and Mark Leary. "The Need to Belong: Desire for Interpersonal Attachments as a Fundamental Human Motivation." *Psychological Bulletin* 117, no. 3 (1995): 497–529.

BBC News. "Prince's Mugabe Handshake Gaff." *BBC News*, April 8, 2005, http://news.bbc.co.uk/2/hi/uk_news/4425385.stm.

Beardsley, Elizabeth, "Understanding and Forgiveness." In *The Philosophy of Brand Blanshard,* edited by P. A. Schilpp, 247–258. La Salle, IL: Open Court, 1980.

Bell, Macalester. "A Woman's Scorn: Toward a Feminist Defense of Contempt as a Moral Emotion." *Hypatia* 20, no.2 (2005): 80–93.

———. "Forgiving Someone for Who They Are (and Not Just What They've Done)." *Philosophy and Phenomenological Research* 77, no. 3 (2008): 625–658.

———. "Anger, Oppression, and Virtue." In *Feminist Ethics and Social and Political Philosophy: Theorizing the Non-Ideal,* edited by Lisa Tessman, 165–183. New York: Springer, 2009.

———. "Globalist Attitudes and the Fittingness Objection." *Philosophical Quarterly* 61, no. 244 (2011): 449–472.

———. "Forgiveness, Inspiration, and the Powers of Reparation." *American Philosophical Quarterly* 49, no. 3 (2012): 205–221.

Ben-Ze'ev, Aaron. *The Subtlety of Emotions.* Cambridge, MA: MIT Press, 2001.

Benedict, Ruth. *The Chrysanthemum and the Sword.* Wilmington: Mariner Books, 2006.

Blanshard, Brand. *Reason and Goodness.* New York: Macmillan, 1961.

Blum, Lawrence. "Stereotypes and Stereotyping: A Moral Analysis." *Philosophical Papers* 33, no. 3 (2004): 251–289.

Brady, Michael S. "Emotions, Perceptions, and Reasons." In *Morality and the Emotions,* edited by Carla Bagnoli, 135–149. Oxford: Oxford University Press, 2011.

Brandt, Richard B. "Moral Valuation." *Ethics* 56, no. 2 (1946): 106–121.

Brennan, Geoffrey, and Philip Pettit. "The Hidden Economy of Esteem." *Economics and Philosophy* 16 (2000): 77–98.

———. *The Economy of Esteem: An Essay on Civil and Political Society.* New York: Oxford University Press, 2004.

Brown, John. "Prison Letters." Reprinted in *American Protest Literature,* edited by Zoe Trodd. Cambridge, MA: Belknap Press of Harvard University Press, 2006.

Burke, Edmund. "Letters on a Regicide Peace." In *The Writings and Speeches of Edmund Burke.* Beaconsfield Edition, vol. 5. Boston: Little, Brown and Company, 1901.

Buss, Sarah. "Appearing Respectful: On the Moral Significance of Manners." *Ethics* 109, no. 4 (1999): 795–826.

Butler, Joseph. "Upon the Forgiveness of Injuries." In *The Whole Works of Joseph Butler*. London: Thomas Tegg, 1826.
Calhoun, Cheshire. "Changing One's Heart." *Ethics* 103, no. 1 (1992): 76–96.
———. "The Virtue of Civility." *Philosophy & Public Affairs* 29, no. 3 (2000): 251–275.
———. "Cognitive Emotions?" In *What Is an Emotion? Classic and Contemporary Readings*, edited by Robert Solomon, 236–247. 2nd ed. New York: Oxford University Press, 2003.
———. "An Apology for Moral Shame." *Journal of Political Philosophy* 12, no. 2 (2004): 127–146.
Stanhope, Philip Dormer, Earl of Chesterfield. *Lord Chesterfield's Letters*. Edited by David Roberts. Oxford: Oxford University Press, 1998.
Colaiaco, James A. *Frederick Douglass and the Fourth of July*. New York: Palgrave Macmillan, 2006.
Crisp, Roger, and Christopher Cowton. "Hypocrisy and Moral Seriousness." *American Philosophical Quarterly* 31, no. 4 (1994): 343–349.
Curzer, Howard J. "Aristotle's Much Maligned *Megalopsychos*." *Australasian Journal of Philosophy* 69, no. 2 (1991): 131–151.
D'Arms, Justin, and Daniel Jacobson. "The Moralistic Fallacy: On the 'Appropriateness' of Emotions." *Philosophy and Phenomenological Research* 61, no. 1 (2000): 65–90.
Damasio, Antonio. *The Feeling of What Happens: Body and Emotion in the Making of Consciousness*. New York: Harcourt Brace and Co., 1999.
Darwall, Stephen L. "Two Kinds of Respect." *Ethics* 88, no. 1 (1977): 36–49.
———. *The Second-Person Standpoint: Morality, Respect, and Accountability*. Cambridge, MA: Harvard University Press, 2006.
Darwin, Charles. *The Expression of the Emotions in Man and Animals*. New York: D. Appleton and Company, 1873.
DeArmond, Michelle. "Inland GOP Mailing Depicts Obama's Face on Food Stamp." *Press Enterprise* (San Bernardino, CA), October 16, 2008.
Deigh, John. "Cognitivism in the Theory of Emotions." *Ethics* 104, no.4 (1994): 824–854.
———. *The Sources of Moral Agency*. New York: Cambridge University Press, 1996.
De Sousa, Ronald. *The Rationality of Emotion*. Cambridge, MA: MIT Press, 1987.
———. "Emotion." In the *Stanford Encyclopedia of Philosophy* http://plato.stanford.edu/entries/emotion, 2010.
Dillon, Robin. "Respect and Care: Toward Moral Integration." *Canadian Journal of Philosophy* 22, no. 1 (1992): 105–132.
———. "Arrogance, Self-Respect, and Personhood." *Journal of Consciousness Studies* 14, no 5/6 (2007): 101–126.

Doris, John M. *Lack of Character: Personality and Moral Behavior*. Cambridge: Cambridge University Press, 2005.

———. "Replies: Evidence and Sensibility." *Philosophy and Phenomenological Research* 71, no. 3 (2005): 656–677.

Dougher, Jamie. "Senior Class Gives Nod to Unsung Founders." *Daily Tarheel* (Chapel Hill, NC), October 12, 2001, http://www.dailytarheel.com/index.php/article/2001/10/senior_class_gives_nod_to_unsung_founders.

Douglas, Lana. "UNC's Confederate Statue Draws New Protest." *News & Observer* (Raleigh, NC), September 2, 2011, http://www.newsobserver.com/2011/09/02/1454360/sam-is-silent-his-detractors-arent.html.

Douglass, Frederick. "What to the Slave is the Fourth of July?" Speech sponsored by the Rochester Ladies' Anti-Slavery Society, Rochester, New York, July 5, 1852.

Driver, Julia. *Uneasy Virtue*. New York: Cambridge University Press, 2001.

"Dr. Phil's Ten Life Laws," http://drphil.com/articles/article/44/.

Du Bois, W. E. B. *The Souls of Black Folk*. Mineola, NY: Dover Publications Inc., 1994.

Ekman, Paul, and Wallace V. Friesen. *Unmasking the Face: A Guide to Recognizing Emotions from Facial Clues*. Englewood Cliffs, NJ: Prentice-Hall, 1975.

———. "A New Pan-Cultural Facial Expression of Emotion." *Motivation and Emotion* 10, no. 2 (1986): 159–168.

Elster, Jon. *Sour Grapes: Studies in the Subversion of Rationality*. Cambridge: Cambridge University Press, 1983.

Folkard, Henry Coleman. *The Law of Slander and Libel*. 7th ed. London: Butterworth & Co., 1908.

Frye, Marilyn. "A Note on Anger." In *Politics of Reality: Essays in Feminist Theory*, 84–94. Trumansburg, NY: Crossing Press, 1983.

Garcia, Ernesto V. "Bishop Butler on Forgiveness and Resentment." *Philosophers' Imprint* http://quod.lib.umich.edu/cgi/p/pod/dod-idx/bishop-butler-on-forgiveness-and-resentment.pdf?c=phimp;idno=3521354.0011.010 11, no. 10 (2011): 1–19.

Garcia, J. L. A. "The Heart of Racism." *Journal of Social Philosophy* 27, no. 1 (1996): 5–45.

———. "Current Conceptions of Racism: A Critical Examination of Some Recent Social Philosophy." *Journal of Social Philosophy* 28 (1997): 5–42.

———. "Philosophical Analysis and the Moral Concept of Racism." *Philosophy and Social Criticism* 25, no. 1 (1999): 1–32.

Gibbard, Allan. *Wise Choices, Apt Feelings: A Theory of Normative Judgment*. Cambridge, MA: Harvard University Press, 1992.

Gottman, John, and Robert Levenson. "How Stable is Marital Interaction Over Time?" *Family Process* 38, no. 2 (1999): 159–165.

Gottman, John, Robert Levenson, and Erica Woodin. "Facial Expressions During Marital Conflict." *Journal of Family Communication* 1, no. 1 (2001): 37–57.

Gottman, John. *What Predicts Divorce?: The Relationship Between Marital Processes and Marital Outcomes.* Hillsdale, NJ: Lawrence Erlbaum Associates, 1994.

Greenlee-Donnell, Cynthia. "UNC-Chapel Hill Examines Race and History." *Independent Weekly*, October 18, 2006, http://www.indyweek.com/indyweek/unc-chapel-hill-examines-race-and-history/Content?oid=1199381.

Greenspan, Patricia. "A Case of Mixed Feelings: Ambivalence and the Logic of Emotion." In *Philosophy and the Emotions: A Reader*, edited by Stephen Leighton. New York: Broadview Press, 2003.

Griswold, Charles. *Forgiveness: A Philosophical Exploration.* New York: Cambridge University Press, 2007.

———. "Debating Forgiveness: A Reply to My Critics." *Philosophia* 38, no. 3 (2010): 457–473.

Haidt, Jonathan. "The Moral Emotions." In *Handbook of Affective Sciences*, edited by Richard J. Davidson, L. Klaus R. Scherer, and H. Hill Goldsmith, 852–870. Oxford: Oxford University Press, 2003.

Haidt, Jonathan, and Dacher Keltner. "Culture and Facial Expression: Open-ended Methods Find More Faces and a Gradient of Recognition." *Cognition and Emotion* 13, no. 3 (1999): 225–266.

Harman, Gilbert. "Moral Philosophy Meets Social Psychology: Virtue Ethics and the Fundamental Attribution Error." *Proceedings of The Aristotelian Society* 99 (1999): 315–331.

Hieronymi, Pamela. "Articulating an Uncompromising Forgiveness." *Philosophy and Phenomenological Research* 62, no. 3 (2001): 529–555.

Hill, Thomas. "Self-Respect Reconsidered." In *Autonomy and Self-Respect*, 19–24. Cambridge, New York: Cambridge University Press, 1991.

———. "The Message of Affirmative Action." *Social Philosophy and Policy* 8, no. 2 (1991): 108–129.

———. "Must Respect be Earned?" In *Respect, Pluralism, and Justice: Kantian Perspectives* 87–118. Oxford: Oxford University Press, 2000.

Hobbes, Thomas. *De Cive.* In *The English Works of Thomas Hobbes of Malmesbury*, vol. 2, edited by William Molesworth. London: John Bohn, 1839.

———. *Leviathan: With Selected Variants from the Latin Edition of 1668.* Edited by Edwin Curley. Indianapolis: Hackett Publishing Company, 1994.

Horsburgh, H. J. N. "Forgiveness." *Canadian Journal of Philosophy* 4, no. 2 (1974): 269–282.

Hume, David. *A Treatise of Human Nature*. Edited by David Norton and Mary Norton. Oxford: Oxford University Press, 2007.
Hurka, Thomas. *Virtue, Vice, and Value*. Oxford: Oxford University Press, 2001.
James, William. "What Is an Emotion?" *Mind* 9 (1884): 188–205.
———. *The Principles of Psychology*, vol. 2. New York: Dover, 1950.
Jones, Karen. "Emotional Rationality as Practical Rationality." In *Setting the Moral Compass: Essays by Women Philosophers*, edited by Cheshire Calhoun, 333–352. New York: Oxford University Press, 2004.
Kant, Immanuel. *Anthropology from a Pragmatic Point of View*. Translated by V. L. Dowdell. Carbondale: Southern Illinois University Press, 1978.
———. *Lectures on Ethics*. Translated by Louis Infield. Indianapolis: Hackett Publishing Company, 1981.
———. *The Metaphysics of Morals*. Translated and edited by Mary Gregor, with an introduction by Roger J. Sullivan. Cambridge: Cambridge University Press, 1996.
———. *Groundwork of the Metaphysics of Morals*. Translated and edited by Mary Gregor, with an introduction by Christine Korsgaard. Cambridge: Cambridge University Press, 1998.
Kelly, Daniel. *Yuck!: The Nature and Moral Significance of Disgust*. Cambridge, MA: MIT Press, 2011.
Keltner, Dacher, and Jonathan Haidt. "Social Functions of Emotions at Four Levels of Analysis." *Cognition and Emotion* 13, no. 5 (1999): 505–521.
Kim, David Haekwon. "Contempt and Ordinary Inequality." In *Racism and Philosophy*, edited by Susan E. Babbitt and Sue Campbell, 108–123. Ithaca, NY: Cornell University Press, 1999.
Kolodny, Niko. "Love as Valuing a Relationship." *Philosophical Review*. 112, no. 2 (2003): 135–189.
———. "Which Relationships Justify Partiality? General Considerations and Problem Cases." In *Partiality and Impartiality: Morality, Special Relationships and the Wider World*, edited by Brian Feltham and John Cottingham, 169–193. Oxford: Oxford University Press, 2010.
Kristjánsson, Kristján. "On the Very Idea of 'Negative Emotions.'" *Journal for the Theory of Social Behavior* 33, no. 4 (2003): 351–364.
Kutz, Christopher. *Complicity: Ethics and Law for a Collective Age*. Cambridge; New York: Cambridge University Press, 2000.
Lange, Carl. "The Emotions." In *The Emotions*, edited by K. Dunlap, 33–90. Baltimore: Williams & Wilkins, 1922. Originally published in 1885.
Lazarus, Richard. *Emotion and Adaptation*. New York: Oxford University Press, 1991.
Lectric Law Library's Legal Lexicon "Contempt of Court."
Lemann, Nicholas. "O Lucky Man: The Diaries of Ronald Reagan." *New Yorker* May 28, 2007. http://www.newyorker.com/arts/critics/books/2007/05/28/070528crbo_books_lemann?currentPage=1.

Little Children. Dir. Todd Field, New Line Cinema 2006.
Liu, Caitlin. "Sleepy Juror Gets Rude Awakening." *Los Angeles Times*, April 20, 2005, http://articles.latimes.com/2005/apr/20/local/me-yawn20.
Lorde, Audre. "The Uses of Anger: Women Responding to Racism." In *Sister Outsider*. Trumansburg, NY: Crossing Press, 1984.
Machiavelli, Niccolò. *The Prince*. Edited by Quentin Skinner and Russell Prince. Cambridge: Cambridge University Press, 1988.
Mason, Michelle. "Contempt as a Moral Attitude." *Ethics* 113, no. 2 (2003): 234–272.
Matsumoto, David. "More Evidence for the Universality of a Contempt Expression." *Motivation and Emotion* 16, no. 4 (1992): 363–368.
McKinnon, Christine. "Hypocrisy, with a Note on Integrity." *American Philosophical Quarterly* 28, no. 4 (1991): 321–330.
McMullin, Irene. "A Modest Proposal: Accounting for the Virtuousness of Modesty." *Philosophical Quarterly* 60, no. 241 (2010): 783–807.
Miller, William Ian. *The Anatomy of Disgust*. Cambridge, MA: Harvard University Press, 1997.
Minas, Anne C. "God and Forgiveness." *Philosophical Quarterly* 25, no. 99 (1975): 138–150.
Molière. *Tartuffe*. In *The Misanthrope, Tartuffe, and other Plays*, edited by Maya Slater. New York: Oxford University Press, 2008.
Monin, Benoit. "Holier than Me? Threatening Social Comparison in the Moral Domain." *International Review of Social Psychology* 20, no. 1 (2007): 53–68.
Montaigne, Michel. "Of the Inconsistency of Our Actions." In *Selected Essays*, translated by Donald M. Frame, 117–126. Roslyn, NY: Walter J. Black, Inc., 1943.
Moravia, Alberto. *Contempt*. Translated by Angus Davidson. New York: New York Review Classics, 2004.
Morris, Herbert. "Persons and Punishment." *Monist* 52, no. 4 (1968): 475–501.
Mubarak, Hosni. "Egypt unrest: Full text of Hosni Mubarak's speech." *BBC News*, February 10, 2011, http://www.bbc.co.uk/news/mobile/world-middle-east-12427091.
Munger, Kristen, and Shelby J Harris. "Effects of an Observer on Handwashing in a Public Restroom." *Perceptual and Motor Skills* 69 (1989): 733–734.
Murphy, Jeffrie. "Shame Creeps Through Guilt and Feels like Retribution." *Law and Philosophy* 18 (1999): 327–344.
———. *Getting Even*. New York: Oxford University Press, 2003.
Murphy, Jeffrie, and Jean Hampton. *Forgiveness and Mercy*. Cambridge: Cambridge University Press, 1988.
Nagel, Thomas. "Concealment and Exposure." *Philosophy & Public Affairs* 27, no. 1 (1998): 3–30.

Narayan, Uma. "Working Together Across Difference: Some Considerations on Emotions and Political Practice." *Hypatia* 3, no. 3 (1988): 31–47.
Newberry, Paul A. "Joseph Butler on Forgiveness: A Presupposed Theory of Emotion." *Journal of the History of Ideas* 62, no. 2 (2001), 233–244.
Nietzsche, Friedrich. *Beyond Good and Evil: Prelude to a Philosophy of the Future*. Translated by Walter Kaufmann. New York: Vintage Books, 1966.
———. *On the Genealogy of Morals*. Translated by Walter Kauffman and R. J. Hollingdale. New York: Vintage Books, 1989.
Nussbaum, Martha C. *Upheavals of Thought: The Intelligence of Emotions*. Cambridge: Cambridge University Press, 2001.
———. "Discussing Disgust: On the Folly of Gross-Out Public Policy." Interview by Julian Sanchez, July 15, 2004, http://reason.com/archives/2004/07/15/discussing-disgust.
———. *Hiding From Humanity: Disgust, Shame and the Law*. Princeton, NJ: Princeton University Press, 2004.
O'Shaughnessy, R. J. "Forgiveness." *Philosophy* 42 (1967): 336–352.
Ortony, Andrew, and Terence Turner. "What's Basic about Basic Emotions?" *Psychological Review* 97, no. 3 (1990): 315–331.
Pettigrove, Glen. "The Standing to Forgive." *Monist* 92, no. 4 (2009): 583–603.
The Philadelphia Story. Dir. George Cukor, Warner Bros. 1940.
Plutchik, Robert. *Emotion: A Psychoevolutionary Synthesis*. New York: Harper & Row, 1980.
Post, Robert. "Hate Speech." In *Extreme Speech and Democracy*, edited by Ivan Hare and James Weinstein, 123–138. New York: Oxford University Press, 2009.
Potter, Nelson. "Kant on Punishment." In *The Blackwell Guide to Kant's Ethics*, edited by Thomas E. Hill, 179–195. Chichester, UK: Wiley Blackwell, 2009.
Prinz, Jesse. "Embodied Emotions." In *Thinking about Feeling: Contemporary Philosophers on Emotions*, edited by Robert Solomon, 44–58. New York: Oxford University Press 2004.
Radzik, Linda. *Making Amends: Atonement in Morality, Law, and Politics*. New York: Oxford University Press, 2009.
Rawls, John. *A Theory of Justice*. Rev. ed. Cambridge, MA: Belknap Press of Harvard University Press, 1999.
Raz, Joseph. *Value, Respect, and Attachment*. The Seeley Lectures. Cambridge: Cambridge University Press, 2001.
Reagan, Ronald. *The Reagan Diaries*. Edited by Douglas Brinkley. New York: HarperCollins, 2007.
Reginster, Bernard. "Nietzsche on *Ressentiment* and Valuation." *Philosophy and Phenomenological Research* 57, no. 2 (1997): 281–305.

Rich, Frank. "Everybody Hates Don Imus." *New York Times*, April 15, 2007, http://www.nytimes.com/2007/04/15/opinion/15rich.html?scp=1&sq=Everybody%20Hates%20Don%20Imus&st=cse.

Richards, Norvin. "Forgiveness." *Ethics* 99, no. 1 (1988): 77–97.

Roberts, Robert C. "What an Emotion Is: A Sketch." *Philosophical Review* 97, no. 2 (1988): 183–209.

———. "Forgivingness." *American Philosophical Quarterly* 32, no.4 (1995): 289–306.

Robinson, Jenefer. *Deeper Than Reason: Emotion and its Role in Literature, Music and Art.* Oxford: Clarendon Press, 2005.

Rorty, Amélie. "Explaining Emotions." In *Explaining Emotions*, edited by Amélie Rorty. Los Angeles: University of California Press, 1980.

Rosenberg, Erika L., and Paul Ekman. "Conceptual and Methodological Issues in the Judgment of Facial Expressions of Emotion." *Motivation and Emotion* 19, no. 2 (1995): 111–138.

Rozin, Paul, and April Fallon. "A Perspective on Disgust." *Psychological Review* 94, no. 1 (1987): 23–41.

Rozin, Paul, Jonathan Haidt, and Clark McCauley. "Disgust." In *Handbook of Emotions*, edited by Michael Lewis and Jeannette Haviland-Jones, 757–776. 2nd ed. New York: Guilford Press, 2000.

Rozin, Paul, Laura Lowery, Sumio Imada, and Jonathan Haidt. "The CAD Triad Hypothesis: A Mapping Between Three Moral Emotions (Contempt, Anger, Disgust) and Three Moral Codes (Community, Autonomy, Divinity)." *Journal of Personality and Social Psychology* 76, no. 4 (1999): 574–586.

Russell, James A. "Negative Results on a Reported Facial Expression of Contempt." *Motivation and Emotion* 15, no. 4 (1991): 281–291.

Scanlon, T. M. *What we Owe to Each Other.* Cambridge, MA: Belknap Press of Harvard University Press, 1998.

———. *Moral Dimensions: Permissibility, Meaning, Blame.* Cambridge MA: Belknap Press of Harvard University Press, 2008.

Scheffler, Samuel. "Valuing" (15–40) and "Morality and Reasonably Partiality" (41–71). In Scheffler, *Equality and Tradition: Questions of Value in Moral and Political Theory.* New York: Oxford University Press, 2010.

Schopenhauer, Arthur. *Essays and Aphorisms.* Translated by Reginald John Hollingdale. London: Penguin Books, 1970.

Shakespeare, William. *King Lear.* Edited by R. A. Foakes. 3rd ed. London: Arden Shakespeare, 1997.

Sherman, Nancy. "Taking Responsibility for our Emotions." *Social Philosophy and Policy* 16, no. 2 (1999): 294–323.

Shklar, Judith. *Ordinary Vices.* Cambridge, MA: Belknap Press of Harvard University Press, 1984.

Slate. *The Complete Bushisms*, http://www.slate.com/articles/news_and_politics/bushisms/2000/03/the_complete_bushisms.html.

Smith, Angela. "Responsibility for Attitudes: Activity and Passivity in Mental Life." *Ethics* 115, no. 2 (2005): 236–271.

Solomon, Robert C. *The Passions: Emotions and the Meaning of Life.* Indianapolis: Hackett Publishing Company, 1976.

———. "The Philosophy of Emotions." In *Handbook of Emotions,* edited by Michael Lewis, Jeannette M. Haviland-Jones, and Lisa Feldman Barrett, 3–16. New York: Guildford Press, 2008.

Solomon, Robert C., and Lori D. Stone. "On 'Positive' and 'Negative' Emotions." *Journal for the Theory of Social Behavior* 32, no. 4 (2002): 417–435.

Steele, Claude M., and Joshua Aronson. "Stereotype Threat and the Intellectual Test Performance of African Americans." *Journal of Personality and Social Psychology* 69, no. 5 (1995): 797–811.

Stocker, Michael, and Elizabeth Hegeman. *Valuing Emotions.* Cambridge: Cambridge University Press, 1996.

Strawson, Peter F. "Freedom and Resentment." *Proceedings of the British Academy* 48 (1962): 187–211.

Sussman, David. "Shame and Punishment in Kant's *Doctrine of Right.*" *Philosophical Quarterly* 58, no. 231 (2008): 299–317.

Szabados, Béla, and Eldon Soifer. *Hypocrisy: Ethical Investigations.* Peterborough, ON: Broadview Press, 2004.

Tangney, June Price, and Ronda L. Dearing. *Shame and Guilt.* New York: The Guilford Press, 2002.

Taylor, Gabriele. *Pride, Shame, and Guilt: Emotions of Self-Assessment.* Oxford: Clarendon Press, 1985.

Tiberius, Valerie, and John D. Walker. "Arrogance." *American Philosophical Quarterly* 35, no. 4 (1998): 379–390.

Tierney, John. "Of Smiles and Sneers." *New York Times,* July 18, 2004, http://www.nytimes.com/2004/07/18/politics/races/18points.html.

UNC University Library. *Slavery and the Making of the University: The College Servants,* http://www.lib.unc.edu/mss/exhibits/slavery/servants.html.

———. *The Carolina Story: A Virtual Museum of University History: African Americans and Segregation,* http://museum.unc.edu/exhibits/segregation/ben-boothe-died-1891.

University of North Carolina at Chapel Hill. *Silent Sentinels of Stone: Old Chapel Hill Cemetery,* http://www.ibiblio.org/cemetery/index.html.

Upton, Candace L. *Situational Traits of Character: Dispositional Foundations and Implications for Moral Psychology and Friendship.* Lanham, MD: Lexington Books of Rowman & Littlefield, 2009.

Velleman, J. David. "Love as Moral Emotion." *Ethics* 109, no. 2 (1999): 338–374.

———. "The Genesis of Shame." *Philosophy & Public Affairs* 30, no. 1 (2001): 27–52.

Wagner, Hugh. "The Accessibility of the Term 'Contempt' and the Meaning of the Unilateral Lip Curl." *Cognition and Emotion* 14, no. 5 (2000): 689–710.

Waldron, Jeremy. "Superseding Historic Injustice." *Ethics* 103, no. 1 (1992): 4–28.

Walker, David. *Appeal to the Coloured Citizens* (1829). Reprinted in *American Protest Literature*, edited by Zoe Trodd. Cambridge, MA: Belknap Press of Harvard University Press, 2006.

Walker, Margaret Urban. *Moral Repair: Reconstructing Moral Relationships after Wrongdoing*. New York: Cambridge University Press, 2006.

Wallace, R. Jay. *Responsibility and the Moral Sentiments*. Cambridge MA: Harvard University Press, 1994.

———. "Hypocrisy, Moral Address, and the Equal Standing of Persons." *Philosophy & Public Affairs* 38, no. 4 (2010): 307–341.

Watson, Gary. "Responsibility and the Limits of Evil: Variations on a Strawsonian Theme." In *Responsibility, Character and the Emotions: New Essays in Moral Psychology*, edited by Ferdinand Schoeman, 256–286. Cambridge: Cambridge University Press, 1987.

Westlund, Andrea. "Anger, Faith, and Forgiveness." *Monist* 92, no. 4 (2009): 507–536.

Wettstein, Howard. "Forgiveness and Moral Reckoning." *Philosophia* 38 (2010): 445–455.

Whiting, Demian. "The Feeling Theory of Emotion and the Object-Directed Emotions." *European Journal of Philosophy* 19, no. 2 (2011): 281–303.

Williams, Bernard. *Shame and Necessity*. Los Angeles: University of California Press, 1993.

Williams, Kipling D., Joseph P. Forgas, William von Hippel, and Lisa Zadro. "The Social Outcast: An Overview." In *The Social Outcast: Ostracism, Social Exclusion, Rejection, and Bullying*, edited by Kipling D. Williams, Joseph P. Forgas, and William von Hippel, 323. New York: Taylor & Francis Group, 2005.

Wood, Allen W. *Kant's Ethical Thought*. Cambridge: Cambridge University Press, 1999.

Yakas, Ben. "Video: 'Very Well-Educated Person' Flips Out on Metro-North Train." *Gothamist* http://gothamist.com/2011/06/16/video_very_well_educated_person_mak.php.

Zagzebski, Linda. *Virtues of the Mind: An Inquiry into the Nature of Virtue and Ethical Foundations of Knowledge*. New York: Cambridge University Press, 1996.

INDEX

Abramson, Kate, 2n.3, 2n.3, 74n.17, 165
Active contempt, 50-51, 51n.66, 53n.72, 145
Adams, Robert, 1, 160–161
Affective openness, 126, 213–214
Affective oughts, 191, 194
   and control 192
   and ought implies can principle, 193
Anger, 57, 102, 184, 194 (*see also* resentment)
   as a response to racism, 205
Anti-contempt ethic, 9, 14, 128, 137, 177, 197, 198, 273
Appiah, Kwame Anthony, 19n.35, 99n.5, 224
Aristotle, 11 n.15, 49 n.61, 138–141, 143-147, 248
   and the *megalopsychos*, 138–141, 143, 145, 147
Arthur, John, 208-213
Augustine, 233-234

Badbeing, 39, 16, 153, 163, 190, 236, 270, 275
Basic emotions, 30–32
Benedict, Ruth, 18, 19 n.36
Ben-Ze'ev, Aaron, 39 n.46, 40–41, 77 n. 21, 94n.36

Blameworthiness, 20
   and voluntary control, 20-21, 209–211
Blanshard, Brand, 87
Burke, Edmund, 1, 272, 276
Buss, Sarah, 218n.29
Butler, Joseph, 228, 235, 242, 243

Calhoun, Cheshire, 35n.36, 132n.53, 218n.29, 218n.30, 219–224, 247-248
Character 67, 89, 100, 187, 236, 241, 245, 248, 250, 252, 255
   and character change, 127
Civility, 198, 216–218, 222, 226
   and integrity, 221
   limits to, 218–224
   and respect, 198, 217
Cognitive theories of emotion, 33–35
Contempt of court, 47–48, 48n.59, 60
Contempt expression, 5, 29–32, 29n.17
Cowton, Christopher, 116n.27
Crisp, Roger, 116n.27
Curzer, Howard, 139n.3

D'Arms, Justin, 14n.28, 36n.39, 61n.86, 64n.1, 72n.15, 96n.1
Darwall, Stephen, 10n.13, 13n.23, 100n.7, 170-171, 183n.84, 185n.90, 274n.2

INDEX

Darwin, Charles, 29-30
Dearing, Ronda L. 40n.47
Deigh, John, 250n.31
Descartes, René, 26
Disesteem, 123-124, 126
Disgust, 52-55, 102, 183, 186-187, 275
Dishonor, 103, 215-216, 224, 272
Disvalue monism, 273
Doris, John, 64n.1, 68-73, 70n.12, 75n.19, 76-77, 79-80, 88
Douglass, Frederick, 206-207, 217-218, 220, 223
Dr. Phil, 239n.19
Du Bois, W.E.B., 203

Egalitarianism, 8, 146
  and anti-egalitarianism, 146-147
Ekman, Paul, 30n.20, 31
Elster, Jon, 106
Envy, 99
Esteem, 99-101, 104-110, 113-120, 122-128, 215
Ethic of contempt, 8, 128, 137, 147, 168, 171, 173, 177, 198, 203, 226, 273
Ethic of resentment, 9n.13, 9-10, 137, 274
Excuses, 150 (*see also* forgiveness and excuses)

Feeling theories of emotion, 26-29
Fitting attitude accounts of value, 65, 90-91
Fittingness Objection, 69-74, 78, 88, 94-95
Forgiveness, 22, 150, 187
  as agential, 235-236
  and apology, 127, 261
  asking for, 254, 257
  and character transformation, 245-247, 260
  and excuses, 237, 242-245
  as interpersonal activity, 257-258
  as non-complicit, 236
  and reasons to forgive, 230, 235, 238-240, 271
  and reconciliation, 22, 227
  and repentance, 240-241, 247, 249, 252-253
  and resentment, 228-229, 231-232, 256
  and shame, 249-251
  and standing, 255, 258
Friesen, Wallace, 30n.20, 31
Frye, Marilyn, 155

Garcia, Ernesto, 228n.2
Garcia, Jorge, 200-203, 206, 208, 210, 213
Garrison, William, 207
Gibbard, Allan, 9n.13, 16n.30, 250n.32, 274n.2
Gottman, John, 12, 195
Griswold, Charles, 231n.7
Guilt, 17, 19, 19n.36, 40, 67, 250

Haidt, Jonathan, 157-158
Hatred, 55
  and malice, 55-56
  and moral hatred, 55, 57
  and simple hatred, 55-57
  and spite, 55-56
Hampton, Jean, 55-57
Harman, Gilbert, 68
Hieronymi, Pamela 153n.26, 236n.14, 236n.15
Hill, Thomas, 81n.26, 169, 259n.38
Honor, 18, 19n.35, 99n.5, 224 (*see also* dishonor)
Hobbes, Thomas, 11-12, 48-49
Hume, David, 41-42, 180
Hurka, Thomas, 161

Integrity, 161-164, 167, 221

Jacobson, Daniel, 14n.28, 36n.39, 61n.86, 64n.1, 72n.15, 96n.1
James, William, 26-28

Kant, Immanuel, 12, 17n.31, 123n.39, 134-135, 137, 168-169, 171-175, 177-180, 182
  and social virtues, 174-177, 202n.11

INDEX

King Lear, 129–130
Kolodny, Niko, 46n.56, 93n.35
Kutz, Christopher, 90n.32

La Rochefoucauld, 272
Lange, Carl, 26
Libel, 7
Little Children, 186n.91
Lord Chesterfield, 4–5
Lorde, Audre, 156–157

Machiavelli, Niccolò, 11
Mason, Michelle, 2n.3, 25n.1, 38n.41, 39, 74, 81n.25, 149n.18, 150n.19, 156n.31, 169
McKinnon, Christine, 117
McMullin, Irene, 124n.40
Memorials, 22, 227, 260, 262–270
Miller, William Ian, 2n.3, 27, 29n.17, 38, 42, 44n.53, 49n.60, 50, 50n.64, 54n.73
Minimally acceptable morality, 23–24, 63, 97, 128, 148, 213
Modesty, 124–125
Montaigne, Michel de, 71, 71n.14
Moral address, 183, 185, 187
 and contempt, 187–188
 and resentment, 185–186
Moral standing, 100, 129
Moral status, 100, 181–182
Moravia, Alberto, 156
Murphy, Jeffrie, 127, 229, 230–232, 235n.12, 240–241, 242n.25, 243, 243n.25, 252

Narayan, Uma, 154
Negative emotions, 2n.2, 9, 161–162, 229, 230, 257
Newberry, Paul, 228n.2
Nietzsche, Friedrich, 55n.75, 138, 141–147
Nussbaum, Martha, 23n.39, 52n.69, 54, 157n.34

Obama Bucks cartoon, 199, 214–216, 220

Passive contempt, 49–51, 51n.66, 53n.72, 141–146

The Philadelphia Story, 151–152, 156, 158, 242, 245
Pride and Prejudice, 158–160

Quasi-perceptual theories of emotion, 35–36

Race-based contempt, 22, 197, 203–204, 206, 208–210, 212–214, 221, 226
 and racism, 197–198, 200–202, 207–208, 210, 215, 263
 and counter-contempt, 197–198, 206, 207, 216
Radzik, Linda, 23n.39, 100n.6
Rationality of emotion, 34, 36
Rawls, John, 249–250, 250n.31
Reflexivity, 41, 43–44, 46, 54
Reginster, Bernard, 142n.9
Relational damage, 108–109, 112–115, 118, 122–123, 125, 130, 194–195, 258, 274
Reparations, 22, 227, 260–262
Resentment, 10, 51, 61, 126, 139, 152, 154–155, 162–163, 275 (*see also* forgiveness and resentment)
 motivational value of, 156, 158
Respect, 22–23, 96, 129, 146, 164, 168, 171–172, 174, 176, 177–178, 202–203, 217–218, 222–225
 and appraisal respect, 170–171, 214
 and moral recognition respect, 170
 and recognition respect, 170–171, 174, 214, 225
Ressentiment, 141–143
Richards, Norvin, 228–231
Roberts, Robert C., 36n.36, 229n.5
Robinson, Jenefer, 51n.65
Rozin, Paul, 52–54, 101–102, 102n.11, 186n.92

Scheffler, Samuel, 120n.35, 167n.43
Schopenhauer, Arthur, 55, 58
Self-contempt, 61–62, 181
Shame, 17n.31, 18–19, 19n.35, 19n.36, 40–41, 67, 81–82, 85, 132, 181, 250, 275 (*see also* forgiveness and shame)

INDEX

Shweder, Richard, 102n.11
Situationism, 67–68
Soifer, Eldon, 131n.51
Status, 37–38, 41, 99–101, 103, 105–106, 108–109, 114, 117, 119, 125–126, 129, 135, 156, 163, 187, 216
  (*see also* moral status)
Steele, Claude, 204
  and stereotype threat, 204
Stereotypes, 204, 212–215
Strawson, P.F., 18n.33, 123n.37, 162n.39
Sussman, David, 17n.31, 123n.39, 183
Szabados, Béla, 131n.51

Tangney, June Price, 40n.47
Tartuffe, 118-121, 125, 127, 131, 155, 273–274
Tiberius, Valerie, 111–114

Valuing, 120–122, 161, 166–167, 168, 194
Velleman, J. David, 132n.53, 169n.48, 206n.15
Vices of superiority, 9, 95–97, 101, 103–105, 107, 109, 118, 120–123, 125–126, 128–133, 136–137, 149, 155, 191, 273
  and arrogance, 97, 109–115, 118, 128, 152, 215
  and hypocrisy, 97, 99, 109–110, 116–121, 127–128, 149, 152, 215
  and race-based contempt, 203, 205, 216
  and racism, 213
  and superbia, 109–110, 116, 118, 122, 125, 127–128, 130–131, 136–137, 148, 158, 163, 191, 194, 219, 259, 272-274

Waldron, Jeremy, 260–261
Walker, John, 111–114
Walker, Margaret Urban, 50n.62, 51n.66, 122n.36, 154n.27
Wallace, R. Jay, 9n.13, 116n.28, 117n.29, 162n.39, 274n.2
Watson, Gary, 183n.84, 185
Westlund, Andrea, 228n.2
Wettstein, Howard, 229n.5
Wilde, Oscar, 239
Williams, Bernard, 66–67, 75, 250n.32
Withdrawal, 13, 44–46, 62, 145, 154, 158, 166, 183–184, 187, 189, 222, 259, 272
Wood, Allen, 13, 177–179
Wrongdoing, 39, 127, 153, 162–163, 190, 236, 260, 270, 275

www.ingramcontent.com/pod-product-compliance
Ingram Content Group UK Ltd.
Pitfield, Milton Keynes, MK11 3LW, UK
UKHW041302180426
11947UKWH00009B/623